RISK REDUCTION: INTERVENTIONS FOR SPECIAL NEEDS OFFENDERS

FOUNDED 1870

ICCA

THESE PAPERS INITIALLY WERE PRESENTED AT THE
SEVENTH ANNUAL RESEARCH CONFERENCE OF THE
INTERNATIONAL COMMUNITY CORRECTIONS ASSOCIATION,
HELD SEPTEMBER 27-29, 1999 IN CINCINNATI, OHIO,
AND HAVE BEEN UPDATED FOR THIS VOLUME.

HARRY E. ALLEN
ADMINISTRATION OF JUSTICE
SAN JOSE STATE UNIVERSITY, SAN JOSE, CALIFORNIA
EDITOR

AMERICAN CORRECTIONAL ASSOCIATION
LANHAM, MARYLAND

Printed in the United States of America by Kirby Lithographic Company, Inc., Arlington, VA.

ISBN 1-56991-148-7

This publication may be ordered from:
American Correctional Association
4380 Forbes Boulevard
Lanham, MD 20706-4322
1-800-222-5646

For information on publications and videos available from ACA, contact our worldwide web home page at: http://www.aca.org or www.corrections.com/aca.

Contact the ICCA home page at: http://www.ICCAWEB.org

Library of Congress Cataloging-in-Publication Data

Risk reduction : interventions for special needs offenders / Harry E. Allen, editor
  p. cm.
"Papers presented at the presented at the Seventh Annual Research Conference of the International Community Corrections Association, held September 27-29, 1999 in Cincinnati, Ohio"–Pref.
  Includes bibliographical references and index.
  ISBN 1-56991-148-7 (pbk.: alk. paper)
  1. Criminals–Rehabilitation–Congresses. 2. Prisoners–Mental health services–Congresses.
  I. Allen, Harry E. II. International Community Corrections Association. Research Conference (7th : 1999 : Cincinnati, Ohio)

  HV9267 .R57 2001
  365'.66–dc21

                                                            2001053557

TABLE OF CONTENTS

FOREWORD

The American Correctional Association is pleased to present another volume in our joint publishing program with the International Community Corrections Association that explores "what works" in corrections.

Continued public acceptance is a crucial goal for community corrections. Identifying risk and lowering recidivism goes a long way toward making community programs safer, more effective, and more attractive to the public as a viable correctional option.

Risk Reduction: Interventions for Special Needs Offenders acknowledges that there are particular challenges associated with certain offenders who are often more difficult to treat. As this book shows, however, these problems are being addressed with promising results. Based on presentations made at the 7th Annual Research Conference of the International Community Corrections Association, this collection of essays illustrates what some of the leading authorities in community corrections are doing to identify risk and lower recidivism.

Utilizing community-based alternatives and treatment programs in corrections can be effective. This is no different for offenders with special needs. Providing humane programs and services for these offenders by responding to their special needs without compromising public safety is an important goal.

I applaud these authors' efforts, and I hope others share in their success by reading about what's working in community corrections.

James A. Gondles, Jr., CAE
Executive Director
American Correctional Association

Introduction

In 1993, The International Community Corrections Association (ICCA) began commissioning researchers to write papers on treatment related topics. The purpose for the papers was simple. ICCA would commission researchers to answer specific "what works" questions. The researcher would conduct a broad multidisciplinary literature review to find answers to the questions. The literature, through the expertise of the researcher, would provide evidence of what worked. Practitioners would use the evidence of "what works" to advocate for the greater use of community correctional programming.

At the time, it was difficult to explain why community-based correctional programs were not better funded and utilized. Practitioners knew their work improved the probability of offenders' success reentering the community.

There was little argument that community-based programming was not making a difference. Offenders were provided with housing. They were fed. Their activities were monitored daily before being released to their own homes and communities. Community agencies helped offenders find employment and to save money as a nest egg for when there were independent. They assisted offenders with educational and job training arrangements. They monitored drug and alcohol use to keep them straight. They connected offenders to human services and support groups, and introduced them to leisure activities. Good programs monitored acquaintances and assisted with visits from family and friends. In the end, community agencies helped offenders find housing and to otherwise readjust to the real world after being incarcerated.

The assistance provided by community correctional agencies gave offenders the basic life skills necessary to live a crime-free life. At the same time, many agencies were providing a greater and more comprehensive array of services. Without community assistance, the majority of the offenders would fail because they lacked the basic skills necessary to cope and succeed in a pro-social world.

Historically, very little research had been done on community corrections programs. Most of the references to successful programs were anecdotal stories about offenders doing well because they were given help
while in a program. Hard evidence was rare. In the world of evidence, a
story about an offender succeeding is not proof that a program works. It
is easy to believe that a program is effective based upon a good story. It is
quite another thing to prove empirically that what was done had a direct
effect on changing the offender's behavior.

There was a belief in 1993 that more money would be made available
for offender reintegration programs if sufficient evidence existed that programs worked. Evidence in this case were outcome studies conducted by
reputable research organizations. Validated independent studies would
help practitioners make the argument that community corrections should
expand to serve a greater percentage of offenders because it increased the
probability of an offender succeeding. Success was equated as less crime
and greater public safety. The evidence to expand community-based interventions would be irrefutable, or so the discussions went.

Correctional providers were not naive to the realities of the world.
They realized that positive research findings were just one element
toward expanding community corrections.There was a multitude of other
political, social, and economic issues to contend with and these realities
had little to do with research. Still, the validation of effectiveness by independent researchers was a good first step.

So, ICCA began to sponsor annual "What Works" research conferences. With each conference, more and more questions were answered.
ICCA took the information forward in the form of regional research conferences. Public and private agencies began to use the information to
advance the quality of existing practices.

In many ways, the community correctional world of 1993 seems much
simpler than it is today. The implication of the literature and its relevance
to community corrections have opened up avenues of treatment options
that had not been realized just years earlier. The offenders have not
changed but the way in which agencies respond to them has been greatly
influenced by the emerging science of treatment. In short, the literature
has revealed some of the secrets of what works and correctional providers
are beginning to implement the findings into practice.

"What Works" research has provided a more comprehensive view of
what needs to be done in order to effectively reintegrate the offender into
a community. "What Works" has given policymakers a research-validated
path to follow and that path continues to unravel before us. As it turns
out, the science of "What Works" has been with us for some time but it has

only been in the last decade when corrections has begun to integrate it in the form of policies and programs.

The papers presented in this book are a good illustration of the science transformation that is taking place in our correctional world. The chapters enclosed would not have "fit" 1993 community correctional constructs. The understanding of the principles of effective interventions that has found its way into our practices has been rapid.

In 1993, the use of standard risk and criminogenic need assessments was at a minimum. Treatment was poorly defined. There were few established cognitive-behavioral curriculums available and even less governmental support to use them if they had been available. Most agencies developed their own internal approaches of what they believed treatment should be.

If we compare and contrast practices from a decade ago to present time, we can see how the landscape has changed. Today, standard risk and the criminogenic need assessments are recognized as a necessity. Increasingly, agencies are beginning to use a multitude of other specialized assessments to better use treatment programs to change offender behavior

Cognitive-behavioral curriculum-based treatments are rapidly becoming the interventions of choice. The last decade has seen the development of a multitude of curriculum that target specific treatment needs. The curriculums used today are beginning laced with practices like motivational interviewing, motivation, relapse prevention, and social learning. These concepts were not part of the correctional discussion a decade ago.

Assessments of today are increasingly being linked to case management strategies and case management is linked to treatment, particularly to cognitive-behavioral curriculum. Assessment processes are becoming so sensitive that we are now seeing curriculum being developed to address levels of treatment intensity as is consistent with the literature.

The concept of evaluation has also changed dramatically. Program effectiveness was once measured by the percentage of persons who completed the program. This is no longer the case. Effectiveness is beginning to be determined by a number of indicators like the change in risk scores of pre-post assessments. Standard cognitive curriculum programs enable programs to measure pre-post change in attitude and assess change in behavior. As community corrections further embraces scientifically validated cognitive-behavioral interventions, it will soon become practice to measure quality program by program, and staff person by staff person.

The chapters presented in this book discuss specialized assessments and interventions with targeted populations of offenders and their families. It would be safe to say that ICCA representatives could not have predicted what the exploration of "What Works" would have taken them in 1993.

Peter Kinziger
Executive Director
International Community Corrections Association

PREFACE

This book is a collection of professional papers presented at the Seventh Annual Research Conference of the International Community Corrections Association, held September 27-29, 1999, in Cincinnati, Ohio. Cincinnati was the cite of the Declaration of Principles established by the National Prison Congress in 1870, where leaders had gathered to discuss the direction that correctional practices should take. They were especially concerned with crowded prison facilities, and they sought answers as to what type of prisons should be built to alleviate the desperate conditions they faced. Many attendees urged the institutionalization of parole, release to the community, reformation, and rehabilitation. While these are mainstays of contemporary corrections, they were radical ideas and practices in the last third of the nineteenth century. The National Prison Congress endorsed the ideas, setting into motion many of the correctional practices now widespread in corrections.

That organization's first meeting in Cincinnati elected Rutherford B. Hayes, then governor of Ohio and later President of the United States, as the first president of the association. At the 1954 Congress of Correction, as the National Prison Congress came to be known, the organization's name was changed to the American Correctional Association (ACA).

Included in the new conceptions, practices, and programs of the founding National Prison Congress were the elements of treatment, rehabilitation, offender change, prison reform, community-based corrections, and sentence reform. The American Correctional Association has been and remains one of the most influential factors in correctional reform. Comprised of seventy chapters and affiliated organizations and with more than 20,000 members, ACA serves as the umbrella organization for all areas of corrections.

The International Community Corrections Association theme for the 1999 research conference was "What Works in Corrections: Risk Reduction Intervention for Special Needs Offenders." At that conference, significant leaders in the field of research, treatment, and community and institutional corrections developed important state-of-the-art compilations of what is known to work in corrections. These papers have been amassed to produce this monograph. They are summaries of contemporary research and practice. Also included in each paper are questions requiring further research, as well as implications for best practices with specific high-need and high-risk groups: drunk drivers, juvenile offenders, psychopathic inmates and clients, spouse abusers, and sex offenders.

The articles provide the reader with a cumulative and broad understanding of the intricacies of special needs and high-risk offenders. Each chapter can stand on its own merit, but collectively, they expand our knowledge of the dimensions of the problems and issues of special needs clients, as well as detail significant approaches for assessment, treatment, and intervention.

Several individuals were extremely helpful in the conception, construction, and compilation of this volume, the brainchild of Peter Kinziger, executive director of the International Community Corrections Association. Sincere thanks are extended to Peter for his efforts here as well as in advancing the level of practice in the field, and to the staff at ACA, especially Alice Fins.

Harry E. Allen
Professor Emeritus
Administration of Justice
San Jose State University
San Jose, California

Preliminary Remarks

1

Harry E. Allen
Professor Emeritus, Administration of Justice
San Jose State University
San Jose, California

It is sometimes difficult to remember that corrections in general, and community corrections in particular, have been the scenes of wide swings in philosophical focus and emphases. In the early twentieth century, the fledgling notion that offenders could be rehabilitated, changed, and reformed began to creep into correctional practice at both the institutional and community levels. It would be folly to assert that corrections then wholeheartedly embraced either the theory or practice of treatment, as programs were implemented in prisons built for the most part for containment and isolation. Treatment innovations were subject to the absolute necessity of maintaining minimum security staffing, and were sometimes aborted when crowding became critical. Thus one may conclude that treatment efforts were sporadic until the middle of the last century.

In the late 1940s and 1950s, the treatment paradigm gained dominance in juvenile correctional systems and, to a large degree, in adult correctional systems (Bazemore *et al.*, 2000). For almost three decades, correctional practitioners and their philosophical allies in criminology advocated diversion, treatment, rehabilitation, community corrections, and individualized programs designed to address causative factors underlying an offender's unlawful behavior.

In 1972, Robert Martinson, father of the "nothing works" perspective in correctional programming, published his now infamous and largely refuted statement that, with few exceptions, nothing had been proven effective in offender treatment. Coupled with the "just deserts" thrust of von Hirsh (1976), the "nothing works" perspective cast significant doubt on rehabilitation, and also served to legitimize the shift to increased punishment. The resulting mind-set fostered what Clear (1994) labeled the "penal harm" movement that advocated harsh punishment and, at least to some extent, characterized treatment as ineffective and irrelevant. Allen and Simonsen (2001) identify some of the major changes taking place in many states as a result of the derailing of the treatment ideology, including abolition of plea bargaining and parole release, setting minimum sentences, and presumptive sentences.

Politicians seeking office, as well as other politicians, jumped on the "get tough" bandwagon; the media frequently portrayed the public as fed up with predatory criminals and crime. Public attitudes were described (erroneously) as repressive and demanding punishment of offenders, hopefully at the least possible cost. Such attitudes also have contributed to the "punitive paradigm" and sudden adoption of "super-max" prisons (Allen and Simonsen, 2001) and three-strikes legislation (Allen and Abril, 1998; Hostetter, 2000; Meehan, 2000).

Revitalizing Rehabilitation

By the early 1980s, more informed and eloquent criminologists and practitioners initiated arguments against the "nothing works" adherents and position. Treatises by Cullen and Gilbert (1982) and Lipsey (1995) allowed us to take critical looks at correctional philosophy, arguing that there is a growing body of empirical evidence that treatment works and, under some circumstances, yields consistently favorable evidence of effectiveness. Meta-analysis, a tool not available to Martinson, has been used to examine outcomes studies of treatment programs as diverse as electronic monitoring and drug court interventions, and for offender populations as problematic as sex offenders and drunk drivers (Latessa, 2000).

Principles of effective intervention have emerged, primarily from the efforts of Andrews and Bonta (1994) and Gendreau (1996). Briefly, effective correctional practices that have an appreciable effect on recidivism rates can be briefly summarized as the following (Latessa, 2000):

- The risk principle: intervention should target higher risk offenders.

- The need principle: programs need to target criminogenic need factors.

- The responsivity principle: offenders, staff, and programs should be matched.

- The treatment principle: treatment should be behavioral in nature.

First, such principles are far from the "free will and voluntary evil" conceptions of offenders that have been current in the last three decades of contemporary American society. Second, differential sentencing and court disposition are consistent with the principles of effective correctional intervention.

The Twenty-first Century

As the nation entered the current millennium, almost 6 million adults were under correctional control, approximately one in every thirty-four adult Americans. More than half (56 percent) were on probation and 12 percent were on parole. All told, more than two in three were in community corrections. The remaining 31 percent were in institutions (10 percent in jail and 21 percent in prisons).

Altogether, we incarcerate more adult residents in this country than any other major Western society, except the Russian Republic (Allen and Simonsen, 2001). Men are incarcerated at a rate of 1,277 per 100,000 population; the incarceration rate of African-American males is four times that of the Russian Republic (3,250 to 690). One must remember that the Russian Republic was formerly a totalitarian country, and is now struggling toward democratization while mired in upheaval and chaos.

While this is not the venue either to pontificate or prescribe programs that can address crime prevention and crime control, it is constructive to identify six promising programs advocated by correctional observers (Allen and Simonsen, 2001):

- House calls by nurses during prenatal and early childhood years (Olds *et al.*, 1998)

- Treatment for mental health and substance abuse problems of juveniles (Bilchik, 1998)

- Mandatory residential treatment programs for drunk driving offenders (Langworthy and Latessa, 1996)

- Family strengthening interventions (Kumpfer and Alvarado, 1998)

- Mandatory substance abuse prevention programs for adults and prisoners, particularly female inmates (Johnson *et al.*, 2000; Maruschack and Beck, 2001)

- Aggressive and mandatory intervention in domestic violence (Brookoff, 1997)

Conclusions

Staunch defenders of rehabilitation, treatment, and reentry (Travis, 2000; Petersilia, 2000) have amassed evidence of treatment effectiveness and efficacy when treatment is defined as diagnosis, classification, delivery of individualized interventions by competent personnel, case monitoring, and long-term follow-up. The articles in this monograph clearly identify the types of treatment interventions that work effectively with special needs, high-risk, and high-needs offenders. Harm reduction, not "just desserts," is a rational and effective strategy.

The biggest challenge facing corrections in this decade is changing expectations that corrections should not be offender-centered. The authors of this monograph have demonstrated that effective treatment of even the most difficult special needs offenders is possible and will reduce recidivism, furthering our efforts to maximize public safety.

References

Allen, H. E. and J. C. Abril. 1998. Fanning the Flames of Fear Revisited: Three Strikes in California. Paper presented at the annual convention of the American Society of Criminology, Washington, D.C.

Allen, H. E. and C. E. Simonsen. 2001. *Corrections in America*. Upper Saddle River, New Jersey: Prentice Hall.

Andrews, D. A. and J. Bonta. 1994. *The Psychology of Criminal Conduct*. Cincinnati, Ohio: Anderson.

Bazemore, G., R. P. P. Smith, and M. Dooley. 2000. Mobilizing Social Support and Building Relationships: Broadening Correctional and Rehabilitative Agendas. *Corrections Management Quarterly*. 4(4):10-21.

Bilchik, S. 1998. *Mental Health Disorders and Substance Abuse Problems Among Juveniles*. Washington, D.C.: United States Department of Justice.

Brookoff, D. 1997. *Drugs, Alcohol, and Domestic Violence in Memphis*. Washington, D.C.: United States Department of Justice.

Clear, T. 1994. *Harm in American Penology: Offenders, Victims and Their Communities*. Albany, New York: SUNY Press.

Cullen, F. T. and K. Gilbert. 1982. *Reaffirming Rehabilitation*. Cincinnati, Ohio: Anderson.

Gendreau, P. 1996. The Principles of Effective Intervention with Offenders. In A. Harland, ed. *Choosing Correctional Options that Work: Defining the Demand and Evaluating the Supply*. Thousand Oaks, California: Sage.

Hostetter, E. 2000. Three Strikes Against Inmates' Families. *Corrections Now*. 5(3):1-3.

Johnson, S., D. J. Hubbard, and E. J. Latessa. 2000. Drug Courts and Treatment: Lessons to Be Learned from the "What Works" Literature. *Corrections Management Quarterly*. 4(4):70-77.

Johnson, S., D. K. Shaffer, and E. J. Latessa. 2000. A Comparison of Male and Female Drug Court Participants. *Corrections Compendium*. 25(6):1-4, 22.

Kumpfer, K. and R. Alvarado. 1998. *Effective Family Strengthening Interventions*. Washington, D.C.: United States Department of Justice.

Langworthy. R. and F. J. Latessa. 1996. Treatment of Chronic Drunk Drivers. *Journal of Criminal Justice*. 24(3):273-281.

Latessa, E. J. 2000. Incorporating Electronic Monitoring into the Principles of Effective Interventions. *The Journal of Offender Monitoring*. 13(4):5-6.

Lipsey, W. M. 1995. What Do We Learn from 400 Research Studies on Effectiveness of Treatment with Juvenile Delinquents? In J. McGuire, ed. *What Works: Reducing Reoffending,* pp. 48-63. New York: Wiley.

Martinson, R. 1972. What Works: Questions and Answers about Prison Reform. *Public Interest.* 35(1):22-54.

Maruschak, L. M. and A. J. Beck. 2001. *Medical Problems of Inmates,* 1997. Washington, D.C.: United States Department of Justice.

Meehan, K. E. 2000. California's Three Strikes Law: The First Six Years. *Corrections Management Quarterly.* 4(4):22-33.

Olds, D., P. Hill, and E. Rumsey. 1998. *Prenatal and Early Childhood Nurse Home Visitation.* Washington, D.C.: United States Department of Justice.

Petersilia, J. 2000. *When Prisoners Return to the Community: Political, Economic, and Social Consequences.* Washington, D.C.: United States Department of Justice.

Travis, J. 2000. *But They All Come Back: Rethinking Prisoner Reentry.* Washington, D.C.: United States Department of Justice.

von Hirsch, A. 1976. Penal Philosophy: How Much to Punish? In M. Tonry, ed. *Oxford Crime and Justice Handbook,* pp. 237-249. New York: Oxford University Press.

REAFFIRMING REHABILITATION: PUBLIC SUPPORT FOR CORRECTIONAL TREATMENT

2

Francis T. Cullen, Ph.D.
  Distinguished Research Professor,
  Department of Criminal Justice
  University of Cincinnati
  Cincinnati, Ohio

Melissa M. Moon, Ph.D.
  Assistant Professor
  Northern Kentucky University
  Highland Heights, Kentucky

The American public is often portrayed as vengeful and uniformly punitive toward lawbreakers. Although citizens do harbor "get tough" views, their corrections-related attitudes are flexible and complex. Thus, the public supports a range of community alternatives to prison, especially for nonviolent offenders. Most notably, by a substantial majority, Americans continue to believe that rehabilitation is an important goal of corrections. They are most strongly supportive of efforts to reform youthful offenders, and they endorse a range of early intervention programs. In the end, Americans are not rigidly punitive, but rather endorse a correctional policy agenda that is reasonable and balanced—that is, an agenda that seeks to exact justice, protect society, and rehabilitate offenders.

When commentators attack offender treatment, they confidently, if not smugly, make two assertions: rehabilitation does not work, and the public does not advocate it anyway. Taken together, these two criticisms seem to deal a fatal blow to rehabilitation as a guiding principle for what to do with lawbreakers. After all, why pursue a policy that not only is ineffective but also violates the "public will" in a democracy? The problem is, however, that both of these criticisms turn out to be misleading, if not false.

Challenging the "Nothing Works" Doctrine

The idea that "nothing works" to change offenders can be traced back to the classic 1974 article by Robert Martinson. Based on a larger report (Lipton, Martinson, and Wilks, 1975) which ran more than 700 pages and was both more complex and judicious in its conclusions, Martinson distilled this message: "With few and isolated exceptions, the rehabilitative efforts that have been reported thus far have no appreciable effect on recidivism" (1974, p. 25). This boldly pessimistic view appeared incontrovertible. It was based on a systematic analysis of 231 studies published between 1945 and 1967. Who, in the end, could argue with the data?

As it turns out, Martinson's results were not as solid as he imagined. Even so, many scholars embraced his study's conclusions without the level of skepticism that they are trained to bring to research findings, especially those voiced so emphatically. But by the time Martinson was writing, many people—including criminologists—had come to mistrust rehabilitation, which, from the early part of the century until the late 1960s, had been the dominant correctional ideology (Rothman, 1980).

Liberals, with visions of *One Flew Over the Cuckoo's Nest* fresh in their minds, doubted rehabilitation because they believed it was a benevolent idea that had been corrupted to mask the coercive mistreatment of offenders in prison. Conservatives blamed rehabilitation for being too lenient toward offenders—teaching them that crime pays—and thus increasing their willingness and ability to prey on the public. Already harboring such antitreatment sentiments, those on the left and right—normally strange bedfellows—both jumped on Martinson's "nothing works" bandwagon (Allen, 1981; Cullen and Gilbert, 1982).

A few scholars, however, took issue with Martinson's ideas, although their protests were faintly heard amidst the cacophony of cheers accorded the "nothing works" doctrine. Ted Palmer (1975), for example, pointed out that almost half of the studies reviewed by Martinson showed a positive treatment effect on recidivism. Gendreau and Ross (1979) offered "bibliotherapy for cynics" by reviewing study after study finding that rehabilitation interventions could diminish the propensity of offenders to return to crime. A closer look at Martinson's own study reveals more reason for doubt. Of the 231 studies reviewed, only 138 contained outcomes that measured recidivism. Of these, fewer than 80 measured actual treatment programs (the others measured sanctions, such as whether an offender was placed on probation). Further, with only three behavior-modification programs in the data set, Martinson's review contained no treatment category for cognitive-behavioral programs (Cullen and Gendreau, 2000). This omission is noteworthy because research has shown that it is precisely these programs that are most effective in reducing recidivism (Andrews and Bonta, 1998, Gendreau, 1996).

In the quarter century following Martinson's classic work, the research has become even more convincing that rehabilitation does work. Perhaps the most compelling evidence has come from the technique of *meta-analysis*. Typically, scholars had summarized studies and counted how many did or did not reduce recidivism; this "vote-counting" method was the strategy used by Martinson. A meta-analysis, however, computes things differently: across a sample of evaluation studies, it measures the average size of treatment's effect on recidivism (much like taking a player's batting average across all games in which he or she participates). Using this statistical approach, recent studies generally find that correctional rehabilitation programs decrease recidivism an average of 10 percent (Losel, 1995; Redondo, Sanchez-Meca, and Garrido, 1999).

Most significantly, there is considerable variation in the "effect size" of programs. Those interventions that conform to certain "principles of effective treatment" (Gendreau, 1996), such as using cognitive-behavioral programs and focusing on high-risk offenders, achieve reductions of recidivism in excess of 25 percent (Andrews and Bonta, 1998; Cullen and Gendreau, 2000). Correctional programs that emphasize punishing and/or closely supervising offenders have been found to have no effect on—or even to increase—recidivism (for example, Cullen, Wright, and Applegate, 1996; Gendreau, Cullen, and Bonta, 1994; Lipsey and Wilson, 1998; Petersilia and Turner, 1993).

The claim is false, then, that rehabilitation does not work. This does not mean, of course, that all programs reduce recidivism or that implementing effective interventions is an easy task. Still, two conclusions are manifest, if not incontrovertible. First, compared with punitive correctional programs, treatment interventions consistently achieve greater savings in crime, thus serving to protect society in important ways. Second, knowledge and technology now exist to make offenders less criminogenic, including serious, violent lawbreakers (Cullen and Gendreau, 2000; Lipsey and Wilson, 1998). Not to use this knowledge in the service of society is inexcusable.

This brings us to the main focus of this paper: the claim that even if rehabilitation "works," the public—wishing to "get tough" with offenders—will not support it. This assertion, however, is misleading. It is based on misunderstandings of how to measure public opinion and on a selective reading of the existing data. When appropriate methodological techniques are used and the full array of studies are considered, we find that the American public's view toward corrections is far more complex and balanced than is typically characterized. Most noteworthy, people want offenders punished *and* rehabilitated. Below, these issues will be explored in more detail, starting with a brief section on the methodology of assessing public opinion, which will set the stage for a more detailed discussion of what the people in the United States really think should be done with offenders.

Why Opinion Polls Overestimate the Public's Punitiveness

It perhaps is not an exaggeration to say that we have now entered an era of instant, or near instant, public opinion polls. When a newsworthy issue arises—maybe a political controversy or a debate over crime-related policies such as "three-strikes-and-you're-out" laws—a major polling organization, usually working on behalf of a television network or national newspaper, rushes out, conducts a survey, and reports "what the citizens think" about the issue at hand. These polls are useful, as far as they go, but because they are initiated on short notice, they tend to ask respondents only one or two questions about the policy issue in question. In fact, even when these surveys are done with more careful planning, they still tend to try to assess people's attitudes through a restricted number of questions. In part, this is because asking a lengthy roster of complicated questions in a telephone poll would be inordinately expensive.

It would be erroneous to assert that these one- and two-question polls tell us nothing useful about what people think about criminal justice issues, such as whether they support capital punishment or would like the courts to hand out stiffer sentences to "criminals." Even so, the limits of this methodological approach, which are *not* stated when the poll results are reported in the media, are substantial. We therefore must ask this salient question: Is it really possible to assess a person's views with one or two questions?

The answer is that these questions tend to measure *global attitudes*—that is, what people think about an issue, such as punishing offenders, in a general way or as a "first impression." These global attitudes are "real" in the sense that they exist, but they are misleading in that they do not exhaust what respondents would say about a policy issue if the full complexity of their thinking were assessed with a series of questions. These crime-related polls also defy straightforward interpretation because they generally ask about how respondents wish "criminals" to be sanctioned by the law. The difficulty, however, is that the word "criminal" tends to inspire visions of the worst kind of offender. Accordingly, questions that fail to specify which offenders they are asking about will tend to elicit more punitive sentiments because many citizens, as they respond to a poll, will have in mind heinous criminals (Roberts and Stalans, 1997).

Opinion polls suffer another problem: when inquiring what should be done with lawbreakers, they usually ask people to answer questions with "yes" and "no" responses or, at most, furnish only a limited number of sanctioning options (for example "put in prison or on probation"). Again, however, such an approach artificially truncates what respondents might actually believe about an issue by forcing them to select between two answers, neither one of which might capture their true views. The most sophisticated surveys furnish respondents with a variety of choices, for in this way they can more finely calibrate the attitudes people hold. As it turns out, when people can choose from a range of possible penalties, they usually lower their punitiveness. They tend to favor interventions that balance the punishment and control of offenders versus the achievement of other correctional and policy goals (for example, reform offenders, save money by not incarcerating all lawbreakers).

A final concern is that most polls published in the media ask questions only about punishment-oriented policies, such as public support for capital punishment, harsher sanctions, and sending habitual offenders to prison for life. Although more subtle, the problem here is that asking *only about punishment policies* is inherently distorting because it does not assess the other side of the coin: what people think about rehabilitation and about less punitive policies such as community corrections.

To portray public opinion about corrections accurately, it is necessary to move beyond the kinds of polls publicized in the media. Instead, we need to consider research that assesses citizens' attitudes through surveys that: 1) use multiple questions, including carefully constructed scales capable of measuring complex opinions; 2) give respondents multiple sentencing or policy options when they are queried about how they would like to penalize lawbreakers; and 3) ask questions that cover the full range of possible views on corrections, including both punishment and rehabilitation. When research meeting these standards is examined, we arrive at a more balanced portrait of what Americans wish the correctional system to accomplish (for example, Cullen, Fisher, and Applegate, 2000; Flanagan and Longmire, 1996; Roberts and Stalans, 1997; Sundt, 1999).

Five Conclusions about Public Opinion on Corrections

In recent years, research on public opinion about punishment and correctional policies has grown considerably (for summaries, *see* Cullen et al., 2000; Roberts and Stalans, 1997; Sundt, 1999). Although many questions remain to be answered, it is now possible to paint a reasonably clear portrait of what Americans think should be done with lawbreakers. The existing research can be organized around five main conclusions.

1. The American Public Is Punitive Toward Crime

Numerous investigations reveal that in the United States, there is a large reservoir of punitive sentiments toward offenders (Scheingold, 1984). Polls on capital punishment, for example, show that throughout the 1990s, between 70 and 80 percent of Americans favored the death penalty for convicted murderers (Cullen et al., 2000; Moore, 1995). Similarly, when asked if they believe that courts in their community "deal harshly enough with criminals," about 80 percent of respondents in poll after poll answered "not harshly enough" (Maguire and Pastore, 1998; Smith, 1998).

Most instructive, it appears—as Warr (1995, p. 23) notes—that "Americans overwhelmingly regard imprisonment as the appropriate form of punishment for most crimes." The 1987 National Punishment Study lends support to this conclusion. Respondents were given vignettes describing an offender, victim, and the nature of the crime committed. They were then asked what sentence they would like to prescribe—much as a judge would do in a courtroom. There were 24 crimes rated, which were presented in nearly 10,000 different vignettes (each vignette was different because it reflected unique combinations of offender, victim, and crime characteristics). Across the vignettes rated, the respondents favored a prison or jail sentence in 71 percent of the cases, with an average sentence of eleven years (Jacoby and Cullen, 1998; Jacoby and Dunn, 1987). A more recent national study employing the vignette methodology reports similar conclusions, with the public "quick to sentence the defendants to prison" (Rossi, Berk, and Campbell, 1997, p. 277; Rossi and Berk, 1997).

2. Public Punitiveness toward Crime is "Mushy"

Additional polls could have been cited above to substantiate the point that Americans believe that lawbreakers should be subjected to harsh punishment. These sentiments are real and likely influence the willingness of citizens to vote for initiatives—such as "three-strikes-and-you're-out" laws—in referendums. Few politicians, it seems, lose elections by promising to "get tough on crime," and there is no mass movement among the public to curtail the coerciveness and inhumanity of the prison system.

These observations are important because at times critics make the mistake of trying to suggest that the punitiveness found in polls does not capture the "real" opinion of the public. Again, we have been critical of the conclusion that the public is *exclusively* punitive in their crime-related sentiments, arguing—like other critics—that faulty methodology obscures the true complexity of what the public thinks should be done with offenders. Still, the surveys that uncover harsh views and support for locking up criminals are not spurious but are measuring beliefs that people harbor. The key issue, however, is that these beliefs are not fixed or rigid but flexible or "mushy" (Durham, 1993).

By "mushy" we mean that public opinion is best viewed as not being locked on a fixed value but rather as operating within a *range* of attitudes. The views that people express thus may vary depending on what factors they are asked to consider and what choices they are given through which to express their opinion. As noted above in the section on methodological considerations, oftentimes the views Americans express become less punitive when they are asked not to answer simple questions but to deliberate about questions that are constructed to approximate real-life policy decisions.

This point—and the "mushiness" of public opinion—can be illustrated through three examples that relate to current policy issues. First, consider the finding that more than seven in ten Americans support the death penalty. This figure is so high and stable (not having changed much in about two decades) that it seems absurd to suggest that the public is not firmly behind the execution of murderers. Even here, however, the support for this punishment option is "mushy" or contingent on what choices people are given. Research is now fairly convincing in showing that when people are not simply asked whether they support the death penalty, but whether they support executing offenders versus giving them life in prison without parole, support for capital punishment falls to about half of those surveyed. When the option is life without parole plus having the offender work to pay restitution to the victim's family, more people select this option than favor the death penalty (Bowers, Vandiver, and Dugan, 1994; McGarrell and Sandys, 1996; Moon, Wright, Cullen, and Pealer, 1999).

A second example comes from research on "three-strikes" laws that mandate life in prison for offenders convicted of a third felony. Polls find more than 70 percent of the public favors this policy when asked if they support "life sentences without parole for criminals with three violent crimes" ("Dick Tracy Wins," 1994, p. A14; Cullen et al., 2000). But do such "global" or first-impression views hold up when people are asked what sentences they wish to hand out in real-life cases that involve real-life people?

To test this issue, Applegate, Cullen, Turner, and Sundt (1996) asked a 1995 sample of Cincinnati residents if they supported passing a "three-strikes" law in Ohio; 88 percent stated they either "strongly" or "somewhat" endorsed this policy. The same sample members, however, were also asked what sentence they would give to an offender described in a vignette who would qualify for a life sentence under the "three-strikes" law being considered in Ohio. Notably, across the vignettes, only 16.9 percent of the sample assigned these "three-strikes" eligible offenders a life sentence. These findings suggest that the public may support a "three-strikes" law in the abstract—perhaps reflecting an underlying view that repeat offenders should not cavalierly be placed on the streets—but that their global views do not translate into the belief that specific offenders should actually be locked away forever.

Third, on the surface, it seems indisputable that Americans want offenders sent to prison. But, again, how firm is that support? Some shakiness in support for the policy of imprisonment may come from the public's belief that prisons are "schools of crime." In an Iowa survey, for example, 60 percent of the respondents stated that the "majority of inmates" would be "more dangerous" when they were released from prison; less than one in ten said "less dangerous," with the remaining sample members answering "don't know" (Doble Research Associates, 1997). Most instructive, however, is research on "intermediate sanctions" and, more generally, on community alternatives to prison. To be sure, citizens do not favor the use of "regular probation," perhaps because they see it as a penalty that is overly lenient and exposes the public to the risk of victimization. They also are reluctant to use community corrections as an option for violent criminals. Nonetheless, there is a growing body of research that shows Americans endorse punishing a range of offenders with intermediate sanctions such as restitution programs, community service, boot camps, intensive supervision probation, and home confinement/electronic monitoring (for a summary, *see* Cullen et al., 2000). Furthermore, there is evidence that although Americans often "prefer" prison as a penalty, they will "accept" community corrections as an alternative—again, so long as it is not simply a sentence of probation (Turner, Cullen, Sundt, and Applegate, 1997). Finally, there is evidence that citizens also support the concept of "restorative justice" in which offenders would remain in the community and work to repair the harm they have done to victims and to the larger community (Doble Research Associates, 1994; Cullen et al., 2000).

3. Public Support for Rehabilitation Is Strong

A number of commentators have observed that Americans harbor punitive attitudes toward offenders and that recent crime policy in the United States is consistent with these views (for example, prison and jail populations approaching two million, calls to make prison life more painful, the reintroduction of chain gangs, and more attempts to control and closely watch offenders in the community). One writer in *The Wall Street Journal* asserts that "public opinion, in its attitude toward crime, is overwhelmingly repressive; 'ordinary people' do not want to reform offenders but instead 'want them punished, as severely and cheaply as possible . . . They favor punishment that is deterrent and retributive'" (Johnson, 1994, p. A10).

As noted, however, this conclusion is misleading. There is now a large body of research revealing that although citizens may be punitive, *they also want the correctional system to rehabilitate offenders* (for example, Cullen et al., 2000; McCorkle, 1993; Sundt, 1999; Thomson and Ragona, 1987).

We can point to three types of surveys that reinforce this contention. First, there has been considerable research conducted on what the public believes should be the "goals of imprisonment." In a 1996 statewide survey in Ohio, respondents were asked what should be the "main emphasis of prisons." Among the options provided, 41.1 percent chose "trying to rehabilitate the individual so that he might become a productive citizen" versus 31.9 percent for "protecting society from future crimes he might commit," 20.3 percent for "punishing the individual convicted of a crime," and 6.7 percent for "not sure" (Applegate, Cullen, and Fisher, 1997). One might argue that taken together, the respondents selecting the two punitive options (protect society and punishment) exceeded the percentage selecting the rehabilitation option. Still, at the very least, four in ten Ohioans endorsed offender treatment as the main purpose of corrections. The picture becomes even more complete when we look at how "important" the respondents believed each prison goal to be (as rated individually). In this case, more than eight in ten Ohio respondents rated rehabilitation as either "very important" (45.1 percent) or "important" (37.3 percent). With these results in mind, it is difficult to suggest that Americans reject offender treatment as an integral goal of the correctional enterprise.

Second, studies have presented survey respondents with a number of statements about various aspects of rehabilitation and then have asked the extent to which they agreed or disagreed with these statements (typically using a six-point Likert scale ranging from "strongly agree" to "strongly disagree"). The results from the Ohio study of Applegate et al. (1997) are illustrative of the sentiments Americans display. More than eight in ten members of the sample agreed that it is important to rehabilitate adults who have committed crimes and are now in the correctional system and felt that it was important to provide treatment for offenders who are in prison and who are supervised by the courts and live in the community. Even when asked about providing treatment services "for offenders who have been involved in a lot of crime in their lives," a majority of the sample—54.2 percent—favored placing these chronic lawbreakers into rehabilitation programs. There is, we must note, some evidence that the public is less supportive of treatment for "violent" offenders (Cullen, Skovron, Scott, and Burton, 1990; Sundt, Cullen, Applegate, and Turner, 1998). More research is needed, however, to determine if these views are first impressions, and therefore would change if respondents were informed of the successful interventions being undertaken with serious and violent criminals (Henggeler, 1997; Lipsey and Wilson, 1998).

Third, research also has explored whether citizens will favor rehabilitation when asked what should be done with offenders described in vignettes. Might support for treatment decline when people are asked not about their global views about rehabilitation but to assess vignettes that more closely approximate real-life cases? As it turns out, this is not the case (McCorkle, 1993). Applegate et al.'s (1997) Ohio research reports that in rating vignettes, high percentages of the respondents supported "the use of rehabilitation" and believed that "it was right to put people [like the offender] in programs that try to cure the particular problem that caused them to break the law."

In summary, the research convincingly shows that regardless of the survey method employed—polls about the goals of prisons, studies using detailed scales consisting of statements assessing various dimensions of rehabilitation, or vignettes describing real-life cases—the American public firmly endorses the correctional system making efforts to reform its wayward population. This finding is important because it means that the strong support for offender treatment cannot be attributed to some methodological artifact but rather, reflects empirical reality.

The public may believe that the state should force offenders to pay for their crimes and should place violent offenders safely behind bars, but they also recognize the utility, if not the morality, of the correctional system making offenders less criminogenic and more likely to be productive citizens. There is a realization, we suspect, both that lawbreakers will eventually return to society and that rehabilitation is one of the few tools at the state's disposal to make these offenders less dangerous, thus helping to protect the commonweal of the community.

4. The Public Especially Supports Juvenile Rehabilitation

In the early 1990s, with juvenile violence rising rapidly, it became common to speak of an epidemic of youthful crime being perpetrated by "super-predators" (Dilulio, 1995). With some justification, calls were made to consider incarcerating chronically dangerous youngsters. Polls appeared showing that a majority of Americans believed that such youthful violent predators, as well as serious property criminals, should be punished the same as adult offenders (Maguire and Pastore, 1995; Triplett, 1996). Again, however, reading only these polls would leave a misleading impression of what Americans wish the correctional system to accomplish with juvenile delinquents. The research is unmistakable that they also want the system to make a concerted effort to rehabilitate wayward youths. Moreover, support for treating youths invariably is found to be even higher than the considerable support the public shows for treating adults (for example, Cullen, Golden, and Cullen, 1983; Gerber and Engelhardt-Greer, 1996; Moon, Sundt, Cullen, and Wright, 2000; Steinhart, 1988).

Several studies illustrate citizens' firm endorsement for "saving children" from a life in crime. In a 1995 study conducted in Cincinnati, for example, Sundt et al. (1998) discovered that more than eight in ten residents believed that the rehabilitation of juveniles was either "very helpful" or "helpful." In the Applegate et al. (1997, p. 247) statewide study of Ohioans, more than 95 percent agreed that "it is important to try to rehabilitate juveniles who have committed crimes and are now in the correctional system." Similarly, in a 1998 survey in Tennessee, almost two in three respondents expressed the belief that rehabilitation should be the "main emphasis of juvenile prisons."

Moreover, virtually all of the respondents—94.5 percent—answered that rehabilitation as the purpose of juvenile imprisonment was "very important" (64.5 percent) or "important" (30 percent). About the same percentage agreed that it was important to treat youthful offenders whether they were in the community or in prison. Three-fourths concurred that "rehabilitation programs should be available even for juveniles who have been involved in a lot of crime in their lives" (Moon et al., 2000, pp. 46-48).

We should note as well that support for a range of early intervention programs aimed at "nipping juvenile crime in the bud" or targeting "at-risk youths for help" are immensely popular with the American public—including, for example, preschool programs, training parents in how to raise their children more effectively, programs to help dysfunctional families, attempts to identify and treat troubled youth early in life, and the implementation of after-school programs (Cullen, Wright, Brown, Moon, Blankenship, and Applegate, 1998). Most instructive, research shows that when asked to choose between spending tax dollars on either early intervention programs or incarcerating more offenders, more than seven in ten Americans favor the early intervention option (Cullen et al., 1998; Fairbank, Maslin, Maullin and Associates, 1997).

5. The Public Wants the Correctional System to Act Responsibly

How can we make sense of all the polling and research data about what the American public wishes the correctional system to accomplish?

Answering this question requires some degree of modesty because a truly definitive study of the varied dimensions of such public views remains to be undertaken. Still, by weaving together various strands of information drawn from an array of surveys, we are safe in conveying the central hope, if not expectation, that citizens have of correctional interventions: they want the system to act *responsibly* in the sanctioning of offenders.

This rather broad conclusion can, of course, be taken to mean many things, but we believe that it involves five main components. First, citizens are opposed to "lenient" sentences—if by this we mean that offenders are merely placed on probation "supervision" that does little to inconvenience their lives or to protect the public. Phrased differently, they want some type of intervention with offenders that is well thought out. Second, the public is "risk averse;" they do not want dangerous offenders walking the streets. They understand that prisons may be "schools of crime," but the immediate and almost certain threat posed by these offenders supercedes the future and potential threat these offenders *may* pose *if they ever get out of prison*. Third, most Americans see prison as a preferred punishment for most criminal offenses, but they also are open to—and sometimes outright in favor of—community sanctions for many offenders who are not seriously violent.

Fourth, and most important for our purposes, Americans clearly favor offenders using their time in the correctional system *productively*. This sentiment is why "warehousing criminals" makes so little sense to them. Restorative justice is popular, we suspect, precisely for this reason: it moves beyond the philosophy of simply "getting tough" with offenders, and explores how the correctional sanction can be put to good use by rectifying the harm that offenders have caused victims, the community, and themselves.

Rehabilitation has the same appeal: it furnishes the opportunity to, in essence, save a life by redirecting offenders from a hopeless life in crime to a life in which they stay out of trouble and perhaps contribute to society in positive way (Nagin, 2000). For juveniles, the stakes are particularly high because so much of their lives lie ahead—undoubtedly an important reason why the public is especially willing to attempt to transform them from lawbreakers into law-abiding citizens. At the very least, rehabilitation promises to enhance public safety by increasing the chances that offenders will leave prison or community supervision being less likely, rather than more likely, to victimize others.

Fifth and finally, it is time to realize that the public has high expectations for the correctional system. Citizens want corrections to accomplish multiple goals. Their collective "will" might be summarized in this way: Offenders harm others—hurt them, take their property, and so on—and thus deserve to be punished. These offenders also may pose an immediate threat to their fellow citizens and thus need to be controlled, either in prison or by strict measures in the community. But offenders also have a life ahead of them in which they can continue to be a burden on society or, alternatively, to contribute to the commonwealth of society. Rehabilitation offers the prospect of returning offenders to their communities as less criminogenic and perhaps even as good citizens. Thus, to not undertake treatment of offenders is a risky, if not unreasonable, policy.

Reaffirming Rehabilitation

Initially, this essay noted two objections to retaining rehabilitation as an integral goal of corrections: it does not work, and the public will not support it. As we have endeavored to document, both of these objections are questionable, if not incorrect. Researchers have done the important service of demonstrating that treatment interventions can substantially reduce recidivism, especially among high-risk, serious offenders. They also have shown that allocating resources to deterrence- or punishment-oriented correctional programs is ill-advised if one's goal is to reduce crime. Further, as we have reviewed, the public is in no way opposed to concerted efforts to involve offenders in treatment programs. Polls which suggest that Americans are *exclusively* punitive are mistaken. The public is too reasonable to hold such a narrow view. They recognize that by *reaffirming rehabilitation*, the correctional system has the potential to improve the lives of offenders and to make society safer.

Again, much work needs to be done to make rehabilitation an effective correctional policy. As noted, research does not state that all treatment interventions are equally effective. There is now an increasing body of knowledge identifying the principles of effective intervention (Andrews and Bonta, 1998; Gendreau, 1996). To build public trust and to deepen support for rehabilitation, it will be incumbent on correctional policymakers and practitioners to use the existing knowledge to develop and sustain the most effective interventions possible. If this challenge is taken seriously, then a new era of corrections is not beyond reach—an era in which the limits of punishment will be more clearly appreciated and the possibilities of rehabilitation more clearly realized.

References

Allen, F. A. 1981. *The Decline of the Rehabilitative Ideal: Penal Policy and Social Purpose*. New Haven, Connecticut: Yale University Press.

Andrews, D. A., and J. Bonta. 1998. *The Psychology of Criminal Conduct*, 2nd edition. Cincinnati, Ohio: Anderson.

Applegate, B. K., F. T. Cullen, and B. S. Fisher. 1997. Public Support for Correctional Treatment: The Continuing Appeal of the Rehabilitative Ideal. *Prison Journal*. 77:237-258.

Applegate, B. K., F. T. Cullen, M. G. Turner, and J. L. Sundt. 1996. Assessing Public Support for Three-strikes-and-you're-out Laws: Global Versus Specific Attitudes. *Crime and Delinquency*. 42:517-534.

Bowers, W. J., M. Vandiver, and P. H. Dugan. 1994. A New Look at Public Opinion on Capital Punishment: What Citizens and Legislators Prefer. *American Journal of Criminal Law*. 22:77-150.

Cullen, F. T., B. S. Fisher, and B. K. Applegate. 2000. Public Opinion about Punishment and Corrections. In M. Tonry, ed. *Crime and Justice: A Review of Research*. Vol. 27:1-79. Chicago, Illinois: University of Chicago Press.

Cullen, F. T. and P. Gendreau. 2000. Assessing Correctional Rehabilitation: Policy, Practice, and Prospects. In J. Horney, ed. *Criminal Justice 2000, Vol. 3: Policies, Processes, and Decisions of the Criminal Justice System*, pp. 109-175. Washington, D.C.: U. S. Department of Justice, National Institute of Justice.

Cullen, F. T. and K. E. Gilbert. 1982. *Reaffirming Rehabilitation*. Cincinnati, Ohio: Anderson.

Cullen, F. T., K. M. Golden, and J. B. Cullen. 1983. Is Child Saving Dead? Attitudes toward Juvenile Rehabilitation in Illinois. *Journal of Criminal Justice*. 11:1-13.

Cullen, F. T., S. E. Skovron, J. E. Scott, and V. B. Burton, Jr. 1990. Public Support for Correctional Treatment: The Tenacity of Rehabilitative Ideology. *Criminal Justice and Behavior*. 17:6-18.

Cullen, F. T., J. P. Wright, and B. K. Applegate. 1996. Control in the Community: The Limits of Reform? In A. T. Harland, ed. *Choosing Correctional Options that Work: Defining the Demand and Evaluating the Supply*, pp. 69-116. Thousand Oaks, California: Sage.

Cullen, F. T., J. P. Wright, S. Brown, M. M. Moon, M. B. Blankenship, and B. K. Applegate. 1998. Public Support for Early Intervention Programs: Implications for a Progressive Policy Agenda. *Crime and Delinquency*. 44:187-204.

Dick Tracy Wins. 1994. *Wall Street Journal*. A14, January 26.

Dilulio, J. J. 1995, November 27. The Coming of the Super-predators. *Weekly Standard*. 23-28.

Doble Research Associates. 1994. *Crime and Corrections: The Views of the People of Vermont*. Englewood Cliffs, New Jersey: Doble Research Associates.

————. 1997. *Crime and Corrections in Iowa: The Views of 451 Participants in a Series of Statewide Forums*. Englewood Cliffs, New Jersey: Doble Research Associates.

Durham, A. M. 1993. Public Opinion Regarding Sentences for Crime: Does it Exist? *Journal of Criminal Justice*. 21:1-11.

Fairbank, Maslin, Maullin and Associates. 1997. *Resources for Youth California Survey*. Santa Monica, California: Fairbank, Maslin, Maullin and Associates.

Flanagan, T. J. and D. R. Longmire, eds. 1996. *Americans View Crime and Justice: A National Public Opinion Survey*. Thousand Oaks, California: Sage.

Gendreau, P. 1996. The Principles of Effective Intervention with Offenders. In A. T. Harland, ed. *Choosing Correctional Interventions that Work: Defining the Demand and Evaluating the Supply*, pp. 117-130. Thousand Oaks, California: Sage.

Gendreau, P., F. T. Cullen, and J. Bonta. 1994, March. Intensive Rehabilitation Supervision: The Next Generation in Community Corrections? *Federal Probation*. 58:72-78.

Gendreau, P. and B. Ross. 1979. Effective Correctional Treatment: Bibliotherapy for Cynics. *Crime and Delinquency*. 25:463-489.

Gerber, J. and S. Engelhardt-Greer. 1996. Just and Painful: Attitudes toward Sentencing Criminals. In T. J. Flanagan and D. R. Longmire, eds. *Americans View Crime and Justice: A National Public Opinion Survey*, pp. 62-74. Thousand Oaks, California: Sage.

Henggeler, S. W. 1997. *Treating Serious Anti-social Behavior in Youth: The MST Approach*. Washington, D.C.: United States Department of Justice, Office of Juvenile Justice and Delinquency Prevention.

Jacoby, J. E. and F. T. Cullen. 1998. The Structure of Punishment Norms: Applying the Rossi-Berk Model. *Journal of Criminal Law and Criminology*. 89:245-312.

Jacoby, J. E. and C. S. Dunn. 1987, November. National Survey on Punishment for Criminal Offenses: Executive Summary. Paper presented at the National Conference on Punishment for Criminal Offenses, Ann Arbor, Michigan.

Johnson, P. 1994. Crime: The People Want Revenge. *Wall Street Journal.* A10, January 4.

Lipsey, M. W. and D. B. Wilson. 1998. Effective Intervention with Serious Juvenile Offenders: A Synthesis of Research. In R. Loeber and D. P. Farrington, eds. *Serious and Violent Juvenile Offenders: Risk Factors and Successful Interventions*, pp. 313-345. Thousand Oaks, California: Sage.

Lipton, D., R. Martinson, and J. Wilks. 1975. *The Effectiveness of Correctional Treatment: A Survey of Treatment Evaluation Studies.* New York: Praeger.

Losel, F. 1995. The Efficacy of Correctional Treatment: A Review and Synthesis of Meta evaluations. In J. McGuire, ed. *What Works: Reducing Reoffending*, pp. 79-111. West Sussex, United Kingdon: John Wiley.

Maguire, K. and A. L. Pastore, eds. 1995. *Sourcebook of Criminal Justice Statistics 1994.* Washington, D.C.: U.S. Department of Justice, Bureau of Justice Statistics.

Maguire, K. and A. L. Pastore, eds. 1998. *Sourcebook of Criminal Justice Statistics 1997.* Washington, D.C.: U.S. Department of Justice, Bureau of Justice Statistics.

Martinson, R. 1974. What Works? Questions and Answers about Prison Reform. *The Public Interest.* 35:22-54.

McCorkle, R. C. 1993. Research Note: Punish and Rehabilitate? Public Attitudes toward Six Common Crimes. *Crime and Delinquency.* 39:240-252.

McGarrell, E. F. and M. Sandys. 1996. The Misperception of Public Opinion toward Capital Punishment. *American Behavioral Scientist.* 39:500-513.

Moon, M. M., J. L. Sundt, F. T. Cullen, and J. P. Wright. 2000. Is Child Saving Dead? Public Support for Juvenile Rehabilitation. *Crime and Delinquency.* 46:38-60.

Moon, M. M., J. P. Wright, F. T. Cullen, and J. A. Pealer. 1999, March. Putting Kids to Death: Specifying Public Support for Juvenile Capital Punishment. Paper presented at the meeting of the Academy of Criminal Justice Sciences, Orlando, Florida.

Moore, D. W. 1995, June. Americans Firmly Support Death Penalty. *Gallup Poll Monthly.* 357:23-25.

Nagin, D. 2000. Measuring the Economic Benefits of Developmental Prevention Programs. Unpublished manuscript. Carnegie Mellon University.

Palmer, T. 1975. Martinson Revisited. *Journal of Research in Crime and Delinquency.* 12:133-152.

Petersilia, J. and S. Turner. 1993. Intensive Probation and Parole. In M. Tonry, ed. *Crime and Justice: A Review of Research.* Chicago, Illinois: University of Chicago Press.

Redondo, S., J. Sanchez-Meca, and V. Garrido. 1999. The Influence of Treatment Programmes on the Recidivism of Juvenile and Adult Offenders: A European Meta-analytic Review. *Psychology, Crime and Law.* 5:251-278.

Roberts, J. V. and L. J. Stalans. 1997. *Public Opinion, Crime, and Criminal Justice.* Boulder, Colorado: Westview.

Rossi, P. H. and R. A. Berk. 1997. *Just Punishments: Federal Guidelines and Public Views Compared.* New York: de Gruyter.

Rossi, P. H., R. A. Berk, and A. Campbell. 1997. Just Punishments: Guideline Sentences and Normative Consensus. *Journal of Quantitative Criminology.* 13:267-290.

Rothman, D. J. 1980. *Conscience and Convenience: The Asylum and its Alternatives in Progressive America.* Boston, Massachusetts: Little, Brown.

Scheingold, S. A. 1984. *The Politics of Law and Order: Street Crime and Public Policy.* New York: Longman.

Smith, T. W. 1998, August. Trendlets: B. Crime and Punishment: An Update. *GSS News.* 12:5.

Steinhart, D. 1988. *Californian Opinion Poll: Public Attitudes on Youth Crime.* San Francisco, California: National Council on Crime and Delinquency.

Sundt, J. L. 1999. Is There Room for Change? A Review of Public Attitudes toward Crime Control and Alternatives to Incarceration. *Southern Illinois University Law Journal.* 23:519-537.

Sundt, J. L., F. T. Cullen, B. K. Applegate, and M. G. Turner. 1998. The Tenacity of the Rehabilitative Ideal Revisited: Have Attitudes Toward Rehabilitation Changed? *Criminal Justice and Behavior.* 25:426-442.

Thomson, D. R. and A. J. Ragona. 1987. Popular Moderation Versus Governmental Authoritarianism: An Interactionist View of Public Sentiments toward Criminal Sanctions. *Crime and Delinquency.* 33:337-357.

Triplett, R. 1996. The Growing Threat: Gangs and Juvenile Offenders. In T. J. Flanagan and D. R. Longmire, eds. *Americans View Crime and Justice: A National Public Opinion Survey*, pp. 137-150. Thousand Oaks, California: Sage.

Turner, M. G., F. T. Cullen, J. L. Sundt, and B. K. Applegate. 1997. Public Tolerance for Community-based Sanctions. *Prison Journal.* 77:6-26.

Warr, M. 1995. Public Perceptions of Crime and Punishment. In J. F. Sheley, ed. *Criminology: A Contemporary Handbook*, 2nd edition, pp. 14-30. Belmont, California: Wadsworth.

WHAT WORKS: EFFECTIVE DWI INTERVENTIONS

3

David S. Timken, Ph.D.
President and Senior Research Scientist
Timken and Associates
Boulder, Colorado

Introduction

Alcohol dependence and alcoholism have become serious health issues in the past twenty years. The latest edition of the *Diagnostic and Statistical Manual (DSM-IVTR)* (American Psychiatric Association) has expanded the number of pages dedicated to alcohol use and abuse, and there is a proliferation of books, articles, and even radio and television shows on the subject of alcoholism and treatment. Most would agree that the best approach for dealing with problem drinking is through treatment.

Driving while intoxicated (DWI), however, is not a disease but a violation of the criminal code and, as such, drunk driving is a crime and dealt with under the auspices of the criminal justice system. The criminal justice system is primarily designed to hold offenders accountable for their actions through punishment (jail, fines, and so forth) and sanctions (suspension/denial of driving privileges, and other options). The dual goals of rehabilitation and treatment then can be introduced into the treatment model. The early attempts at intervention with drunk driving focused solely on punishment, with deterrence as the only goal.

To better understand the current problems, the following sections will be offered: an overview of the DWI problem; background information specifically related to education and treatment for alcohol and other drug traffic offenders; a discussion of problem areas including staff, offender evaluation, education programs, and treatment approaches; research-based effective approaches in the aforementioned areas; and conclusions including recommendations for future research.

Background

Traffic accidents remain among the leading causes of death among the population aged one to forty-four (Peters et al., 1998). The figures for 1997 indicate that 38.7 percent of those fatalities (41,967 people) occurred in alcohol-involved crashes. This percentage has held constant over the past three years. The figures further show that an additional 10 percent of all those injured in traffic accidents (327,000 people) were injured in alcohol-related crashes. Some 78.5 percent of those drivers fatally injured had a Blood Alcohol Concentration (BAC) of > .10. This is high enough to qualify as legally intoxicated in forty-eight states. The other two states have not set a legal limit (National Highway Traffic Safety Administration, 1998). A disproportionate number of those drivers fatally injured had prior DWI convictions (Fell, 1994). These studies have made it clear that license suspension and other sanctions typically applied to DWI offenders did not adequately reduce drinking and driving behavior. A 1996 a study by Kennedy et al. found that drivers in as many as 25 percent of alcohol-involved fatal crashes were driving while their license was suspended or denied. An informal study places that at nearer to 54 percent.

The risk of arrest for drinking and driving is relatively low. An estimated 46.5 million people drove after drinking in 1996 (Townsend et al., 1998), and many of these individuals drove more than once during the year. The arrest records indicate that only 1.4 million DWI arrests were made in 1995. The odds of being arrested for each incident of drinking and driving have been estimated at anywhere from 1 in 82 (Liu et al., 1997) to 1 in 2000 (Anda et al., 1986; Maull et al., 1984). Recent figures place this at approximately 1 in 1,100 (Transportation Research Board, 1995).

Over the past few years, several large-scale studies have characterized the drinking-driver population using self-report, traffic fatality reports, driving records, and blood alcohol concentrations collected both at the crash site and in random roadside sobriety checkpoints. Several generalizations can be drawn from this research. The demographic factors most commonly associated with drinking and driving are gender, age, and race or ethnicity. White men in their twenties and early thirties are responsible for the greatest number of accidents from drinking and driving. In 1997, persons aged twenty-one to twenty-four had the highest arrest rates (1,695 per 100,000) while those over sixty-five had the lowest arrest rates (78 per 100,000). It does appear though, that non-white and non-Asian subgroups are overrepresented among drinking drivers (Jones and Lacey, 1998; Liu et al., 1997; Lund and Wolf, 1991; Townsend et al., 1998). Also overrepresented among drinking drivers are those who are single, unemployed, those having no college degree, and those with personalities characterized by verbal hostility, assaultiveness, impulsivity, and sensation seeking (Jones and Lacey, 1998; Lund and Wolf, 1991; Wilson, 1992).

Often, DWI offenders are distinguished from the wider population of drivers by several identifying characteristics. Such offenders are more likely to acknowledge driving aggressively and competitively than are comparative groups of drivers (Donovan et al., 1985). A survey of DWI offenders' driving records shows more prior accidents and tickets than nondrinking drivers (Jonah and Wilson, 1986). Therefore, it is not surprising that a large proportion of DWI offenders have criminal records. In 1985, a study of Massachusetts DWI offenders (Argeriou et al., 1986) found that more than half of a random sample had prior criminal records for offenses other than DWI and, among repeat DWI offenders, that number grew to more than two-thirds. Using the INSLAW scale of criminal careers to rate the criminal records of a random sample of males in Louisiana, Gould and Gould (1992) found that 4.3 percent of first-time DWI offenders scored within the "career criminal" range, while 30 percent of the multiple DWI cases scored in this range. It would seem that a "criminal career" might be stopped in its tracks if successful intervention could take place early.

Drinking behavior is one of the best predictors of drinking and driving incidents (Gruenewald et al., 1996; Wilson, 1984). In 1997, Liu et al. estimated that on an average, adults in the United States acknowledge driving while intoxicated about 0.65 times per year. Binge drinkers (those who drank five or more drinks on at least one occasion in the last thirty days) commit nearly six times that number of drinking/driving incidents, and those who report drinking two or more drinks per day appear responsible for more than ten times as many drinking/driving incidents (Liu et al., 1997).

There is a strong association between drinking drivers and binge drinkers, and it is not surprising that some estimates suggest that 30 to 50 percent of DWI offenders could be classified as alcoholic (Vingilis, 1983). These numbers may not reflect the depth of the problem because seldom have such estimates been made for representative samples of offenders, using clinically valid procedures for assessing alcohol dependence or abuse (Beirness and Simpson, 1997).

One reasonably strong study done in New York (Nochajski et al., 1994) reported that 28 percent of first-time DWI arrests and 45 percent of repeat DWI arrests were found by clinical assessment to meet DSM-III criteria for alcohol dependence disorders. Recent Colorado data (Colorado Department of Human Services, Alcohol and Drug Abuse Division, 1997-1998) show that, at a maximum, only 20 percent of alcohol and other drug traffic offenders could be classified as social or nonproblem drinkers. Even studied alone, a history of multiple DWI arrests seems to be evidence enough of a serious drinking problem.

A single DWI arrest puts an offender at a significantly higher risk for additional offenses, arrests, and convictions. Therefore, a large percentage of DWI arrests are individuals with prior DWI arrests and convictions. Recent studies have found that approximately 35 percent of all DWI convictions are for drivers with DWI convictions in the previous five years (Peck et al., 1993; Fell, 1994; Yu and Williford, 1991). Donovan et al. (1990) examined the driving records of 39,000 Washington state drivers, and found that in a three-year follow-up period, 27.8 percent of the drivers with prior DWI offenses were rearrested for the same offense. Put another way, when compared with drivers with no recent DWI convictions, drivers with prior offenses were almost fourteen times more likely to be rearrested for DWI within three years. Many more DWI offenders continue to drink and drive without being caught. This problem is often discussed during semistructured interviews after arrest, and 54 percent of those questioned acknowledged continuing to drink and drive, often with a suspended license (Donovan et al., 1990).

In addition to the risk of arrest, DWI offenders are at a highly increased risk of being in an alcohol-related crash. A North Carolina study (Brewer et al., 1994) reported on all driver fatalities between 1980 and 1989. The study compared drivers with BACs of > .20 (he called them "the intoxicated drivers") with drivers with BACs of < .20 (called "the less intoxicated drivers"). In the BAC > .20 group, 26 percent had prior DWI offenses in the past five years, compared with only 3.1 percent of the drivers with BACs of < .20. They also found that the BACs of the intoxicated group tended to be higher for those with more previous arrests. This suggests that there is a subset of drivers that is at increased risk for DWI arrests, as well as alcohol-involved crashes. These are the drivers who cause the greatest concern.

The demographics associated with DWI recidivism are similar to those for drinking and driving. Age, gender, ethnicity, and years of education are all important, but actually explain only a small part of the problem. The number of prior DWI arrests/convictions and the severity of the alcohol problems have consistently been shown to be among the most powerful predictors of DWI recidivism (Beerman et al., 1988; Donovan et al., 1990; National Highway Traffic Safety Administration/ National Institute on Alcohol Abuse and Alcoholism, 1996; Peck, 1991). A typological analysis (Peck et al., 1993) showed that prior driving record (which included accidents, traffic convictions, and DWI offenses during a five-to-seven year period) and the severity of the alcohol problem accounted for the greatest risk of subsequent DWI recidivism.

Carefully administered and monitored studies of the effects of rehabilitation on the recidivism risks of DWI offenders began in the early 1970s with the funding of thirty-five Alcohol Safety Action Projects (ASAPs) by the National Highway Traffic Safety Administration (National Highway Traffic Safety Administration, 1972, 1983; Nichols and Ross, 1989; Voas, 1991). Scores of studies followed. In general, these studies supported the claims that brief (two-to-six session) education programs, sometimes supplemented with group counseling or other treatment, reduce subsequent DWI arrests when compared to no treatment controls, but have little effect on subsequent traffic crashes (Nichols, 1990). They also found that the effect of these programs seemed to diminish as the prior number of offenses increased.

There were numerous concerns about the quality of treatment and the integrity of the implementation in the original Alcohol Safety Action Projects. These concerns led to the funding of eight new Alcohol Safety Action Projects in 1975. Each one of these Alcohol Safety Action Projects provided the same rehabilitative therapy, Power Motivation Training, and researchers went to great length to ensure fidelity to the model. Even with all the extra measures taken, results for these eight Alcohol Safety Action Projects were discouraging (Stewart and Ellingstad, 1989). No evidence could be produced that Power Motivation Training reduced crash or arrest recidivism, increased abstinence, diminished alcohol consumption, or had any of a number of other possible positive effects (Struckman-Johnson and Ellingstad, 1978 a,b). There was even some evidence to indicate that Power Motivation Training might actually lead to worse outcomes (Stewart and Ellingstad, 1989).

In 1981, Reis began the Comprehensive Driving-Under-the-Influence (CDUI) Treatment Evaluation Program in California (Reis, 1982a, 1982b). This was an experimental study of education and treatment interventions for first-time and repeat offenders in Sacramento County. First-time offenders were randomly assigned to one of the following groups: 1) a no-intervention control group, 2) a four-session group driver education program, or 3) a home-study educational program. Multiple offenders were randomly assigned to one of the following: 1) a no-intervention control group (legislation was obtained allowing this group to avoid suspension), 2) an active intervention such as therapeutic counseling, 3) therapeutic counseling with chemotherapy (disulfiram), or 4) biweekly contacts without counseling or chemotherapy.

The first-time offender part of the study found small reductions in DWI recidivism for both educational programs. However, a more impressive 20 to 30 percent reduction was found among the multiple offenders who were in the groups that received both the biweekly contacts and the group counseling, compared to the control group, which received neither. Later studies, however, have cast doubt on the impressive treatment effects reported in the Reis study (Peck et al., 1993). It appeared that none of the rehabilitation conditions led to significantly reduced recidivism rates after controlling for driving record, or other driver characteristics.

The research design of the original Comprehensive Driving-Under-the-Influence studies further limits their value. The control group had no license restrictions and the intervention groups did. Therefore, any reduction in recidivism could be attributed to this sanction. There have been many studies, most of them recent, that provide enough evidence to show that when rehabilitation is offered in lieu of license actions, offenders are more likely to reoffend than comparable groups who receive only license sanctions (Hagen, 1978; Sadler and Perrine, 1984; Nichols, 1990; Peck et al., 1985; Tashima and Peck, 1986; Nichols and Ross, 1989; Voas, 1986). A study in 1983 found that when alcohol- and drug-education replaced license sanctions for a group of DWI offenders, the education group had higher recidivism rates than the sanctions group (Popkin et al., 1983). A later study showed that combining education with license suspension led to lower recidivism rates than suspension alone. This study was done with a group of first-time DWI offenders in North Carolina (Popkin et al., 1988).

All the studies previously cited leave little doubt that license suspension is an important component of the sanctions received by multiple DWI offenders. With this in mind, several studies have taken place that compare rehabilitation and licensing sanctions with other punitive actions, such as jail or licensing sanctions alone. A study of more than 29,000 first offenders looked at the outcomes for those sentenced to jail, license suspension, or license restriction with mandated rehabilitation (Tashima and Peck, 1986). The study participants were followed for a period of time after the sanctions took place. The rehabilitation group had the lowest rates of minor traffic offenses, the lowest rate of major traffic offenses, and the lowest rate of total convictions. These figures are ambiguous, however, because the persons sentenced to jail in the first place tended to have worse driving records than those in the other groups.

In 1987, Siegal examined the recidivism rates for DWI offenders who had participated in a weekend intervention program (court mandated), in comparison to jail or suspended sentence. Weekend intervention programs provide the opportunity to assess the offender's alcohol and other drug problems, allow individualized treatment plans to be formed, and also allow the offender to keep his or her job (Siegal, 1987). The weekend intervention program consisted of a seventy-two-hour jail sentence that took place over a weekend. The offenders received careful assessment and referral. Siegal found that repeat offenders assigned to the weekend intervention program had almost 20 percent fewer subsequent DWI offenses than offenders sentenced to jail and almost 30 percent fewer offenses than those offenders who received a suspended sentence. The results were not so impressive for first-time offenders who were assigned to the weekend-intervention program. They had lower recidivism rates than other first-time offenders, but it was not significant (9.2 percent versus 12.7 percent).

A comprehensive meta-analysis of the effects of rehabilitation on DWI drivers that reviewed 105 studies all meeting minimum standards of rigor was published in 1995 (Wells-Parker et al., 1995). The average effect was a 7 to 9 percent reduction in recidivism. Considering that the studies used (from the seventies and early eighties) frequently assessed the effects of treatment in the absence of license sanctions, the average reduction might well be on the lower end. As previously noted, we now know that this form of intervention is ineffective. Wells-Parker and colleagues related that multimodal treatment approaches coupled with aftercare appeared to be the most effective for repeat offenders. While they were unable to identify "best practices" in treatment, they did find an average reduction rate of 7 to 9 percent. Even this reduction in recidivism over a large population of offenders translates into a considerable number of avoided DWI incidents, crashes, and arrests.

There are several objectives when imposing sanctions on DWI offenders. They may simultaneously seek to 1) protect the public, both driving and nondriving, 2) hold the offender responsible for his or her actions, taking into account both the victim and society at large, and 3) provide education and/or treatment to the DWI offender with a combination of retribution, deterrence, incapacitation, rehabilitation, and restorative justice. A combination of sanctions is often needed to achieve these goals. Evidence suggests that the exclusive use of criminal sanctions is not effective when dealing with drunk drivers. Incarceration may have a short-term deterrent effect on first time DWI offenders, but it does not appear to have long-term impact (Hingson, 1996). The use of incarceration alone may even increase recidivism (Mann et al., 1991).

Because of these studies, there has been some research examining the effectiveness of probation for DWI offenders, and this appears to be promising. Probation is not a single program or strategy; rather the conditions of probation vary widely from case to case and court to court. There is little data on the effectiveness of particular probation programs of varying length and scope as conditions. Probation sentences have been demonstrated to reduce recidivism significantly, but not among those at highest risk of recidivism (National Highway Traffic Safety Administration/National Institute on Alcohol Abuse and Alcoholism, 1996). It appears safe to conclude that "punishment only" sanctions are not as effective for those who habitually drink and drive as are a combination of punishment and treatment. Incarceration continues to be the sanction most frequently imposed on most persistent DWI offenders.

Licensing sanctions also have shown to be mildly effective. The courts and state departments of motor vehicles share the responsibility for managing DWI offenders when license sanctions have been imposed. Departments of motor vehicles maintain critical records and have administrative power to suspend and deny a driver's license and vehicle registration, and are also responsible for monitoring the records to determine when an offender is eligible for reinstatement. License suspension is effective in reducing DWI recidivism and the ensuing risk of crashes among drinking drivers. The optimum suspension appears to be from twelve to eighteen months (National Highway Traffic Safety Administration/ National Institute on Alcohol Abuse and Alcoholism, 1996).

Other related sanctions also appear to have some positive effect on DWI recidivism. Vehicle impoundment, license plate impoundment and tagging, and/or use of ignition interlocks may all be somewhat effective both during and following the sanction period.

There is considerable evidence to show that electronically monitored home detention programs that allow offenders to leave the house for employment and treatment services reduce both drinking and drunk driving (Baumer and Mendelsohn, 1992). DWI offenders on home monitoring are more likely to complete their home detention sentences successfully and are less likely to experience contact with the criminal justice system during the year following their release.

Drivers who persist in drinking and driving, as evidenced by more than one DWI arrest, are more likely to have been through several mandated treatment programs (Simpson and Mayhew, 1991; Simpson et al., 1996). In 1997 Justice Department surveys, DWI offenders represented 14 percent of all adults on probation, and nearly two-thirds of those DWI offenders reported previous attendance at alcohol or drug treatment. These offenders tend to think of treatment as a high cost "waste of time" that holds very little benefit for them. They often see little need for change and may remain unconvinced that treatment is necessary or helpful (Wieczorek et al., 1997).

In general, treatment for the DWI population has concentrated on separating drinking behavior from driving, and has been based on a disease orientation model that suggests treatment needs be based only on level of drinking or use severity (Timken et al., 1995). This emphasis has resulted in inadequate assessment with little, if any, focus on personality or risk-taking behavior. The result of this has been little assessment information incorporated into treatment plans. A further result, and perhaps more damaging, is "one-size-fits-all" treatment plans that lead to frequent recycling of DWI offenders through the treatment system.

A further complication in treatment has been a lack of understanding of and training in techniques that both the alcohol and criminal justice literature have shown to be effective (Miller and Hester, 1995; Beck et al., 1993; Andrews and Bonta, 1994). Miller's work shows that confrontational strategies produce poorer outcomes when compared to motivational strategies and that the more counselors confront, the more clients have been shown to be drinking at follow up (Miller and Rollnick, 1991). Thus, implementation of alternative techniques may indeed be helpful.

It is important for offenders to complete the treatment program. One study (Nochajski et al., 1993) found, when evaluating a treatment and evaluation program for high risk drinking drivers in Erie County, New York, that among those individuals who completed the program the DWI recidivism rate over a twenty-four-month follow-up phase was 14 percent. This compared with a rate of 34 percent for those who dropped out of the program before finishing it.

A study of a diversion program in Monroe County, New York also supports the positive impact of treatment completion. At the three-year follow up, those who completed the program had a 50 percent reduction in the DWI recidivism rate. Those who dropped out before completion had only a 24 percent reduction in the same figures. Finally, there was a nine-year follow up. The recidivism rate had, as expected, increased, in fact nearly doubled over time; however, there was still a significantly lower recidivism rate for those who completed the program, as compared to those who began and dropped out, as well as those offenders who did not participate at all (Darbey, 1993).

In 1999, the recidivism rates for DUI/DWAI (Driving While Ability Impaired) clients completing treatment in Colorado in 1998 were compared with recidivism rates for those offenders who did not complete recommended treatment. The group who did not complete treatment had a recidivism rate of 14 percent compared with 7.3 percent for the group completing treatment. These rates would most likely go up some if the groups were followed for a longer period of time; however, one would expect that the group that completed treatment would continue to do better than the other group.

All the studies reported above indicate that treatment completion contributes to lower DWI recidivism rates. Additional research designed to evaluate factors hypothesized to have a positive effect on treatment compliance and treatment completion is definitely needed (Peck et al., 1993; Nichols, 1990). Recently demonstrated to have a positive effect on treatment attendance and treatment outcome with alcoholics and DWI offenders is client motivation and readiness for change (Miller and Hester, 1995; Miller and Rollnick, 1991; Timken et al., 1995).

Another factor that may have an effect on treatment dropout rates is the type of treatment. It has been demonstrated that treatment for DWI has been based primarily on the disease model that emphasizes total abstinence (Timken et al. 1995). The disease model views alcohol problems as either present or absent, and tends to believe that there is one "right" treatment to fit all. A problem here is that DWI offenders often reject the disease model, do not see a need for total abstinence and, therefore, drop out of treatment before they gain any real benefit from that treatment. It would appear, therefore, that an approach to treatment that accepts both moderation and abstinence goals, focuses on reducing negative effects of alcohol rather than on the alcohol itself, and acknowledges the fact that alcohol problems fall on a continuum may be more acceptable to DWI offenders and therefore may encourage more offenders to stay and complete treatment.

Major Problem Areas

The background information provided a number of insights in the area of DWI intervention problems. Four broad categories have been identified. They are as follows: program staff, DWI offender evaluation, education programs, and treatment approaches.

Program Staff

Problems with clinicians, educators, and other staff who provide DWI offender evaluation, education, and treatment have certainly contributed to poor outcomes in the areas of recidivism and program compliance (Timken and Wanberg, 1999; Timken et al., 1995).

Many individuals doing evaluation and treatment have little experience. It has been a common practice for DWI programs to use new staff who have little preparation and/or background in working with alcohol and other drug traffic offenders. Working with the various DWI populations is considered to be "entry level," with the result being that the staff person is in almost immediate difficulty (Timken, unpublished informal study). Coupled with the lack of experience is the issue of training. A large number of staff have had only minimal training and usually lack information on offenders, including DWI behavior. The focus is usually on substance misuse with little, if any, attention paid to driving behavior. The models of addiction and treatment approaches in which many staff are trained are generally those that are least efficacious. Myth rather than science continues to prevail (Miller et al., 1995; Finney and Monahan, 1996). Staff members often have difficulty in balancing their responsibilities between offenders and public safety. Many cannot easily "wear two hats."

Reviews have found that many DWI programs lack structure on the part of staff (Lindstrom, 1992; Timken, unpublished informal study). Approaches used are frequently found to be confrontational and static

(Lindstrom, 1992; Miller and Rollnick, 1991; Timken et al., 1995). Many programs have been found to be neither goal- nor problem-focused. This, coupled with the nonempathic approach of many staff, results in an increase in resistance from the clients who are none too happy to be there in the first place (Miller and McCrady, 1993). This population far too frequently is combined with a lack of clinical supervision, which compounds and perpetuates the problems. In many ways, it is a wonder that there are not more problems regarding outcomes with these populations.

DWI Offender Evaluation

There are a number of continuing difficulties found in this arena. They can be categorized as administrative, systemic, and clinical. All have contributed to outcome deficiencies.

Administrative problems center around fees for services and record keeping. The former have either been inadequate to cover costs, or have been nonexistent. The literature is clear in this area, demonstrating that DWI offenders who pay for all or part of any intervention have better outcomes (National Highway Traffic Safety Administration, 1979; National Highway Traffic Safety Administration, 1983; Timken, unpublished survey, continuing).

Record insufficiencies have contributed by not having adequate data for either program management or outcome studies. Offender resistance is increased when records are unavailable or inaccurate.

The major systemic problem is not having the initial components of DWI offender evaluation (such as screening, placement, and referral) performed by an agency, practitioner, and so forth, totally independent of the education and/or treatment program. "Incestuous" type arrangements lead to perceived as well as actual conflicts of interest.

There are a number of clinical problems that have plagued and continue to plague DWI offender evaluations in independent screening and referral systems as well as in the education and treatment programs. Labeling or classifying alcohol and other drug traffic offenders increases resistance and is not needed for changes in behavior (Miller and Rollnick, 1991; Timken and Wanberg, 1999). Programs have used a number of instruments over the years in screening, diagnosis, and assessment of DWI offenders, but often they have been used for the wrong purpose and, many times, have been totally relied on rather than combining the results of instrumentation with clinical judgment. Both clinical judgment and reliable and valid instrumentation normed for the various DWI offender populations must be used if accurate offender evaluations are to be done (Miller et al., 1995; National Highway Traffic Safety Administration, National Institute on Alcohol Abuse and Alcoholism, 1997; Timken, 1999).

Education and treatment programs in systems where the screening, referral, and initial placement decisions have been made independently (in other words, by a probation department) often have failed to complete offender evaluations by not performing an in-depth differential assessment and/or by not incorporating the overall results of the evaluation in an individualized treatment plan. There are also concerns as to whether instrumentation is appropriate for adolescents as well as adult males, women, and various ethnic groups.

The areas of screening and assessment generally have been found in DWI intervention programs to measure only substance misuse. Frequently, antisocial behavior, mental health issues, and driving risk have been ignored, as have physical health, motivation, relapse potential, and environmental concerns. All of these are needed if accurate matching for placement decisions is to be made. The majority of the time, assessments are not a process, nor do they occur at more than one point in time, such as at admission. Reiterative assessments in DWI programs are few and far between (Timken et al., 1995).

Finally, there continues to be little being done in the area of follow-up. What has changed? What is needed? These questions need to be answered as part of the DWI offender evaluation package.

Education Programs

The quality of studies concerning DWI education programs leaves much to be desired. They have, for the most part, been quasi-experimental at best, with questionable methodology and statistical techniques. Major problem areas, in addition to the above, can be categorized in two broad areas: administrative and clinical.

Fees have often been waived and the waivers were seldom based on the ability to pay. Record keeping in terms of administrative data collection and clinical charting remains often scanty and inaccurate. Reviews by the author have found a "mixed bag," which made auditing very difficult.

Class sizes have often been too large. Thirty or more offenders have been found in programs designed for nonproblem drinkers, and fifteen-to-twenty people have been seen in groups supposedly interactive in nature, and designed for offenders with clinical alcohol and other drug problems. Outdated films and materials are common, and interaction with a therapeutic orientation is often lacking or minimal. A number of programs have been found to show so many films that there is virtually no presentation from a professional.

There is generally a lack of models for different types of offenders. Disease-oriented programs continue to be in vogue, and there is a paucity of programs designed for women, adolescents, and various ethnic groups. Topics generally deal largely with alcohol and other drug issues, and far too little time is spent on driving behavior, and what might be done to prevent a recurrence other than life-long abstinence from alcohol and other drugs (Timken et al., 1995; Timken, unpublished review).

Evaluations of the offender at admission as well as during the program and at discharge are often minimal and, when done, the process is less than sterling. There continues to be lack of matching to offender type in many of these programs and a large number of the programs continue to be an end in themselves, and are not combined with actual treatment to provide a continuum of care. A recent Colorado study (Deyle, 1997) found that DWI offenders classified as problem drinkers, who were sent to a didactic, brief education program rather than to a combination interactive education and lengthy treatment program, recidivated at a rate of more than 20 percent compared to 7 percent for those offenders appropriately matched.

The number of programs using manuals has grown over the years, but there continues to be a lack of fidelity to the prescribed written model. Length of programs varies greatly. They range from one day for the sessions designed for the social or nonproblem drinker, to approximately three months for those designed to educate the problem-drinking driver. The longer, supposedly interactive programs often lack a true therapeutic orientation and remain confrontational in nature. Coupled with these problems is the fact that formal, well-designed evaluations of DWI educational programs are scarce, and there has been little recently published work in the area.

DWI Treatment

Problems common to those found in DWI education programs have also plagued actual treatment programs. Fiscal management concerns are widespread. Many offenders are of low income (Colorado Department of Human Services, Alcohol and Drug Abuse Division, 1996 unpublished data) and have difficulty paying even a part of their treatment costs. Other offenders, who can pay, refuse to do so. These situations, coupled with management inadequacies and the failure of courts to enforce payment, have led to some of the difficulties.

Record keeping problems in clinical, data collection, and general collection venues have been widespread. Reviews, such as those done with educational programs by the author, have found wide variations among programs in the area of management.

Group size has generally been too large for optimum therapeutic benefit (Yalom, 1975; Timken, unpublished review). Groups have been found to have twelve-to-fifteen offenders, and this has made group process difficult if not impossible. Coupled with this are inadequacies in DWI evaluation (*see* the section on education for detail) and inadequate lengths of stay. The latter, for a variety of reasons, often comes nowhere close to the time frames mentioned for best clinical practice and optimum outcomes (Nichols and Ross, 1989; National Highway Traffic Safety Administration, 1979; N. Hoffman, personal communication, April 22, 1999; Timken et al., 1995).

As with education programs, there continues to be a lack of models for different types of drinking/drugging drivers. Twelve-step oriented programs are still prevalent, and a number of programs do not combine treatment with education as the literature suggests (Wells-Parker et al., 1995). There have also been far too few programs designed for women, minorities, and adolescents. Frequently, a label has been placed on a group with no real gender, ethnic, or age specificity (Timken, unpublished review). Far too often, there is no real effort made toward placement in the correct setting (Timken, unpublished review). Few programs have used the American Society of Addiction Medicine or similar criteria; however, this appears to be changing.

The programs have also paid far too little attention to behaviors other than alcohol and other drug misuse. Driving behavior as well as types of maladaptive behavior other than alcohol and other drug use and misuse, including criminality, has been slighted. Critical lifestyle and personality variables that create, shape, perpetuate, and maintain the maladaptive behavior have also largely been ignored.

Adjuncts to treatment, including medications to alleviate or attenuate alcohol and other drug use, mutual-help groups, ignition interlocks, electronic monitoring, and victim impact panels, among others, have either been used inconsistently or improperly, or have been ignored altogether. Treatments have seldom been manualized (deduced to a workbook or other such written approach), and when they have been, this author has found little fidelity to the programs' prescriptions. Fortunately, this has begun to change and more programs are beginning to pay some attention to recent research in the area.

Effective DWI Intervention Programming

The following discussion will focus on the following components: staff and related issues; DWI offender evaluation; DWI education programs; treatment approaches for alcohol and other drug related traffic offenders; and data systems. The first four will include and discuss findings taken from the general alcohol and other drug education and treatment literature and the overall criminal justice field as well as from the DWI area. This is being done due to the general clinical "carry-over" and the fact that a significant percentage of DWI offenders have other involvement in the criminal justice system (Parrish, 1999). The problem behavior theory and subsequent research by the Jessors and their colleagues (Jessor and Jessor, 1977; Jessor, 1987) also support this approach.

Staff and Related Issues

Optimally, providers of DWI intervention services should have a master's degree in the behavioral sciences with a clinical emphasis. This is particularly important if the individual is to be either the sole clinician working with either education or therapy clients, or performing evaluations (Monti et al., 1989). However, when this is not feasible, the individual should be certified, licensed, and so forth, according to the specific state standards for individuals providing services for those with substance misuse problems. Such approval should not be at entry level. Persons falling in the latter category should only work with clients as cofacilitators under close supervision.

Training must be competency based and include not only a general background with alcohol and other drug basics and issues, but also in the approaches that have been shown to be the most effective, such as cognitive behavioral, Community Reinforcement Approach, and so forth (Andrews and Bonta, 1994; Miller et al., 1995; Finney and Monahan, 1996; Gendreau, 1996; Wieczorek, 1995; Wanberg and Milkman, 1998; Monti et al., 1989). There should be training in relapse prevention since a large number of offenders are recidivists (Colorado Department of Human Services, Alcohol and Drug Abuse Division, 1999; Parrish, 1999).

Individuals working in the DWI intervention field also should be familiar with the criminal justice literature, particularly that of Bonta and

Andrews, and Gendreau (Andrews and Bonta, 1994; Gendreau, 1996). Evidence of training in the areas of cultural competency and diversity, women's treatment, and age-related issues and differences is also of great import (Wanberg and Milkman, 1998).

Specific training also is required in the use of the offender evaluation instruments the program has chosen. Staff providing education services need to demonstrate knowledge of the materials along with presentation and, in the case of interactive or therapeutically oriented education, group process competency.

A serious attempt should be made not only to match the DWI clinical staff person to clients but also in terms of milieu (Lindstrom, 1992; Wieczorek, 1995). Philosophy should also be considered. Clinicians with one frame of reference should not be trying to practice an approach in which they neither believe nor have had adequate training.

Regardless of the area in which a DWI interventionist is working—evaluation, education or treatment—the type of interviewing skills that are most salient are those falling under the rubric of motivational enhancement (Miller and Rollnick, 1991; Wanberg and Milkman, 1998; Timken and Wanberg, 1999). In this approach, motivation is understood to be the result of an interaction between the alcohol and other drug-related traffic offender and those around him or her. This means that the clinician can do things to influence motivation positively or negatively. The DWI staff must understand that motivation is something one does, rather than something one has.

The change model on which motivational enhancement/interviewing is based is the transtheoretical model developed by Prochaska and DiClemente (1982, 1986). It consists of the following stages; precontemplation (the entry point), contemplation, preparation or determination, action, maintenance (permanent exit point), and relapse. DWI offenders most often fall in either the precontemplation or contemplation stages (Timken, 1993 and 1997; Packard, 1996). Staff needs to be familiar with this and realize that any intervention must be based on where the client is in regard to change, rather than where the clinician wants the person.

Motivational interviewing requires that the clinician be able to ask open-ended questions, provide accurate, skilled reflections and summaries, provide appropriate affirmation, and do so in a nonconfrontational but yet directive manner. A role model from television in using this approach is Lt. Columbo.

The key to increasing motivation change is FRAMES (Bien et al., 1993; Miller and Sanchez, 1994). This acronym stands for the following:

F = Feedback. Personal feedback does have strong motivational effects.

R = Responsibility. The emphasis is on the offender's personal responsibility and freedom of choice.

A = Advice. Giving the offender clear and direct advice concerning the need for change and how to accomplish it.

M = Menu. Providing alternatives from which the offender can choose. The choices may be few within the criminal justice system.

E = Empathy. An empathic style is common to a variety of interventions that are shown to provide positive outcomes (Bien et al., 1993; Chafetz, 1961; Orford and Edwards, 1977; Valle, 1981). Hostile confrontational approaches have been shown to be associated with poor results (Lieberman, Yalom, and Miles, 1973).

S = Self-efficacy. There is no motivation when there is no degree of optimism (Bandura, 1982). Clinician expectations of progress can powerfully influence outcome.

A major concept for the DWI interventionist to learn is the importance of creating salient dissonance between the offenders' behavior and meaningful life goals. The staff must also learn and practice techniques that reduce resistance. Miller and Rollnick (1991) describe five principles underlying motivational interviewing. They are: express empathy, develop discrepancy, avoid argumentation, roll with resistance, and support self-efficacy. Related to these are the traits of an effective clinician as described by Truax and Carkhuff (1967). Warmth, genuineness, and respect in addition to empathy are important characteristics to learn and maintain for DWI staff.

There are many benefits from having staff thoroughly trained in motivational enhancement/interviewing practices (Miller and Rollnick, 1991; Packard, 1993; Timken, 1993). Among them are: providing a model that demonstrates how to increase DWI offender compliance with a case plan; reframing "denial" as "ambivalence"; demonstrating to the clinician how to manage ambivalence about change; increasing rapport; correlating with compliance (thus, the clinician does not have to work as hard); assisting in focusing more accurately on the client; providing affirmation to the client; empowering the client to be involved in the intervention(s); emphasizing client responsibility; and producing better outcomes.

Staff must learn and be comfortable with the fact that they must "wear two hats." One involves responsibility to the individual client where the clinician confronts the offender with his or her own behavior. The other is confronting the individual with society. The former considers the goals and agenda of the clients: their needs and expectations in the change process. The latter starts with the agenda of society and the community representing it. It is expressed through the legal system. Therapeutic interventions are client-centered, whereas, correctional treatments are society-centered. Staff must be able to address the needs of each of these and be able to express both to the offender (Wanberg and Timken, 1999).

The final point to be made about having effective staff to provide DWI services concerns clinical supervision. Clinical supervision needs to be provided to all staff on a regularly scheduled basis. This author recommends monthly sessions conducted by someone who not only meets state alcohol and other drug standards as a clinical supervisor, but also has a thorough working knowledge of DWI offenders and background knowledge of offenders in general. Review of programs in Colorado by the author has found this area to be lacking, particularly in programs that are a component of an incarceration facility.

DWI Offender Evaluation

Comprehensive evaluation of DWI offenders is a critical component of the intervention process. It should drive decisions as to whether education or treatment would be needed and, if so, what type and level of services are needed. Finally, it should also be able to provide information as to intervention effects, both immediate and longitudinally.

The overall purpose of DWI offender evaluation is to provide information about the nature and extent of the problems experienced by the individual to render appropriate decisions concerning the scope and type of approaches most likely to be beneficial. Matching of alcohol and other drug traffic offenders to particular education and/or treatment programs increases the overall efficiency and effectiveness of the intervention system (Simpson et al., 1996). A component of the process must include evaluation of the social, environmental, attitudinal, interpersonal, and psychological factors that contribute to the individual's DWI behavior (Timken et al., 1995).

The factors influencing risk for DWI recidivism need to be determined as part of the evaluation. They are as follows: history of alcohol and other

drug use; level of social and family functioning; history of previous evaluations, education, and treatment; history of arrests and legal
interventions associated with alcohol and other drug use; ability to
become qualified for and obtain employment, as well as the ability to perform on the job; and ability to function in an education setting (Popkin et
al., 1988).

Social, environmental, interpersonal and individual factors combine
to shape the DWI offender's risk behaviors. Individuals who evidence
interrelated problem behaviors are frequently characterized by a lack of
social stability, conceptual rigidity, an external locus of control and poor
problem solving skills and, in general, lack the skills needed for adaptive
functioning (Institute of Medicine, 1990). Their deficits are cognitive,
interpersonal, and social. Cognitive factors include their driving-related
attitudes, attitudes toward law enforcement, and their cognitive set: the
manner in which they view their lives, themselves, and others.
Interpersonal factors include poor social relations, some of which are
characterized by high levels of aggression and risk-taking. Social factors
include lifestyle, social network, and occupational and leisure functioning. All need to be evaluated in the process.

Evaluation of offender programs has produced findings that support
procedures for referral and matching of DWI clients (Siegal, 1985; Jeune
et al., 1988; Huebert, 1990; Parsons et al., 1993). Overall, evaluation
should consist of two parts: 1) administration of standardized instru-
ment(s) and completion of a biopsychsocial history; and 2) a personal
interview using motivational techniques by a trained clinician (National
Highway Traffic Safety Administration, 1996; Timken et al., 1995).

Multifaceted comprehensive evaluations need to be process oriented.
They should evaluate offender status throughout education or treatment
in the areas of motivation for change, behavioral coping skills, and
psychopathology. Data from the evaluation need to be used as a continuous feedback loop, providing staff with information that can help guide
and individualize the course of the program. It must be reiterative in
nature (Timken et al., 1995). Evaluation-as-intervention has been shown
to increase motivation in alcohol and other drug populations, and shows
promise for improving the level and nature of the offender's involvement
in education and treatment (Miller and Rollnick, 1991).

The evaluation of DWI offenders should contain the following components: screening, diagnosis, determination of motivation, assessment,
placement, referral, and follow-up. Screening, placement, and referral
should be done independently of education or treatment programs to

avoid any real or potential conflicts of interest. Diagnosis, level of motivation, assessment and follow-up are the responsibility of the education and treatment providers, although follow-up can and in many cases should be independent.

Screening is the process, either binary or differential, which indicates whether a substance abuse problem exists. The differential process and associated instruments will provide detail and screen in additional areas such as driving risk, mental health issues, antisocial behavior, perceptual defensiveness and motivation (Miller et al., 1995; Allen and Columbus, 1995; Timken, 1999).

Diagnosis is the process of determining whether an individual meets currently established criteria for substance abuse or dependence according to the current edition of the *Diagnostic and Statistical Manual* (DSM) of the American Psychiatric Association. Results must be included in the education or treatment plan (Miller et al., 1995; Allen and Columbus, 1995; Timken, 1999).

Motivational determination is the process of determining the individual's motivation in regard to the stage-of-change (Miller et al., 1995; Timken, 1999).

Assessment is the process of gaining an understanding of the offender's unique situation via systematic collection and analysis of data on a number of dimensions including: functional and dysfunctional aspects of psychological patterns and family and social structures including histories of physical, emotional, and sexual abuse; biological systems including current physical and mental health status and family health histories; offender and family alcohol and other drug use/abuse histories; factors affecting offender, family, and community safety including criminal and driving risk; leisure time activities; education and vocational history; religious or spiritual life; legal status; life skill acquisition; treatment history; cultural factors including racial and ethnic background; age; gender; sexual orientation; linguistic abilities; and personal strengths. Results also must be incorporated into any treatment plan (Miller et al., 1995; Allen and Columbus, 1995; Timken, 1999).

Placement is the process of determining what level and setting is needed and what is/are likely to be most effective. It is based on diagnosis, motivation, and assessment. Along with screening and referral, this should be done, at least on a preliminary basis, by an independent agency such as a probation department to avoid any conflict of interest, whether perceived or real. The two placement criteria recommended in this paper use the dimensions set forth by the American Society of Addiction Medicine (1996). The dimensions include the following:

1) Acute intoxication and/or withdrawal potential

2) Biomedical conditions and complications

3) Emotional/behavioral conditions and complications

4) Treatment acceptance/resistance (motivation)

5) Relapse/continued use potential

6) Recovery/living environment

Use of these dimensions will enable the clinician to select the correct level(s) and setting(s) of care, such as education, outpatient or inpatient, or various combinations. At this point, specific programs may be considered (Timken and Wanberg, 1999).

The placement process also involves determining whether any adjuncts to education or treatment should be recommended. The following adjuncts should be considered in the referral process: medications for alcohol/drug control such as Antabuse (disulfiram), Naltrexone, Methadone, and LAAM; random urine and breath screens; victim impact panels; ignition interlocks; electronic monitoring; self-mutual help groups (Alcoholics Anonymous, Rational Recovery, and so forth); and certainly intensive probation supervision. None of these are meant to replace education or treatment, but to complement them in combination with other sanctions, including fines, jail, community service, and driver license restraint actions.

The referral process itself must involve the offender as much as possible. The more people believe they have some control in making a decision that affects them, the more likely it is that they are going to comply. The greater the degree of ownership that can be instituted within DWI offenders, the less resistance will be encountered. Use of the FRAMES model is particularly critical in this process (Timken and Wanberg, 1999).

Things to be considered in making a specific referral include the following:

- appropriateness of education or treatment (will intervention have any chance of success?)

- clinical appropriateness including adjuncts as well as setting and level of care

- accessibility or proximity to education or treatment provider

- ethnicity

- gender

- age

- sexual orientation

- costs

- driving privilege status

- court obligations

- client choice (Timken and Wanberg, 1999).

Follow-up is the part of the evaluation where measures are conducted to see whether any change in the DWI offender has occurred. Minimally, the offender's use of alcohol or other drugs and driving behavior should be evaluated. If the treatment goals include hope for change on other dimensions (such as employment, relationships, stability, health, and so forth), these can and should also be measured. The process of treatment may also be measured (Miller et al., 1995; Finney, 1995; Tonigan, 1995).

The final part of this section on DWI offender evaluation provides the author's recommendations on specific instruments for each of the component parts of the evaluation. An additional category of driving risk instruments is listed due to the emphasis of the paper. It is neither an exhaustive nor an extensive, all-inclusive list. Rather, it is a limited menu of instruments from which clinicians/agencies may select without becoming overwhelmed by volume.

Contents of the listings were selected by the author on the basis of research and clinical experience (Miller et al., 1995; Allen and Columbus, 1995; Lacey et al., 1997; Timken, 1999). The decision to include each instrument and the placement criteria was based on the following.

1) The instrument must be directly related to alcohol and/or other drug problems, and directly or indirectly related to risky behaviors associated with driving problems.

2) The instrument must be available in English.

3) The instrument must be quantitative (placement criteria excepted).

4) Psychometric characteristics must be adequate (placement and in some cases, follow-up instruments excepted).

5) There must be a consensus of opinion by experts concerning utility.

6) The literature must support the instrument.

All screening, diagnostic, motivation, and assessment instruments listed have acceptable reliability and validity data associated with them, and all have been, to some degree, independently evaluated. They are listed alphabetically, within category.

Simple Screening

- Mortimer-Filkins(M-F), (National Highway Traffic Safety Administration, 1971)

- Research Institute on Addictions Self-Inventory (RIASI), (Nochajski and Wieczorek, 1995)

Differential Screening

- Adult Substance Use and Driving Survey (ASUDS), (Wanberg and Timken, 1998)

- Driver Risk Inventory (DRI), (Lindeman, 1987)

- Lovelace Institute's Comprehensive Screening Instrument (LCSI), (Lapham et al., 1996)

Diagnostic Instruments

- Diagnostic Interview Schedule (DIS), (Robins et al., 1981)

- DSM-IV Brief Interview for Substance Abuse or Dependence, (Timken, 1996a)

- DSM-IV Checklists for Substance Abuse or Dependence, (Timken, 1996b)

- Structural Clinical Interview for DSM-IV Personality Disorders (SCID-II) (Alcohol), (Spitzer et al., 1996)

- Substance Use Disorder Diagnosis Schedule (SUDDS), (Harrison and Hoffman, 1985)

Motivation Measurement Instruments

- Adult Self Assessment Questionnaire (AdSAQ), (Wanberg and Milkman, 1993)

- Stages of Change Readiness and Treatment Eagerness Scale (SOCRATES), (Miller and Tonigan, 1991, 1996)

- University of Rhode Island Change Assessment (URICA), (Prochaska and DiClemente, 1991)

Assessment Instrumentation

- Adult Clinical Assessment Profile (ACAP), (Wanberg, 1999)

- Alcohol Use Inventory (AUI), (Horn, Wanberg, and Foster, 1987, 1990)

- Comprehensive Drinker Profile (CDP), (Miller and Marlatt, 1984)

- Drug Use Self Report (DUSR), (Wanberg and Horn, 1991)

- Substance Use Disorder Diagnosis Schedule (SUDDS), (Harrison and Hoffman, 1985)

Driving Risk Instruments

- Driving Assessment Survey (DAS), (Wanberg and Timken, 1990)

- Driver Risk Inventory (DRI), (Lindeman, 1987)

- Adult Substance Use and Driving Survey (ASUDS), (Wanberg and Timken, 1998)

- Lovelace Institutes Comprehensive Screening Instrument (LCSI), (Lapham et al., 1996)

- Sensation Seeking Scale (SSS), (Zuckerman, 1964)

Placement Criteria

The Alcohol Drug Driving Safety Program Placement Criteria for Substance Abusing Drivers (ADDS-PC), (Timken, 1997)

American Society of Addiction Medicine Patient Placement Criteria for the Treatment of Substance-Related Disorders (American Society of Addictive Medicine-PPC-II), (American Society of Addictive Medicine, 1996)

Follow-up Instrumentation

- Addiction Severity Index (ASI), (McClellan et al., 1985, 1996)

- Alcohol Use Inventory (AUI), (Horn, Wanberg, and Foster, 1987, 1990)

- Drinker Inventory of Consequences (DrInC), (Miller, 1994)

- Life Activity Inventory (LAI), (Ellingstad and Struckman-Johnson, 1978)

It must be noted that a number of instruments used in the other components are also useful in regard to follow-up. (For more detail concerning any of the above instruments, consult the author, the Internet, or the library.)

Education Programs for DWI Offenders

DWI education programs combined with the arrest and other legal system experience are often sufficient to deter further DWI behavior. However, the content, format, and materials in such programs have varied widely and have not vigorously been assessed (National Highway Traffic Safety Administration, 1996).

The major objectives of educational programs are to increase knowledge, change attitudes, and reduce recidivism. Educational programs may be strictly limited to didactic presentations on the medical and legal consequences of drinking and driving, be interactive and group-process oriented, or be a combination of both. A review of studies by the National Highway Traffic Safety Administration indicated that the didactic type programs reduced DWI recidivism by approximately 10 percent for the nonproblem offender and that only the therapeutically oriented schools had any impact on offenders with some degree of alcohol and other drug problems (National Highway Traffic Safety Administration, 1996; Mann et al., 1988; Nichols et al., 1978). A Colorado study (Deyle, 1997) found similar results and, as previously mentioned, noted the drastic recidivism

differences when offenders were incorrectly matched to the type of education program.

It can be concluded that the didactic programs are ineffective or
harmful for DWI offenders with problems, and that only the therapeutic
programs combined with long-term treatment can benefit the more problematic group (Mann et al., 1988). Further confirmation was found by
Wells-Parker et al. (1995) in their meta-analytic study. Reviews of treatment effectiveness by Miller et al. (1995) and Finney and Monahan (1996)
found educational programs to be one of the least effective approaches
in the treatment of alcoholism.

Effective educational programs must be properly managed. Sound fiscal procedures need to be strictly maintained, and record keeping in
terms of administration, data, and clinical charting needs to be accurate
and current.

Size of the class depends on the type of school. Reviews by the
author (Timken, 1998) have found that twenty offenders per didactic
group and twelve per therapeutically oriented classes are about the maximum if program goals are to be accomplished. Films or videotapes, if
used, should be kept to a minimum and, along with all materials, should
be current.

Harm reduction may certainly be included in programs designed for
both the nonproblem offender and the alcohol and other drug problem
offender (Marlatt et al.,1995), and attention must be paid to women's and
adolescents' needs as well as ethnic issues. Programs designed for special populations need to be truly designed for them and not "just the
same old stuff" relabeled for the particular group in question.

Evaluation of offenders (following the format described in the
Evaluation section of this paper) must be done for all education clients.
Confirmation is needed that offenders assigned to didactic formats are
appropriately matched, and individualized plans need to be developed
for those clients with some degree of problem who are in the therapeutically oriented sessions. Both types of programs need to be manualized to
insure consistency of the intervention and fidelity to the model.

Motivational enhancement should be part of any type of DWI education. Miller and Rollnick (1991) found that motivational enhancement
techniques promoted a spirit of "collaboration" with clients. Poor motivation may contribute to poor compliance and outcome. Use of the
FRAMES approach in educational settings is as important as it is in
offender evaluations and treatment. Several studies have demonstrated
the efficacy of preparing clients for treatment (Brown and Miller, 1993;

Conners et al., 1998). Consistent with Prochaska and DiClemente's (1982) model of stages of behavior change, motivationally based DWI education programs are designed to help an individual move from considering change to attempting change.

There are no set prescriptions for length of stay or content. Reviews of select programs by the author have led to the development of curricula outlines for both didactic or Level I programs for the nonproblem offender and a therapeutically oriented curriculum for those individuals with some level of problem. The latter, for many reasons, must be combined with long-term treatment.

It is recommended that the Level I (didactic) program be conducted over a six-week period (one session per week) and the Level II (therapeutically oriented) be conducted over a twelve-week period (one session per week). Modifications may be made in order to provide the therapeutically oriented program in either eight or ten weeks as well as the recommended twelve weeks.

The following content/topic outline for DWI education is part of a comprehensive education and treatment program entitled Driving With Care (Wanberg, Milkman, and Timken, in press). It is a well-researched program based on many years of clinical as well as research practice by the authors. Both educational components and the treatment program are cognitive-behaviorally based with emphasis on harm reduction and public health. The Motivational Enhancement aspects developed by Miller and Rollnick during the last decade are integral as are some parts of the Community Reinforcement Approach set forth by Meyers and Smith is 1995.

Driving With Care – Level II Education

Lesson 1:   Program Orientation—Developing a Working Relationship

Lesson 2:   Alcohol and Other Drug Impaired Driving—The Laws and Beyond the Law

Lesson 3:   How Thinking, Attitudes, and Beliefs Control Actions

Lesson 4:   Understanding How Behavior Is Learned and Changed—Learning Self-control and Driving With Care

Lesson 5:   Alcohol and Other Drugs: How Do the Facts and Ideas About Alcohol and Other Drug Use Fit You?

Lesson 6: Alcohol and Other Drug Use Patterns—How Do They Fit You?

Lesson 7: Problem Outcomes of Alcohol and Other Drug Use— Patterns of Misuse and Abuse—How Do They Fit You?

Lesson 8: Preventing Recidivism and Relapse

Lesson 9: Developing Careful Driving Attitudes—Behaviors

Lesson 10: Preventing Recidivism and Relapse—Building Personal Values and Prosocial Attitudes

Lesson 11: Preventing Recidivism and Relapse—Managing Stress and Emotions.

Lesson 12: Preventing Recidivism and Relapse—Building Healthy Family and Social Relations

Closure: Review and Reflection

The Level I program uses material taken from the therapeutically oriented twelve-session program and places it in a six-session format designed to be used with nonproblem drinking drivers. However, unlike the majority of educational programs for social or nonproblem drinkers, it is very experiential in nature.

Effective Treatment

It is believed that those coerced into education or treatment for a substance-related offense are not motivated, less likely to comply, and have poorer outcomes. These individuals are viewed by treatment and some criminal justice system personnel as "doing their time" with little probability of benefit. This perception is based on the belief that substance-misusing offenders cannot be helped until they "want to change" and have to be intrinsically motivated (Hartnoll, 1992).

Fortunately, the literature has found few differences between persons mandated and "volunteers" in treatment regarding compliance and outcomes (Brecht et al., 1993; DeLeon, 1988; Stitzer and McCaul, 1987). In fact, when differences were found, they often favored the mandated clients (Mark, 1988). With the coerced clients, the better outcomes were obtained when there was greater probability of losing a valued outcome, such as a job, marriage, or a driver's license (Mark, 1988).

The general treatment of alcohol problems literature, as previously cited, has found that the most effective approaches involve cognitive-behavioral, motivational enhancement, or combinations of them with environmental modification, such as community reinforcement (Miller et al., 1995; Finney and Monahan, 1996).

DWI offenders are a distinct population; nonetheless, they exhibit some of the same thinking and behavior patterns common to other types of offenders (Wanberg and Milkman, 1998; Timken, 1999). Because of this, there is every reason to believe that the efficacious criminal justice treatment approaches may be successfully applied to the DWI offender population.

There is a significant amount of research to demonstrate the efficacy of the treatment of offenders (Andrews, 1995; Andrews et al., 1990; Izzo and Ross, 1990; Lipsey, 1989; Lipsey, 1992; Lipsey and Wilson, 1993; Lipton, 1994; McGuire and Priestly, 1995; Van Voorhis, 1987). This literature closely parallels that of the treatment of general alcoholism in demonstrating the efficaciousness of the cognitive behavioral approaches with offenders.

The literature shows, as does the general alcohol treatment literature, that some of the most popular and widely used approaches have had little if any improved outcomes, including reducing recidivism. Included in the group of rather noneffective approaches are general counseling, confrontational interventions, boot camps, and community service. While the general alcohol and other drug treatment literature indicates that much improvement in drinking and other drug-related behaviors might be achieved in brief periods of time, people with more severe problems need lengthier, more intense interventions (Miller et al., 1995). The criminal justice literature indicates that long-term (in other words, one year) programs are needed because of the necessity to change criminal as well as alcohol and other drug behavior (Andrews and Bonta, 1994).

DWI treatment programs exemplify the health-legal approach to handling the problem of alcohol and other drug-impaired driving. There are numerous approaches to the treatment of DWI offenders. No one approach has emerged as the most effective for all types of offenders (Wells-Parker et al.,1995). There is no reason to believe that the alcohol and other drugs and behavior problems associated with these people are much different from those of other offender populations. The focus with DWI groups must be on a specific type of illegal behavior, such as impaired driving.

The heterogeneity of the DWI populations makes comprehensive evaluation and matching to various levels, settings, and approaches to rehabilitation of prime importance (Simpson et al., 1996). Eliany and Rush (1992) found that 50 to 65 percent of offenders receiving treatment showed evidence of improvement at follow-up. The meta-analysis by Wells-Parker and colleagues (1995) found that, on average, DWI treatment programs reduced recidivism and crashes by 7 to 9 percent when compared to no treatment. Programs that combined education, treatment, and monitoring were found to be more effective for offenders with some level of alcohol and other drug problem.

Recidivism may be reduced and other outcomes improved if treatment for the problem drinkers is in the range of nine to twelve months or even longer (National Highway Traffic Safety Administration, 1996; Timken et al., 1995). The more serious the problems of both alcohol and other drug misuse and maladaptive driving, the more comprehensive the intervention should be in terms of length and intensity.

The extensive literature review by Wanberg and Milkman (1998) indicates that the key cognitive behavioral methods necessary for use with offenders are as follows:

- Preparing for treatment; understanding the therapeutic relationship and using motivational enhancement

- Providing information and knowledge about alcohol and other drugs and using the process of cognitive-behavioral change; changing alcohol and other drug-related beliefs

- Using feedback on alcohol and other drug use patterns and appraisals revealed in assessment

- Coping and social skills training

- Problem solving

- Using cognitive aversive reaction and advantage/disadvantage analysis

- Learning relaxation training and stress management

- Employing community reinforcement and contingency management

- Challenging expectancies

- Offering self-efficacy training

- Challenging automatic thoughts

- Changing dysfunctional assumptions

- Employing imagery techniques

- Managing drug cravings

- Learning relapse prevention, including harm reduction

- Recording and journaling

Since cognitive-behavioral approaches appear to be the choice for alcohol and other drug traffic offenders, the providers need to use well-designed manuals with specific details on how to provide each session. The manuals also need to contain supporting information as well as background material and all other required materials for program delivery. Participant workbooks for offenders also need to be developed and used.

The goals of DWI treatment in combination with education should include: 1) increasing motivation for change in the offender's lifestyle and alcohol and other drug misuse pattern; 2) using environment and social interventions to increase motivation and reinforce behavior change once it occurs; and 3) developing offender self-efficacy in the areas of problem solving, communication skills, conflict management skills, stress-management skills and conceptual flexibility linked to the maintenance of prosocial behaviors.

DWI treatment, as with DWI education, must be driven by the results of offender evaluation. All components of the evaluation need to be included when determining the setting as well as the individualized-treatment plan (for more details refer to the section on Offender Evaluation).

Settings for treatment can range from different intensities of outpatient treatment to various settings and intensities of residential care, including hospital and therapeutic communities. While the general rule is to use the least restrictive environment that is clinically appropriate, best practice requires that a range of services providing a continuum of care be available.

The levels and settings of care as set forth in the Colorado Alcohol Drug Driving Safety Placement Criteria for Alcohol and other Drug Related Traffic Offenders (ADDS-PC) (Timken, 1997) is a viable model that specifically tailors the majority of the American Society of Addictive

Medicine PPC-II to alcohol and other drug-related traffic offenders. The Colorado Alcohol Drug Driving Safety Placement Criteria for Alcohol and other Drug Related Traffic Offenders PC is as follows:

- Level I Education (Didactic)

- Level II Education (Therapeutic)

- Level II Education, and Weekly Outpatient Treatment

- Intensive Outpatient, Level II Education, and Weekly Outpatient Treatment

- Day Care, Level II Education, and Weekly Outpatient Treatment

- Halfway House, Level II Education, Intensive Outpatient Treatment and/or Weekly Outpatient Treatment

- Transitional Treatment, Level II Education, Intensive Outpatient Treatment and/or Weekly Outpatient Treatment

- Intensive Residential Treatment; Level II Education, Intensive Outpatient Treatment, and/or Weekly Outpatient Treatment

- Hospital, Level II Education, Intensive Outpatient Treatment, and/or Weekly Outpatient Treatment

- Therapeutic Community and Level II Education

- No Treatment - Refer for Indepth Psychological Exam Due to Severity, Mental Illness, Cognitive Problems, or Psychopathy

To be effective, treatment programs must be managed properly from an administrative as well as a clinical perspective. They, as with education programs, must maintain sound fiscal procedures and record keeping in the clinical charting, management of information, and general record keeping area. Group size should not exceed twelve due to the need for therapeutic process and management, particularly in terms of assuring that all group members are participating and meeting group as well as individual goals.

While this number of group members is larger than recommended (Chaney et al., 1978; Yalom, 1975), the volume of DWI offenders in most jurisdictions mandates the larger number. Smaller groups of six-to-ten would be preferable but generally this is not practical.

Both open (enter at any time) groups and closed (members stay together as a group from beginning to end, such as cohorts of offenders) have been used (Chaney et al., 1978; McCrady et al., 1985). Closed groups have the advantage of being able to build on earlier sessions and maximize group cohesion, and they may be easier to manage clinically (Yalom, 1975). Conducting closed groups may be more administratively difficult because of the volume of cases. One approach to this problem is to have the first phase of a nine-to-twelve-month program closed, followed by an open group format for the remainder of the program.

Intensity of treatment can range from one to five times per week depending on which level(s) and setting(s) of care are assigned. However, as previously noted, the overall length of stay in a program combining therapeutic education with treatment should be an absolute minimum of nine months for offenders with more moderate problems in the alcohol and other drug and driving areas to twelve or more months for those with more severe problems.

Attention must be paid in treatment programming to gender, ethnic group, and age. Special populations need to have programs designed to meet their specific needs, and these programs need to be run by staff with training and demonstrated competency with the particular age group, gender, and/or ethnic group in question.

Adjunctive Intervention

The adjuncts to be briefly discussed are not intended to replace education or treatment but to complement them. They are categorized and reviewed under the following headings: medications to have an impact on alcohol or other drug use, driver- based sanctions, and vehicle-based sanctions.

Medications which may be used to have an impact on alcohol and other drug use are disulfiram (trade name Antabuse), naltrexone (trade name Revia, Trexan), Methadone, and LAAM. There are a significant number of medications currently being tested as part of the government approval process but only those mentioned above are currently approved and will be discussed.

Disulfiram disturbs the normal process of metabolism. If drinking occurs after taking the drug, the result is a group of symptoms which include: flushing, nausea, vomiting, headache, accelerated heart rate, fall in blood pressure, and difficulty in breathing (Keller et al., 1982). The idea behind the use of disulfiram is that the client knows illness will follow the use of alcohol while the drug is in his or her system. It works as a deterrent. There are suggested guidelines as to the characteristics of offenders who generally respond favorably to the drug (Mendelson and Mello, 1979; Baekland et al., 1975; Miller, 1980; Brewer, 1995; Fuller et al., 1986). Alcohol and other drug traffic offenders should be seriously considered for disulfiram when the BAC is > .20, there are multiple alcohol and other drug-related arrests, there is failure of previous treatment(s), there is loss of control, or the offender requests the drug. It and other medications are most likely to succeed where compliance can be closely monitored (Chick, 1992).

One study done in 1993 (Azrin) found that alcoholics who have a family member to closely monitor their taking of the drug (especially spouses) have much higher rates of sobriety without the need for additional psychological counseling. In contrast, alcoholics who take disulfiram but do not have close family ties have an increased need for psychological counseling, and different types or intensities of treatment. For this population, careful assessment and re-assessment during the course of treatment appears to be necessary.

Naltrexone (Revia, Trexan) has been used successfully in treating opioid dependence since 1984. It is not an aversion type of treatment for alcohol problems. Persons with alcohol problems who take naltrexone generally have lower levels of craving, fewer drinking days, and lower rates of relapse as compared to a placebo (Brewer, 1995). In the treatment of opioid dependence, the drug blocks the effects of opioids by competing with them for opioid receptors in the brain. There are general guidelines, such as those published by Colorado (Colorado Department of Human Services, Alcohol and Drug Abuse Division, 1999) for use, but to date there is nothing concerning usage directly related to alcohol and other drug traffic offenders. Anecdotally, it would appear that the drug might be considered when the offender evaluation process identifies craving as a major component. As with disulfiram, naltrexone is more effective if its use is closely monitored.

Methadone and LAAM are the two primary drugs used to assist in the treatment of opioid dependence. They are synthetic narcotic analgesic compounds used to "block" the effects of opioids and do not, in proper dose, create euphoria, sedation, or analgesia (Lowinson et al., 1997). When combined with treatment, the drugs provide consistently positive, cost-effective outcomes (Harwood et al., 1988; Rufener et al., 1977; Gordon, 1976). There is scant information in the area of DWI offenders, but it appears that if the individual client does indeed have a diagnosis of opioid dependence, then these drugs ought to be considered. The Colorado Alcohol Drug Driving Safety Placement Criteria for Alcohol and other Drug Related Traffic Offenders has tables based on the American Society of Addictive Medicine Placement Criteria that provide guidelines as to the use of these drugs.

Driver-based sanctions other than medication are random urine/breath testing, victim impact panels, electronic monitoring (ELMO), self/mutual help support groups, driver license restraint actions, incarceration, and probation supervision.

Random urine testing should be used when the offender has either been convicted of DWI and drugs other than alcohol were involved and/or where there is evidence that drugs other than alcohol are being or have been used by the offender. Testing may be done either as an assessment method or for compliance. If used as a means to determine whether some level of drug problem exists, the procedures should run for a period of four-to-six weeks. A good random program will be able to ascertain with a high degree of validity whether a problem exists during the month or so of testing. Compliance testing on the other hand, should be for an extended period, perhaps even the full length of supervision. Frequency, though, may be decreased if the offender is "clean" for a period of six months or longer.

The test of choice for offenders is the NIDA-5 protocol. The drugs tested for are cocaine, opioids, THC, amphetamines, and PCP. This is far sounder than trying to test for one or two drugs because of the nature of dual- or poly-drug abuse by offenders whose "taste in drugs" may change. Regardless of any circumstances, urine testing should not be done when alcohol is the drug being monitored. It is water-soluble and one would have to be somewhat lucky if an offender were to be tested at the time when alcohol was in the body.

Breath testing on a random basis should be used as a compliance tool for offenders who are required to abstain from alcohol or who are not to drink to impairment. It may be used when disulfiram is medically contraindicated or in conjunction with disulfiram if alcohol use is suspected while the offender is taking the drug.

Breath testing also may be done on a twice-daily basis for high-risk offenders who either have a history of noncompliance and/or are suspected of surreptitious drinking. Use of either approach, most particularly the latter, is time consuming and can be quite problematic. Law enforcement agencies as well as treatment programs may be used to perform the breath testing.

Victim impact panels are mainly available in larger population centers. Mothers Against Drunk Driving (MADD) originated these groups which are composed of victims and offenders who describe the impact of DWI on their lives. Offenders are sentenced to the victim impact panel and are required to attend the two (or so) hour session on a one-time basis.

A review of the literature found there is little measurable and consistent impact of a victim impact panel on recidivism (Shinar and Compton, 1995). Fors and Rojek (1999) did, however, report that at a twelve-month follow-up, arrest rates were lower for the victim impact panel group than the comparison. The differences were greater for white men, twenty-six to thirty-five years, with only one prior arrest and lower levels of severity. There are two recent studies that provide some evidence that victim impact panels have a negative impact on repeat offenders by increasing recidivism (Woodall et al., 2000; C'de Baca et al., 2000). However, more studies need to be done to make a final determination as to the effectiveness of the programs. There is some thought that these "one shot" meetings are just not enough to change behavior of most alcohol and other drug traffic offenders. However, participation may be constructive in other ways, particularly in terms of an overall restorative justice effect.

Referring offenders to a victim impact panel should be decided on an individualized basis. Do not, as a matter of course, refer all offenders. Persistent offenders are the least likely to benefit, whereas twenty-six-to-thirty-five-year-old white males with minimal alcohol and other drug problems appear to benefit the most.

Electronic monitoring systems are available in several types. They include radio frequency and programmed contact. The latter may be combined with a breath test and a camera.

DWI offenders fare better than other types of offenders on electronic monitoring (Baumer and Mendelsohn, 1992). Recidivism rates in such programs were 3.5 percent less than those in comparison groups (Jones et al., 1996). This same study indicated that savings of nearly $1 million were achieved with DWI offenders placed on electronic monitoring, as compared to those jailed.

Currently, this adjunct should be used either as an alternate to jail or as a step-wise program for persistent offenders needing very close scrutiny and control after jail. It certainly can be used in combination with other adjuncts for the higher-risk individuals who have a history of treatment failure and other forms of noncompliance. To be effective, it also has to be used longer than the jail sentence it replaces or complements.

Self/mutual help/support groups are not limited to Alcoholics Anonymous (AA) and there are several that fit in this category. Included are Narcotics Anonymous (NA), Cocaine Anonymous (CA), Rational Recovery (RR), Women for Sobriety (WFS), Moderation Management (MM), Men for Sobriety (MFS), and Self Management and Recovery Training (SMART). Narconon, while sounding similar to these adjuncts, is actually a program operated by the Church of Scientology.

Alcoholics Anonymous (AA) is the most popular and well known of the self/mutual help group approaches to alcoholism treatment. However, its effectiveness is not supported by much scientific evidence at this time (Miller and McCrady, 1993). The AA method appears to be the most helpful in conjunction with other types of therapy (Miller, 1980; Emrick et al., 1993). Recent work indicates AA (as well as other such groups) has a "booster effect" on treatment if the client is a good match (Project Match Research Group, 1997).

Over a period of several years, studies have suggested that certain types of alcoholics respond better to AA and other self/mutual help groups than others (Mendelson and Mello, 1979; Pattison and Kaufman, 1982; Miller, 1980; Kinney and Leaton, 1995; Hester and Miller, 1995; Emrick et al., 1993). Those who join, remain, and are successful in AA are usually alike in terms of class, race, and social identity or education. They are usually social people and can function within a relatively large group of people. Successful participants have usually suffered a loss of social status while retaining psychological competency (Mendleson and Mello, 1979; Kurtz, 1993). In addition, they tend to be religiously oriented and guilt prone. Alcoholic clients who fit these criteria will usually benefit from a referral to and subsequent association with AA and/or other self/mutual help groups (Project Match Research Group, 1997).

Offenders who attend support groups before, during, or after treatment have more favorable outcomes in regard to substance use (Emrick, 1989). Outcomes are also more favorable for those who attend more than one meeting per week and for those who have a sponsor, lead meetings, and work through steps six through twelve after completing treatment. Taking steps four or five is not consistently related to outcome, nor is telling one's story or doing twelve step work (Tonigan and Toscova, 1993).

Just as there are clients who should benefit from self/mutual help groups, there are those who should not be referred to this adjunct. These clients prefer talking with professionals. They tend to be deeply introspective and view alcoholism as a psychological problem. These clients typically wish to talk to "as few people as possible about alcoholism and will choose to keep the battle against alcoholism separate from social activities" (Emrick, 1987; Nace, 1997). Other types of clients who do not do well in AA are those who have a high degree of psychiatric symptoms or who are chronic skid-row alcoholics. Clients who are not willing to accept abstinence as a goal, preferring controlled drinking, will also make poor AA referrals (Poley et al., 1979; Bean, 1975).

It is appropriate to use a support group as an optional part of the treatment menu if the offender appears to be a good match in terms of characteristics and readiness for change. Precontemplators, contemplators, and perhaps even those in the determination stage are not ready and will not be able to affiliate and engage. Usually they will increase their resistance and not be compliant. When recommending a support group, make sure the client understands that it is an option, and that involvement may well mean better outcomes and that if one type of group does not seem to help or be attractive, there are options. Offenders in cognitive behavioral programs often find that Rational Recovery is the best "fit" for them. Also, if the client is a first-time offender, minimally to moderately involved with alcohol but either does not need or want to be abstinent, Moderation Management would be a good choice.

License restraint actions do have specific as well as general effects on recidivism (Blomberg et al., 1987; Sadler and Perrine, 1984; Mann et al., 1988; McKnight and Voas, 1991; Williams et al., 1991; Voas and Tippets, 1993; Stewart et al., 1989). Peck et al. (1985) found that combining license revocation with treatment provided better outcomes than either alone.

Jail provides a public safety benefit while the offender is incarcerated. Very short jail terms, such as a few days, do provide some positive impacts on recidivism (Compton, 1986; Falkowski, 1984; Grube and Kearney, 1983). Lengthier sentences, though, are not related to lower recidivism. Instead, they have been found to be associated with higher crash and recidivism rates (Joksch, 1988; Martin et al., 1993; Ross and Klette, 1995; Mann et al., 1991; Homel, 1988; Friedman et al., 1995; Nichols and Ross, 1989).

Intensive supervision probation program evaluations are scarce, but those done reveal very favorable results (Voas and Tippetts, 1990; Jones et al., 1996). Street enforcement of the rules and swift, sure punishment along with allowing greater access to treatment are the essential elements of these programs.

Vehicle-based Sanctions

The vehicle-based sanctions include interlocks, autotimers and fuel locks, stickers, special plates, electronic driver's licenses, vehicle plate/ registration actions, vehicle impoundment, and vehicle immobilization.

Ignition interlocks are designed to prevent a vehicle from starting if the operator has a measurable amount of alcohol in a breath sample. They are breath-testing machines attached to the ignition of vehicles. The research indicates that the use of interlocks in combination with treatment is one of the most promising adjuncts in the area of recidivism reduction (EMT Group, 1990; Morse and Elliott, 1990; Jones, 1993; Popkin et al., 1993; Beirness, 1996; Marques and Voas, 1995). However, their efficaciousness declines rapidly once the devices are removed from the vehicles. Keeping the interlocks installed after treatment for a period of time and perhaps coupling the extended use with brief "booster" counseling sessions may solve the problem.

Autotimers and fuel locks are two devices that allow offenders to drive on a limited basis. Unlike ignition interlocks, there have been no published outcome reports, and while the technologies show some promise, their effectiveness has not been demonstrated.

Special sticker programs were tried in Washington and Oregon. Evaluations by Voas and Tippetts (1994) provided mixed results. In Washington, there was no impact on offenses or crashes, but there were positive findings in Oregon.

Special license plates have been tried in three states, but the author was unable to find any published outcome studies. The *electronic driver's license* is a new technology and is being tested in Sweden (Goldberg, 1995). Preliminary results appear favorable, but no definitive outcomes have been published.

Registration and plate seizure is allowed in ten states, but there has been only one published outcome study. The Minnesota Department of Public Safety (1990) found that was effective in reducing recidivism and repeat offenders. The recidivism rate for offenders with plates seized was 50 percent lower than for the control group (Rogers, 1994).

Few jurisdictions impound vehicles. The question as to whether these programs positively impact recidivism and crashes remains largely unanswered. Logistical problems along with management may well turn out to be major concerns (Voas, 1991). One program in Ohio evaluated by Voas et al. (1996) combined impoundment with immobilization. It was found that recidivism rates for DWI were significantly reduced and held beyond the expiration of the penalty.

Forfeiture is the strongest and least-applied vehicle sanction. Little evaluation has been done, but the results are similar to impoundment, in other words, a 50 percent reduction in recidivism.

Treatment Models

The following section of the paper will present two manual-driven treatment approaches that, when combined with therapeutic education, can be very appropriate for DWI offenders who have some degree of alcohol and other drug problems. The two approaches were specifically designed for offenders. Strategies for Self-improvement and Change (Wanberg and Milkman, 1998) was originally designed for felons, but it also can be used for a certain type of offender, such as the individual whose DWI is but one aspect of overall criminal behavior. Both of the programs are based on sound research and incorporate the elements and philosophy that the literature indicates is necessary for providing positive outcomes for DWI offenders.

These manual-driven treatments use combinations of cognitive-behavioral, motivational enhancement, harm reduction, and the Community Reinforcement Approach. They may be presented in a range of from five to twelve or more months and have the flexibility to be offered in different intensities. The beginning phases can be presented in residential settings, including incarceration facilities, and are designed to be used with a broad menu of adjuncts.

Strategies for Self-improvement and Change includes three phases— challenge to change, commitment to change, and taking ownership of change. Specific protocols for assessment are included, and each phase has modules with step-by-step lesson/session plans.

Challenge to change—the first phase—includes six modules and eighteen sessions. The modules are: 1) building trust and rapport; 2) building on desire and motivation to change; 3) building the knowledge base for change; 4) using self-disclosure and receiving feedback: pathways to self-awareness and change; 5) preventing relapse and recidivism: identifying high-risk situations, and 6) knowing how people change: understanding the process of self-improvement and change. These modules contain the first eighteen sessions.

Commitment to change—the second phase—has three modules and includes sessions nineteen through forty. The modules are: developing commitment to change; performing an in-depth assessment: looking at the areas of need and change; and strengthening basic skills for self-improvement and change; acting on the commitment to change.

The final phase—taking ownership for change—also contains three modules: learning relapse and recidivism prevention: a review and learning strategies for self-control and lifestyle balance; strengthening our ownership of change: developing the skills of critical reasoning and settling conflicts; and maintaining self-improvement and change: developing a healthy lifestyle or manner of living. Sessions forty-one through fifty are contained in this final phase.

For use with criminal offenders who have had a DWI, *Strategies for Self-improvement and Change* would need to include evaluation instruments described in the evaluation section of this paper and modify the participants' workbook to be more DWI-specific to criminal offenders.

Driving with Care (Wanberg, Milkman, and Timken, in press), based in part on *Strategies for Self-improvement and Change* (Wanberg and Milkman, 1998), contains a complete long-term treatment component specifically designed for DWI offenders. Both *Strategies for Self-improvement and Change* and *Driving with Care* should be used in conjunction with the Level II educational component that is part of the overall *Driving with Care* program for DWI offenders. It also combines cognitive behavioral approaches with motivational enhancement and contains harm reduction techniques along with aspects of the Community Reinforcement Approach espoused by Meyers and Smith in 1995.

The program can be presented in open-group as well as closed-group format, and the length of stay ranges from five to ten months depending on the severity of the DWI offender's drinking and driving problem. In terms of contact hours, the range is from forty-two to eighty-six actual hours of group time. It is assessment driven and requires a large amount of work on the part of the offender to complete the program exercises. A workbook is given to each participant and time is set aside during the group session for completing at least part of the weekly assignment. There are four treatment tracks of differing length. All persons admitted must complete the number of tracks, which the assessment (including BAC level and number of prior offenses) indicates is needed. The least severe who are in need of treatment must complete the first track, while those with the greatest severity and who are still amenable to treatment must complete all four tracks.

Included in the twenty-first through the forty-third sessions will be topics covering the following that are designed to complement and enhance the material found in the Level II education component of *Driving with Care*. They are learning communication skills and tools, tools of self-disclosure, the process and stages of change, ways to change self-disclosure, coping and social skills, managing and changing negative thoughts, thinking errors, how to manage craving and urges, assertiveness skills, anger management, how to understand values and moral development, critical reasoning and decision making, conflict resolution, alternatives to maladaptive behaviors, how to maintain change, and additional material on recidivism and relapse prevention.

There are other approaches that could certainly be used with DWI offenders. Both Strategies for *Self-improvement and Change* and *Driving with Care* can be used with first-time offenders, as well as repeat and persistent or hardcore offenders, but a number of cognitive-behavioral programs, such as those developed by Monti et al. (1989) and Carroll (1998), could be modified to be appropriate in terms of length and content for DWI offenders. Community Reinforcement Approach (Meyers and Smith, 1995) or Community Reinforcement Approach with Vouchers (Budney and Higgins, 1998) also could be adapted to provide an excellent approach for DWI offenders. Either cognitive behavioral therapy or the Community Reinforcement Approach, when combined with therapeutically oriented education, could provide an effective treatment within a nine-month time frame. There is also the Risk Modification Training (RMT) program (Packard et al., 1993) which was specifically designed for DWI offenders.

Data and Related Systems

DWI education and treatment programs must be efficacious and there must be proof of this. Process and outcome evaluation are both necessary. Programs, therefore, must gather and maintain appropriate data that will enable the evaluation process. Optimally, counselor as well as program information should be kept.

Any education or treatment data system should be compatible with the state alcohol and other drug traffic offender management information system in which it is located. Communication between all contributors and consumers of traffic safety data must be maintained. All participants need to fully understand the entire system in general as well as all of the individual aspects of the system. Comprehensive DWI tracking systems need to be developed and maintained.

Current DWI education and treatment need to be further examined and better approaches developed. DWI outcomes need further examination in terms of subgroups, and combined sanctions require further evaluation (Wieczorek, 1995). Data elements concerning the following need to be gathered on all DWI offenders.

1. offender evaluation

2. prior education and treatment history

3. education and treatment approach

4. medication and dose

5. intensity and length of stay

6. progress in program

7. discharge as well as admission status

8. adjuncts

9. counselor data

10. demographic and identifier information

Information on DWI offenders may be used to measure what is happening and what has happened to individuals as well as specific or overall populations. The data can be used internally as a management tool as well as for clinical process and outcome measurers. There must be the ability to link this information with other data elements from other components of the overall DWI management system, such as law enforcement, prosecution, the judicial system, and the motor vehicle department.

An overall DWI tracking system should provide the means to accomplish two specific ends. First, the "critical path" of each offender should be trackable and monitored from arrest through dismissal or sentence completion. The system should monitor all offenders and ensure that sanctions are completed, thereby imposing some deterrent-based sanctions that may encourage them to avoid repeating the offense (Timken, 1998).

Second, the DWI tracking system should provide aggregate data on various demographic groups. This will allow legislators, policy makers, the judiciary system, treatment professionals, researchers, and so forth, to evaluate the current DWI environment and to design countermeasure programs, statutes, regulations, and policies to reduce recidivism and crashes, and rehabilitate DWI offenders. In essence, a DWI tracking system can combine case management and evaluation.

Summary and Conclusions

Progress in the effectiveness of DWI interventions has been made over the last thirty years. The traffic safety data indicates that while DWI incidents remain a problem in terms of incidence and crashes, there has been a trend toward improvement. The prominent starting point toward the development of effective interventions began with the Alcohol Safety Action Projects (ASAP) and continues today with local, state, regional, national, and international efforts.

While there are many questions that remain to be answered, research strongly suggests that if certain methods and instruments are used, a significant number of DWI offenders can be helped, with the result being a reduction in recidivism and alcohol and other drug-related crashes.

DWI programs can be effective if they:

- are well managed administratively and clinically

- are conducted by highly trained experienced staff

- provide tailored services for women, minorities, adolescents, and older offenders

- incorporate comprehensive, process-oriented offender evaluations, including screening, diagnosis, motivation measurement, assessment and follow-up

- provide evaluation that uses standardized, psychometrically sound instruments and interviews leading to individualized treatment plans

- specify placements based on the evaluations in accord with widely accepted criteria, such as the American Society of Addictive Medicine PPC-II

- conduct educational programs tailored according to severity of the alcohol and other drug and driving-risk problem

- take into consideration personality and others factors contributing to high-risk driving besides alcohol and other drug use

- provide therapeutically oriented education programs combined with treatment monitoring for offenders with alcohol and other drug problems

- conduct education and treatment programs based on outcome research which are of sufficient duration, such as nine to twelve or more months

- combine these long-term programs with appropriate medications, offender-based and vehicle-based sanctions

- develop and maintain data systems which can be used both internally and externally for process and outcome evaluations, as well as for program management

Even though progress has been made and there is sufficient literature to be fairly prescriptive, there are a number of questions which need to be answered or at least clarified. These include the following:

- What are the specific impacts of combining incarceration with education and treatment?

- What are the effects of different lengths, type, and scope of probation on recidivism?

- Would use of the drug court model provide better outcomes than the traditional model?

- What is the optimal duration for various vehicle sanctions?

- What can be done to ensure program completion by offenders?

- What is the most appropriate content and length for educational programs?

- What are the most important variables for matching offenders to treatment?

- Will outcomes differ if there is separate examination by subgroups?

- Can outcomes achieved by long-term treatments be equaled or improved by implementing well-designed programs of much shorter duration, such as ninety days?

- What is the optimal combination of vehicle and driver-based sanctions with treatment for various subgroups of offenders?

- What are the relevant characteristics of various interventions?

- Does each intervention practiced maintain fidelity to the written protocol?

- What are the most clinically relevant subgroups of DWI offenders?

- Why do some people become persistent offenders and what is/are the developmental pathway(s)?

The problem of DWI has gained international attention, and the past few years in particular have seen a proliferation of research projects. There is evidence to support the use of all of the interventions discussed above; however, at the present, there is no definitive answer to the "DWI problem." There is clearly much work yet to be done.

References

Allen, J. P. and M. Columbus, eds. 1995. *Assessing Alcohol Problems: A Guide for Clinicians and Researchers. Treatment Handbook Series #4.* Bethesda, Maryland: National Highway Traffic Safety Administration and the National Institute on Alcohol Abuse and Alcoholism.

American Psychiatric Association. 2000. *Diagnostic and Statistical Manual of Mental Disorders, IV-TR.* Washington, D.C.: American Psychiatric Association.

American Society of Addiction Medicine. 1996. *American Society of Addiction Medicine Patient Placement Criteria for the Treatment of Substance-Related Disorders (ASAM PPC-II).* Chevy Chase, Maryland: American Society of Addiction Medicine.

Anda, R. F., P. L. Remington, and D. F. Williamson. 1986. A Sobering Perspective on a Lower Blood Alcohol Limit. *Journal of the American Medical Association (JAMA).* 256: 3213.

Andrews, D. A. 1995. The Psychology of Criminal Conduct and Effective Correctional Treatment. In J. Mcguire, ed. *What Works: Reducing Reoffending*, pp. 35-61. New Jersey: Wiley.

Andrews, D. A., Bonta, J. 1994. *The Psychology of Criminal Conduct.* Cincinnati, Ohio: Anderson Publishing Co.

Andrews, D. A., K. I. Zinger, R. D. Hoge, P. Gendreau, and F. T. Cullen. 1990. Does Correctional Treatment Work? A Clinically-relevant and Psychologically-informed Meta-analysis. *Criminology.* 28(3):369-404.

Argeriou, M., D. McCarty, and E. Blacker. 1986. Criminality among Individuals Arraigned for Drinking and Driving in Massachusetts. *Journal of Studies on Alcohol.* 46(6):525-530.

Azrin, N. H. 1993. Disulfiram and Behavior Therapy: A Social-biological Model of Alcohol Abuse and Treatment. In C. Brewer, ed. *Treatment Options in Addiction: Medical Management of Alcohol and Opiate Abuse.* London: Gaskell.

Baekeland, F., L. Lundwell, B. Kissen, and T. Shanahan. 1975. Correlates of Outcome in Disulfiram Treatment of Alcohol. *Journal of Nervous and Mental Disease.* 157:99-107.

Bandura, A. 1982. Self-efficacy Mechanism in Human Agency. *American Psychologist.* 37(2):122-147.

Baumer, T. L. and R. I. Mendelsohn. 1992. Electronically Monitored Home Confinement: Does it Work? In J. Petersilia, A. J. Lurigio, and J. M. Byrne, eds. *Smart Sentencing: The Emergence of Intermediate Sanctions*, pp. 54-67. Thousand Oaks, California: Sage.

Bean, M. H. 1975. Alcoholics Anonymous, Parts I and II. *Psychiatric Annals.* 5, 7-61.

Beck, A. T., F. D. Wright, C. F. Newman, and B. S. Liese. 1993. *Cognitive Therapy of Substance Abuse.* New York: The Guilford Press.

Beerman, K.A., M. M. Smith, and R. L. Hal. 1988. Predictors of Recidivism in DUIs. *Journal of Studies on Alcohol.* 49(3):443-449.

Beirness, D. J. 1996, January. Alcohol Ignition Interlocks: A Link Between Punishing and Helping Systems. Paper presented at the Transportation Research Board Human Factors Workshop on New Strategies for Dealing with the Persistent Drinking Driver. Washington, D.C.

Beirness, D. J. and H. M. Simpson. 1997. *Study of the Profile of High-Risk Drivers.* Ottawa, Ontario: Traffic Injury Research Foundation of Canada.

Bien, T. H., W. R. Miller, and S. Tonigan. 1993. Brief Interventions for Alcohol Problems: A Review. *Addiction.* 88:315-336.

Blomberg, R. D., D. F. Preusser, and R. G. Ulmer. 1987. *Deterrent Effects of Mandatory License Suspension for DWI Conviction.* DOT HS 807 138. Final Report. Washington, D.C.: U.S. Department of Transportation, National Highway Traffic Safety Administration.

Brecht, M. L., M. D. Anglin, and J. C. Wang. 1993. Treatment Effectiveness for Legally Coerced Versus Voluntary Methadone Maintenance Clients. *American Journal of Drug and Alcohol Abuse.* 19:89-106.

Brewer, C. 1995. Recent Developments in Disulfiram Treatment. *Alcohol and Alcoholism.* 8(4):383-395.

Brewer, R. D., P. D. Morris, T. B. Cole, S. Watkins, M. J. Patetta, and C. Popkin. 1994. The Risk of Dying in Alcohol-related Automobile Crashes among Habitual Drunk Drivers. *New England Journal of Medicine*. 331:513-517.

Brown, J. M. and W. R. Miller. 1993. Impact of Motivational Interviewing on Participation and Outcome in Residential Alcoholism Treatment. *Psychology of Addictive Behaviors*. 7(4):211-218.

Budney, A. J. and S. T. Higgins. 1998. Manual II. A Community Reinforcement Plus Vouchers Approach: Treating Cocaine Addiction. *Therapy Manual for Drug Addiction*. Washington, D.C.: U.S. Department of Health and Human Services, National Institutes of Health.

Carroll, K. M. 1998. Manual I. A Cognitive Behavioral Approach: Treating Cocaine Addiction. *Therapy Manual for Drug Addiction*. Washington, D.C.: U.S. Department of Health and Human Services, National Institutes of Health.

C'de Baca, J., S. C. Lapham, S. Paine, and B. J. Skipper. 2000. Victim Impact Panels: Who Is Sentenced to Attend? Does Attendance Affect Recidivism of First-time DWI Offenders? *Alcoholism. Clinical and Experimental Research*. 24(9):1420-1426.

Chafetz, M. E.1961. A Procedure for Establishing Therapeutic Contact with the Alcoholic. *Quarterly Journal of Studies on Alcohol*. 22:325-328.

Chaney, E. R., M. R. O'Leary, and G. A. Marlatt. 1978. Skill Training with Alcoholics. *Journal of Consulting and Clinical Psychology*. 46(5):1092-1104.

Chick, J. 1992. Emergent Treatment Concepts. *Annual Review of Addictions Research and Treatment*. 297-312.

Colorado Department of Human Services, Alcohol and Drug Abuse Division. 1996, 1997, 1998, 1999. Data Reports. Denver, Colorado: Department of Human Services.

————. 1999a. Naltrexone Policy. Denver, Colorado: Department of Human Services.

Compton, R. 1986. Preliminary Analysis of the Effect of Tennessee's Mandatory Jail Sanction on DWI Recidivism. In *Research Notes*, June. Washington, D.C.: National Highway Traffic Safety Administration.

Conners, G. J., K. S. Walitzer, and K. H. Derman. June, 1998. Preparing Clients for Alcoholism Treatment: Effects of Preparatory Interventions. Presented at the Annual Meeting of the Research Society on Alcoholism, Hilton Head, South Carolina.

Darbey, B. R. 1993. *Pre-trial Services Corporation Felony Driving While Intoxicated Diversion Program: An Examination of Program Outcomes*. Rochester, New York: Pre-Trial Services Corporation.

DeLeon, G. 1988. Legal Pressure in Therapeutic Communities. *Journal of Drug Issues.* 18:625-640.

Deyle, R. 1997. The Effectiveness of Education and Treatment in Reducing Recidivism among Convicted Drinking Drivers. Denver, Colorado: Alcohol and Drug Abuse Division of the Colorado Department of Human Services.

Donovan, D. M., H. R. Queisser, P. M. Salzberg, and R. L. Umlauf. 1985. Intoxicated and Bad Drivers: Subgroups within the Same Population of High Risk Men Drivers. *Journal of Studies on Alcohol.* 46(5):375-382.

Donovan, D. M., R. L. Umlauf, and P. M. Salzberg. 1990. Bad Drivers: Identification of a Target Group for Alcohol-related Prevention and Early Intervention. *Journal of Studies on Alcohol.* 51(2):136-141.

Eliany, M. and B. Rush. 1992. *How Effective Are Alcohol and Other Drug Prevention and Treatment Programs? A Review of Evaluation Studies.* Ottawa, Ontario: Health and Welfare, Canada.

Ellingstad, V. S. and D. L. Struckman-Johnson. 1978. *Life Activity Inventory (LAI).* Washington, D.C.: National Highway Traffic Safety Administration.

Emrick, C. D. 1987. Alcoholics Anonymous: Affiliation Processes and Effectiveness as Treatment. *Alcoholism: Clinical and Experimental Research.* 11, 416-423.

————. 1989. Alcoholics Anonymous: Membership Characteristics and Effectiveness as Treatment. *Recent Developments in Alcoholism.* 7, 37-53.

Emrick, C. D., J. S. Tonigan, H. Montgomery, and L. Little. 1993. Alcoholics Anonymous: What is Currently Known. In B. S. McCrady and W. R. Miller, eds. *Research on Alcoholics Anonymous*, pp. 41-76. Piscataway, New Jersey: Rutgers University Center of Alcohol Studies.

EMT Group. 1990. *Evaluation of the California Interlock Pilot Program For DWI Offenders.* Sacramento, California: EMT Group.

Falkowski, C. L. 1984. *The Impact of Two-day Jail Sentences for Drunk Drivers in Hennepin County, Minnesota.* DOT HS 806 839. Final Report. Washington, D.C.: National Highway Traffic Safety Administration.

Fell, J. C. 1994. Current Trends: Drivers with Repeat Convictions or Arrests for Driving While Impaired. *MMWR Weekly.* 43(41):759-761.

Finney, J. W. 1995. Assessing Treatment and Treatment Processes. In J. P. Allen and M. Columbus, eds. *Assessing Alcohol Problems: A Guide for Clinicians and Researchers*, pp. 123-142. Bethesda, Maryland: National Institute on Alcohol Abuse and Alcoholism.

Finney, J. W. and S. C. Monahan. 1996. The Cost Effectiveness of Treatment for Alcoholism: A Second Approximation. *Journal of Studies on Alcohol.* 57(3):229-243.

Fors, S. W. and D. G. Rojek. 1999. The Effect of Victim Impact Panels on DUI/ DWAI Rearrest Rates: A Twelve-month Follow-up. *Journal of Studies on Alcohol.* 60(4): 514-520.

Friedman, J., C. Harrington, and D. Higgins. 1995. *Reconvicted Drinking Driver Study.* AL 90-004. Albany, New York: New York State Governor's Traffic Safety Committee.

Fuller, R. K., L. Branchey, and D. R. Brightwell. 1986. Disulfiram Treatment of Alcoholism. *Journal of the American Medical Association.* 256:1449-1455.

Gendreau, P. 1996. Offender Rehabilitation: What We Know and What Needs to Be Done. *American Association for Correctional Psychology.* 23(1):144-161.

Goldberg, F. 1995. Electronic Driving Licenses: Key to a New Traffic Safety System. In C. N. Kloeden and A. J. McLean, eds. *Proceedings of the 13th International Conference on Alcohol, Drugs and Traffic Safety*, Vol. 2, pp. 683-687. Adelaide, South Australia: University of Adelaide, Road Accident Research Unit.

Gordon, N. B. 1976. Influence of Narcotic Drugs on Highway Safety. *Accident Analysis and Prevention.* 8:3-7.

Gould, L. A. and K. H. Gould. 1992. First-time and Multiple-DWI Offenders: A Comparison of Criminal History Records and BAC Levels. *Journal of Criminal Justice.* 20(6):527-539.

Grube, J. W. and K. A. Kearney. 1983. A "Mandatory" Jail Sentence for Drinking and Driving. *Evaluation Review.* 7(2):235-245.

Gruenewald, P. J., P. R. Mitchell, and A. J. Treno. 1996. Drinking and Driving: Drinking Patterns and Drinking Problems. *Addiction.* 91(11):1637-1649.

Hagen, R. E. 1978. The Efficacy of Licensing Controls as a Countermeasure for Multiple DUI Offenders. *Journal of Safety Research.* 10(3):115-122.

Harrison, P. A.and N. G. Hoffman. 1985. *Substance Use Disorder Diagnosis Schedule.* St. Paul, Minnesota: New Standards, Inc.

Hartnoll, R. 1992. Research and the Help-seeking Process. *British Journal of Addiction.* 87(6):429-437.

Harwood, H. J., R. L. Hubbard, J. J. Collins, and J. V. Rachal. 1988. The Costs of Crime and the Benefits of Drug Abuse Treatment: A Cost-benefit Analysis. *NIDA.* 86: 209-235.

Hester, R. K. and W. R. Miller. 1995. *Handbook of Alcoholism Treatment Approaches: Effective Alternatives, Second Edition.* Boston: Allyn and Bacon.

Hingson, R. 1996. Prevention of Drinking and Driving. *Alcohol Health and Research World.* 20(4):219-229.

Homel, R. 1988. *Policing and Punishing the Drinking Driver: A Study of General and Specific Deterrence.* New York: Springer Verlag.

Horn, J. L., K. W. Wanberg, and F. M. Foster. 1987, 1990. *Alcohol Use Inventory (AUI).* Minneapolis, Minnesota: National Computer Systems.

Huebert, K. 1990. *Impact: Measuring Success.* Edmonton, Alberta: Alberta Alcohol and Drug Abuse Commission.

Institute of Medicine. 1990. *Broadening the Base of Treatment for Alcohol Problems.* Washington, D.C.: National Academy Press.

Izzo, R. L. and R. R. Ross. 1990. Meta-analysis of Rehabilitation Programs for Juvenile Delinquents. *Criminal Justice and Behavior.* 17(1):134-142.

Jessor, R. 1987. Risky Driving and Adolescent Problem Behavior: An Extension of Problem Behavior Theory. *Alcohol, Drugs and Driving.* 3(3-4):1-11.

Jessor, R. and S. L. Jessor. 1977. Problem Behavior and Psychosocial Development: A Longitudinal Study of Youth. New York: Academic Press.

Jeune, R. K. Huebert, W. Slavik, C. Brown, and B. Wah. 1988. *Impact: Program Development Studies.* Edmonton, Alberta. Alcohol and Drug Abuse Commission.

Johah, B. A. R. J. Wilson. 1986. Impaired Drivers Who Have Never Been Caught: Are They Different from Convicted Drivers? Society of Automotive Engineers Technical Paper Series. 860195.

Joksch, H. C. 1988. *The Impact of Severe Penalties on Drinking and Driving.* Washington, D.C.: AAA Foundation for Traffic Safety.

Jones, B. 1993. The Effectiveness of Oregon's Ignition Interlock Program. In H. D. Utzelmann, G. Berghaus, and G. Kroj, eds. *Alcohol, Drugs and Traffic Safety.* T92, Band 3 1460-5. Cologne, Germany: Verlag.

Jones, R. K. and J. H. Lacey. 1998. Alcohol Highway Safety: Problem Update. Washington, D.C.: Final Report for the National Highway Traffic Safety Administration.

Jones, R. K., J. H. Lacey, and J. C. Fell. 1996. Alternative Sanctions for Repeat DWI Offenders. In *49th Annual Proceedings of the Association for the Advancement of Automotive Medicine*, pp. 307-315. Des Plaines, Illinois: Association for the Advancement of Automotive Medicine.

Keller, M., M. McCormack, and B. Efron. 1982. *A Dictionary of Words about Alcohol*. Piscataway, New Jersey: Rutgers Center of Alcohol Studies.

Kennedy, B. P., N. E. Isaac, and J. D. Graham. 1996. The Role of Heavy Drinking in the Risk of Traffic Fatalities. *Risk Analysis*. 16(4):565-569.

Kinney, J. and G. Leaton. 1995. Loosening the Grip: *A Handbook of Alcohol Information*. St. Louis, Missouri: Mosby Year Book.

Kurtz, E. 1993. Research on Alcoholics Anonymous: The Historical Context. In B. S. McCrady and W. R. Miller, eds. *Research on Alcoholics Anonymous: Opportunities and Alternatives*, pp. 13-26. Piscataway, New Jersey: Rutgers Center of Alcohol Studies.

Lacey, J. H., R. K. Jones, and C. H. Wiliszowski. 1997. *Validation of Problem Drinking Screening Instruments for DWI Offenders*. Winchester, Massachusetts. Prepared for the U.S. Department of Transportation by Mid-America Research Institute of New England.

Lapham, S. C., K. W. Wanberg, D. S. Timken, and K. J. Barton. 1996. *The Lovelace Institute's Comprehensive Screening Instrument (LCSI)*. Albuquerque, New Mexico: Behavioral Health Research Center of the Southwest.

Lieberman, M. A., I. D. Yalom, and M. D. Miles. 1973. *Encounter Groups: First Facts*. New York: Basic Books.

Lindeman, H. 1987. *Driver Risk Inventory (DRI)*. Phoenix, Arizona: Behavior Data Systems, Inc.

Lindstrom, L. 1992. *Managing Alcoholism: Matching Clients to Treatments*. New York: Oxford University Press.

Lipsey, M. W. 1989. The Efficacy of Intervention for Juvenile Delinquency: Results from 400 Studies. Paper presented at the 41st annual meeting of the American Society of Criminology, Reno, Nevada.

————. 1992. Juvenile Delinquency Treatment: A Meta-analytic Inquiry into the Variability of Effects. In T. D. Cook, H. Cooper, D. S. Cordray, H. Hartman, L. V. Hedges, R. J. Light, T. A. Louis, and F. Mosteller, eds. *Meta-analysis for Explanation*, pp. 83-127. New York: Russell Sage Foundation.

Lipsey, M. W. and D. B. Wilson. 1993. The Efficacy of Psychological, Educational and Behavioral Treatment: Confirmation from Meta-analysis. *American Psychologist*. 48(12):1181-1209.

Lipton, D. S. 1994. The Correctional Opportunity: Pathways to Drug Treatment for Offenders. *Journal of Drug Issues*. 24(1-2):331-348.

Liu, S., P. Z. Siegel, R. D. Brewer, A. H. Mokdad, D. A. Sleet, and M. Surdual. 1997. Prevalence of Alcohol-impaired Driving: Results from a National Self-reported Survey of Health Behaviors. *Journal of the American Medical Association (JAMA)*. 277(2): 122-125.

Lowinson, J. H., J. T. Payte, H. Joseph, I. J. Marion, and V. P. Dole. 1997. Methadone Maintenance. In J. H. Lowinson, P. Ruiz, R. B. Millman and J. G. Langrod, eds. *Substance Abuse: A Comprehensive Textbook*, pp. 405-425. Baltimore, Maryland: Williams and Wilkins.

Lund, A. K. and A. C. Wolf. 1991. Changes in the Incidence of Alcohol-impaired Driving in the United States, 1973-1986. *Journal of Studies on Alcohol*. 52(4):293-301.

Mann, R. E., E. R. Vingilis, D. Gavin, E. Adlaf, and L. Anglin. 1991. Sentence Severity and the Drinking Driver: Relationships with Traffic Safety Outcome. *Accident Analysis and Prevention*. 23(6):483-491.

Mann, R. E., E. R. Vingilis, and K. Stewart. 1988. Programs to Change Individual Behavior: Education and Rehabilitation in the Prevention of Drinking and Driving. In M. D. Laurence, J. R. Snortum, and F. E. Zimring, eds. *Social Control of the Drinking Driver*, pp. 248-269. Chicago: University of Chicago Press.

Mark, F. O. 1988. Does Coercion Work? The Role of Referral Source in Motivating Alcoholics in Treatment. *Alcoholism Treatment Quarterly*. 5(3):5-22.

Marlatt, G. A., J. S. Baer, and M. E. Larimer. 1995. Preventing Alcohol Abuse in College Students: A Harm Reduction Approach. In G. M. Boyd, J. Howard, and R. A. Zucker, eds. *Alcohol Problems among Adolescents: Current Directions in Prevention Research*, pp. 147-172. Hillsdale, New Jersey: Erlbaum.

Marques, P. R. and R. B. Voas. 1995. Case-managed Alcohol Interlock Programs: A Bridge Between the Criminal and Health Systems. *Journal of Traffic Medicine*. 23(2):77- 85.

Martin, S. E., S. Annan, and B. Forst. 1993. The Special Deterrent Effects of a Jail Sentence on First-time Drunk Drivers: A Quasi-experimental Study. *Accident Analysis and Prevention*. 25(5):561-568.

Maull, K. I., L. S. Kinning, and J. K. Hickman. 1984. Culpability and Accountability of Hospitalized Injured Alcohol-impaired Drivers. *Journal of the American Medical Association (JAMA)*. 252(14):1880-1883.

McClellan, A. T., B. Fureman, G. Parikh, and A. Bragg. 1985, 1996. *Addiction Severity Index (ASI)*. Philadelphia, Pennsylvania: The University of Pennsylvania/Veterans Administration Center for Studies on Addiction.

McCrady, B. S., L. Dean, E. Dubreuil, and S. Swanson. 1985. The Problem Drinkers Project: A Programmatic Application of Social Learning Based Treatment. In G. A. Marlatt and J. R. Gordon, eds. *Relapse Prevention: Maintenance Strategies in the Treatment of Addictive Behaviors*, pp. 417-471. New York: Guilford Press.

McGuire, J. and P. Priestley. 1995. Reviewing "What Works": Past, Present and Future. In J. McGuire, ed. *What Works: Reducing Reoffending*, pp. 3-34. New York: Wiley.

McKnight, A. J. and R. B. Voas. 1991. The Effect of License Suspension upon DWI Recidivism. *Alcohol, Drugs and Driving.* 7(1):43-54.

Mendelson, J. and N. Mello. 1979. *The Diagnosis and Treatment of Alcoholism*. New York: McGraw Hill.

Meyers, R. J. and J. E. Smith. 1995. *Clinical Guide to Alcohol Treatment: The Community Reinforcement Approach*. New York: Guilford Press.

Miller, W. R., ed. 1980. *The Addictive Behaviors*. New York: Pergamon.

Miller, W. R., R. J. Benefield, and J. S. Tonigan. 1993. Enhancing Motivation for Change in Problem Drinking: A Controlled Comparison of Two Therapist Styles. *Journal of Consulting and Clinical Psychology*. 61(53):455-461.

Miller, W. R., J. M. Brown, T. L. Simpson, N. H. S. Handmaker, T. H. Bien, L. F. Luckie, H. A. Montgomery, R. K. Hester, and J. S. Tonigan. 1995. What Works? A Methodological Analysis of the Alcohol Treatment Outcome Literature. In R. K. Hester and W. R. Miller, eds. *Handbook of Alcoholism Treatment Approaches: Effective Alternatives*, pp. 12-44. Boston: Allyn and Bacon.

Miller, W. R. and R. K. Hester. 1986. Matching Problem Drinkers with Optimal Treatments. In W. R. Miller and N. Heather, eds. *Treating Addictive Behaviors: Processes of Change*, pp.175-204. New York: Plenum Press.

Miller, W. R. and G. A. Marlatt. 1984. *The Comprehensive Drinker Profile (CDP)*. Albuquerque, New Mexico: Department of Psychology, University of New Mexico.

Miller, W. R. and B. S. McCrady. 1993. The Importance of Research on Alcoholics Anonymous. In B. S. McCrady and W. R. Miller. *Research on Alcoholics Anonymous: Opportunities and Alternatives*, pp 3-12. Piscataway, New Jersey: Rutgers Center of Alcohol Studies.

Miller, W. R. and S. Rollnick. 1991. *Motivational Interviewing*. New York: Guilford Press.

Miller, W. R. and V. C. Sanchez. 1994. Motivating Young Adults for Treatment and Lifestyle Change. In G. Howard, ed. *Issues in Alcohol Use and Misuse by Young Adults*, pp. 55-82. Notre Dame, Indiana: University of Notre Dame Press.

Miller, W. R. and J. S. Tonigan. 1991, 1996. *Stages of Change Readiness and Treatment Eagerness Scale (SOCRATES)*. Albuquerque, New Mexico: Department of Psychology, University of New Mexico.

Miller, W. R., S. Tonigan, and R. Longabaugh. 1995. The Drinker Inventory of Consequences (DrInC!): An Instrument for Assessing Adverse Consequences of Alcohol Abuse. *NIAAA Project Match Monograph Series, Vol. 4*. Bethesda, Maryland: National Institute on Alcohol Abuse and Alcoholism.

Minnesota Department of Public Safety. 1990. *Mandatory Plate Impoundment: An Evaluation of the Implementation of the Mandatory Surrender of Registration Plates of Vehicles Operated by Repeat DWI Offenders*. St. Paul, Minnesota: Minnesota Depart of Public Safety.

Monti, P.M., D. B. Abrams, R. M. Kadden, and N. L. Cooney. 1989. *Treating Alcohol Dependence: A Coping Skills Training Guide*. New York: Guilford Press.

Morse, B.J. and D. S. Elliott. 1990. *Hamilton County Drinking and Driving Study: 30 Month Report*. Boulder, Colorado: University of Colorado Institute of Behavioral Science.

Nace, E.P. 1997. Alcoholics Anonymous. In J. H. Lowinson, P. Ruiz, R. B. Millman, and J. G. Langrod, eds. *Substance Abuse: A Comprehensive Textbook, Third Edition*. Baltimore, Maryland: Williams and Wilkins.

National Highway Traffic Safety Administration. 1971. *Court Procedures for Identifying Problem Drinkers, Vol. 1 and 2*. Prepared for National Highway Traffic Safety Administration by the University of Michigan Highway Safety Research Institute, Ann Arbor, Michigan.

———. 1972. *Alcohol Safety Action Programs: Evaluation of Operations, Vol. I, II*. Washington, D.C.: National Highway Traffic Safety Administration.

———. 1979. *Summary of National Alcohol Safety Action Projects*. Washington, D.C.: National Highway Traffic Safety Administration.

———. 1983. *A Guide to Self-sufficient Funding of Alcohol Traffic Safety Programs (Contract HS 432)*. Washington, D.C.: National Highway Traffic Safety Administration.

———. 1996. *A Guide to Sentencing DUI Offenders (DOT HS 808-365)*. Washington, D.C.: National Highway Traffic Safety Administration.

———. 1998. Traffic Safety Facts, 1997. *Public Information Fact Sheet*. Washington, D.C.: National Highway Traffic Safety Administration.

Nichols, J. L. 1990. Treatment vs. Deterrence. *Alcohol Health and Research World*. 14(1):44-51.

Nichols, J. L. and H. L. Ross. 1989. The Effectiveness of Legal Sanctions in Dealing with Drinking Drivers. In *The Surgeon General's Workshop on Drunk Driving: Background Papers*, pp. 93-112. Rockville, Maryland: Office of the Surgeon General, U.S. Department of Health and Human Services.

Nichols, J. L., E. B. Weinstein, V. S. Ellingstad, and D. L. Struckman-Johnson. 1978. The Specific Deterrent Effect of ASAP Education and Rehabilitation Programs. *Journal of Safety Research*. 10:177-187.

Nochajski, T. H., B. A. Miller, W. F. Wieczorek, and R. Whitney, R. 1993. The Effects of a Drinker-driver Treatment Program: Does Criminal History Make a Difference? *Criminal Justice and Behavior*. 20(2):174-189.

Nochajski, T. H., B. A. Miller, and K. A. Parks. 1994. Comparison of First-time and Repeat DWI Offenders. Paper presented at the annual meeting of the Research Society of Alcoholism, Maui, Hawaii, June 18-23, 1994. Buffalo, New York: Research Institute on Addictions.

Nochajski, T. H. and W. Wieczorek. 1995. *Research Institute on Addictions Self Inventory (RIASI)*. Buffalo, New York: Research Institute on Addictions.

Orford, J., and G. Edwards. 1977. *Alcoholism: A Comparison of Treatment and Advice, with a Study of the Influence of Marriage*. Maudsley Monograph, 26. Oxford: Oxford University Press.

Packard, M. 1993, 1996. Unpublished handouts.

Packard, M. A., D. S. Timken, and B. Bogue. 1993. *Risk Modification Training (RMT): Treating the Multiple Offender*. Boulder, Colorado: Sage Institute.

Parrish, M. R.. ed. 1999. Half Million Drunk Drivers Reported Under Supervision. *Criminal Justice Drug Letter*. June, p.4.

Parsons, M., I. Wnek, and K. M. Huebert. 1993. *A Unique Intervention Program for Repeat Impaired Driving Offenders*. Edmonton, Alberta: Alberta Alcohol and Drug Abuse Commission.

Pattison, E. M. and E. Kaufman. 1982. *Encyclopedia Handbook of Alcoholism*. New York: Gardiner Press.

Peck, R. C. 1991. The General and Specific Deterrent Effects of DUI Sanctions: A Review of California's Experience. *Alcohol, Drugs and Driving*. 7(1):13-42.

Peck, R. C., G. W. Arstein-Kerslake, and C. J. Helander. 1993. Psychometric and Biographical Correlates of Drunk-driving Recidivism and Treatment Program Compliance. *Journal of Studies on Alcohol*. 55(6):667-678.

Peck, R. C., D. D. Sadler, and M. W. Perrine. 1985. The Comparative Effectiveness of Alcohol Rehabilitation and Licensing Control Actions for Drunk Driving Offenders: A Review of the Literature. *Alcohol, Drugs, Driving.* 1(4):15-39.

Peters, K. D., K. D. Kochanek, and S. L. Murphey. 1998. Deaths: Final Data for 1996. *National Vital Statistics Reports.* 47:26.

Poley, , W., G. Lea, and G. Vibe. 1979. *Alcoholism: A Treatment Manual.* New York: Plenum Press.

Popkin, C. L., L. K. Li, J. H. Lacey, J. R. Stewart, and P. F. Waller. 1983. An Initial Evaluation of the North Carolina Alcohol and Drug Education Traffic Schools. *Technical Report, Vol I.* Chapel Hill, North Carolina: Highway Safety Research Center, University of North Carolina.

Popkin, C. L., J. Beckmeyer, and C. Martell. 1993. An Evaluation of the Effectiveness of Interlock Systems in Preventing DWI Recidivism among Second-time DWI Offenders. In H. D. Utzelmann, G. Berghaus, and G. Kroj, eds. *Alcohol, Drugs and Traffic Safety*, T- 92, Band 3:1466-1470. Cologne, Germany, Verlag.

Popkin, C. L., J. R. Stewart, and J. H. Lacey. 1988. A Follow-up Evaluation of North Carolina's Alcohol and Drug Education Traffic Schools and Mandatory Substance Abuse Assessments. *Final Report.* Chapel Hill, North Carolina: Highway Safety Research Center, University of North Carolina.

Prochaska, J. O. and C. C. DiClemente. 1982. Transtheoretical Therapy: Toward a More Integrative Model of Change. *Psychotherapy: Theory, Research and Practice.* 19(3):276- 288.

———. 1986. Toward a Comprehensive Model of Change. In W. R. Miller and N. Heather, eds. *Treating Addictive Behaviors: Processes of Change*, pp. 3-27. New York: Plenum Press

———. 1991. *University of Rhode Island Change Assessment (URICA).* Baltimore, Maryland: University of Maryland.

Project MATCH Research Group. 1997. Matching Alcoholism Treatments to Client Heterogeneity: Project MATCH Posttreatment Drinking Outcomes. *Journal of Studies on Alcohol.* 58(1):7-29.

Reis, R. E. 1982a. *The Traffic Safety Effectiveness of Education Programs for First Offense Drunk Drivers*, DOT Contract HS-6-01414. Washington, D.C.: National Highway Traffic Safety Administration.

———. *The Traffic Safety Effectiveness of Education Programs for Multiple Offense Drunk Drivers*, DOT Contract HS-6-01414. Washington, D.C.: National Highway Traffic Safety Administration.

Robins, L. N., J. E. Helzer, J. Croughan, J. B. W. Williams, and R. L. Spitzer. 1981. *Diagnostic Interview Schedule (DIS)*. Bethesda, Maryland: National Institute of Mental Health, Division of Biometry and Epidemiology.

Rogers, A. 1994. Effect of Minnesota's License Plate Impoundment Law on Recidivism of Multiple DWI Violators. *Alcohol, Drugs and Driving*. 10(2):127-134.

Ross, H. L. and H. Klette. 1995. Abandonment of Mandatory Jail for Impaired Drivers in Norway and Sweden. *Accident Analysis and Prevention*. 27(2):151-157.

Rufener, B. L., J. V. Rachal, and A. M. Cruze. 1977. Management Effectiveness Measures for NIDA Drug Abuse Programs, Cost Benefit Analysis. Publication No. (ADM) 77-423. Rockville, Maryland: National Institute on Drug Abuse.

Sadler, D. D. and M. W. Perrine. 1984. The Long-term Traffic Safety Impact of a Pilot Alcohol Abuse Treatment as an Alternative to License Suspensions. *Volume 2: An Evaluation of the California Drunk Driving Countermeasure System*. Sacramento, California: Department of Motor Vehicles.

Shinar, D, and R. P. Compton. 1995. Victim Impact Panels: Their Impact on DWI Recidivism. *Alcohol Drugs and Driving*. 11(1):73-87.

Siegal, H. A. 1985. Impact of Driver Intervention Program on DWI Recidivism and Problem Drinking. *Final Report*, Contract No. DTNH 22 83 C 05150. Washington, D.C.: National Highway Traffic Safety Administration.

———. 1987. Intervention: A Successful Technique for Repeat Offenders. In P. C. Noordzij and R. Roszbach, eds. *Alcohol, Drugs and Traffic Safety—T86*. Excerpta Medica. International Congress Series 721. Amsterdam: Elsevier.

Simpson, H. M. and D. R. Mayhew. 1991. *The Hard Core Drinking Driver*. Ottawa, Ontario: The Traffic Injury Research Foundation of Canada.

Simpson, H. M., D. R. Mayhew, and D. J. Beirness. 1996. *Dealing with the Hard Core Drinking Driver*. Ottawa, Ontario: The Traffic Injury Research Foundation of Canada.

Spitzer, R. L., J. B. Williams, M. Gibbon, M. B. First. 1996. *Structured Clinical Interview for DSM-IV Personality Disorders (SCID-II) (Alcohol Section)*. New York: Biometrics Research Department, New York State Psychiatric Institute.

Stewart, K. and V. S. Ellingstad. 1989. Rehabilitative Countermeasures for Drinking Drivers. In *Surgeon General's Workshop on Drunk Driving: Background Papers*, pp. 234-246. Rockville, Maryland: Office of the Surgeon General, U.S. Department of Health and Human Services.

Stewart, K., P. Gruenewald, and T. Roth. 1989. *An Evaluation of Administrative Per Se Laws*. Final report on grant 86-IJ-CX-0081. Washington, D.C.: National Institute of Justice.

Stitzer, M. L. and M. E. McCaul. 1987. Criminal Justice Interventions with Drug and Alcohol Abusers. In E. K. Morris and C. J. Braukmann, eds. *Behavioral Approaches to Crime and Delinquency: A Handbook of Application: Research and Concepts.* New York: Plenum Press.

Struckman-Johnson, D. L. and V. S. Ellingstad. 1978a. *The Short Term Rehabilitation Study, Vol. III: Site Specific Analyses of Effectiveness.* Report HFL-78-9. Vermillion, South Dakota: Human Factors Laboratory, University of South Dakota.

————. 1978b. *The Short Term Rehabilitation Study, Vol. IV: Program Level Analysis of Effectiveness.* Report HFL-78-9. Vermillion, South Dakota: Human Factory Laboratory, University of South Dakota.

Tashima, H. and R. C. Peck. 1986. An Evaluation of the Specific Deterrent Effects of Alternative Sanctions for First and Repeat DUI Offenders. *Vol. III: An Evaluation of the California Drunk Driving Countermeasures System.* Sacramento, California: Department of Motor Vehicles.

Timken, D. S. Unpublished informal study of treatment staff personnel.

————. Unpublished review of DWI programs in Colorado, ongoing informal study.

————. Unpublished survey, continuing. Is the outcome changed when offenders pay for treatment?

————. 1993. *Motivational Interviewing: Preparing Offenders to Change Drinking and Driving Behaviors.* Boulder, Colorado: Timken and Associates.

————. 1996a. *DSM-IV Brief Interview for Substance Abuse or Dependence.* Boulder, Colorado: Timken and Associates.

————. 1996b. *DSM-IV Checklists for Substance Abuse or Dependence.* Boulder, Colorado: Timken and Associates.

————. 1997. *The Alcohol Drug Driving Safety Program Placement Criteria for Substance Abusing Drivers (ADDS-PC).* Boulder, Colorado: Timken and Associates.

————. 1998. Review of Treatment Programs in Colorado. Unpublished.

————. 1999. *ADAD Approved Instrumentation for Substance Abusing Adults.* Denver, Colorado: Alcohol and Drug Abuse Division of the Colorado Department of Human Services.

Timken, D. S., M. A. Packard, M.A., E. Wells-Parker, and B. Bogue. 1995. Rehabilitation of the Persistent Drinking/Drugging Driver. In *Transportation Research Circular.* 437:63-68.

Timken, D. S. and K. W. Wanberg. 1999. *Alcohol and Drug Driving Safety Program Screening and Referral Guidelines*. Denver, Colorado: Office of Probation Services, Colorado Judicial Department.

Tonigan, J. S. 1995. Issues in Alcohol Treatment Outcome Assessment. In J. P. Allen and M. Columbus. *Assessing Alcohol Problems: a Guide for Clinicians and Researchers*, pp. 143-154. Bethesda, Maryland: National Institute on Alcohol Abuse and Alcoholism.

Tonigan, J. S. and R. T. Toscova. 1993. Mutual-help Groups: Research and Clinical Implications. In W. R. Miller and N. Heather, eds. *Treating Addictive Behaviors, 2nd ed.*, pp. 285-298. New York: Plenum Press.

Townsend, T. N., J. Lane, C. S. Dewa, and A. M. Brittingham. 1998. *Driving after Drug or Alcohol Use Report*. Rockville, Maryland: Substance Abuse and Mental Health Services Administration.

Transportation Research Board. 1995. Human Factors Workshop on New Strategies for Dealing with the Persistent Drinking Driver. In *Transportation Research Circular*, No. 30.

Truax, C. and R. Carkhuff. 1967. *Toward Effective Counseling and Psychotherapy.* Boston: Aldine Press.

Valle, S. K. 1981. Interpersonal Functioning of Alcoholism Counselors and Treatment Outcome. *Journal of Studies on Alcohol* 42:783-790.

Van Voorhis, P. 1987. Correctional Effectiveness: The Cost of Ignoring Success. *Federal Probation*. 51(1):56-62.

Vingilis, E. R. 1983. Drinking Drivers and Alcoholics: Are They from the Same Population? In R. Smart, F. Glasser, and Y. Israel, eds. *Research Advances in Alcohol and Drug Problems, Vol. 7*, pp. 299-342. New York: Plenum Press.

Voas, R. B. 1986. Evaluation of Jail as a Penalty for Drunk Driving. *Alcohol, Drugs and Driving: Abstracts and Reviews*. 2(2):47-70.

————. 1991. Enforcement of DUI Law. *Alcohol Drugs and Driving*. 7(3-4):173-196.

Voas, R. B. and A. S. Tippetts. 1990. Evaluation of Treatment and Monitoring Programs for Drunken Drivers. *Journal of Traffic Medicine*. 18(1):15-26.

————. 1993. Are Licensing Sanctions Effective at Reducing Impaired Driving? Paper presented at National Transportation Research Board Meetings, January, 1993.

————. 1994. *Assessment of Impoundment and Forfeiture Laws for Drivers Convicted of DWI: Phase II Report.* Washington, D.C.: National Highway Traffic Safety Administration.

Voas, R. B., A, S. Tippetts, and E. Taylor. 1996. The Effect of Vehicle Impoundment and Immobilization on Driving Offenses of Suspended and Repeat DWI Drivers. Presented at the 40th Annual Proceedings of the Association for the Advancement of Automotive Medicine, October, 7-9, 1996. Vancouver, British Columbia.

Wanberg, K. W. 1999. *The Adult Clinical Assessment Profile (ACAP)*. Arvada, Colorado: Center for Addictions Research and Evaluation (CARE).

Wanberg, K. W. and J. L. Horn. 1991. *The Drug Use Self Report (DUSR)*. Arvada, Colorado: Center for Addictions Research and Evaluation (CARE).

Wanberg, K. W. and H. B. Milkman. 1993. *Adult Self Assessment Questionnaire (AdSAQ)*. Arvada, Colorado: Center for Addictions Research and Evaluation.

Wanberg, K. W. and H. B. Milkman. 1998. *Criminal Conduct and Substance Abuse Treatment: Strategies for Self-improvement and Change*. Thousand Oaks, California: Sage Publications.

Wanberg, K. W., H. B. Milkman, H. B., and D. S. Timken. In Press. Driving with care: Alcohol and other drugs and driving safety education, Level I education, Level II education, and impaired driving offender treatment: Strategies for self-improvement and change: Level II therapy.

Wanberg, K. W. and D. S. Timken. 1990. *Driving Assessment Survey (DAS)*. Arvada, Colorado: Center for Addiction Research and Evaluation (CARE).

————. *Adult Substance Use and Driving Survey. (ASUDS)*. Arvada, Colorado: Center for Addictions Research and Evaluation (CARE).

————. *A User's Guide to the Adult Substance Use and Driving Survey (ASUDS)*. Arvada, Colorado: Center for Addictions Research and Evaluation (CARE).

Wells-Parker, E., R. Bangert-Drowns, D. L. McMillen, and M. Williams. 1995. Final Results from a Meta-analysis of Remedial Interventions with Drink/Drive Offenders. *Addiction*. 90:907-926.

Wieczorek, W. F. 1995. The Role of Treatment in Reducing Alcohol-related Accidents Involving DWI Offenders. In R. R. Watson, ed. *Drug and Alcohol Abuse Reviews, Vol. 7: Alcohol, Cocaine, and Accidents*. Totowa, New Jersey: Humana Press.

Wieczorek, W. F., C. Callahan, and M. Morales. 1997. Motivation for Change among DWI Offenders. In C. Mercier-Guyon, ed. *Alcohol, Drugs and Traffic Safety*—T97, pp. 1069-1075. Annecy, France: CERMT.

Williams, A. F., K. Weinberg, and M. Fields. 1991. The Effectiveness of Administrative License Suspension Laws. *Alcohol, Drugs and Driving*. 7(1):55-62.

Wilson, R. J. 1984. *A National Household Survey on Drinking and Driving: Knowledge, Attitudes and Behaviour of Canadian Drivers.* Montreal, Canada: Road Safety and Motor Vehicle Directorate.

———. 1992. Convicted Impaired Drivers and High-risk Drivers: How Similar Are They? *Journal of Studies on Alcohol.* 53(4):335-344.

Woodall, W. G., H. Delaney, E. Rogers, and D. Wheeler. June, 2000. *A Randomized Trial of Victim Impact Panels' DWI Deterrence Effectiveness.* Poster session presented at the 23rd Annual Scientific Meeting of the Research Society on Alcoholism, held in Denver Colorado.

Yalom, I. D. 1975. *The Theory and Practice of Group Psychotherapy, 2nd ed.* New York: Basic Books.

Yu, J., and W. R. Williford. 1991. Calculating DWI/DWAI Recidivism with Limited Data: Using State Driver License Files for Drinking and Driving Research. *Journal of Drug Education.* 21(4):285-292.

Zuckerman, M. 1964. Sensation Seeking Scale (SSS). Dimensions of Sensation Seeking. 1971. Additional items published with original test. *Journal of Consulting and Clinical Psychology.* 36(1):45-52.

THE SPOUSAL ASSAULT RISK ASSESSMENT (SARA) GUIDE: RELIABILITY AND VALIDITY IN ADULT MALE OFFENDERS*

4

Stephen D. Hart
Professor of Psychology
Department of Psychology, Simon Fraser University
Burnaby, British Columbia

P. Randall Kropp
Clinical and Forensic Psychologist
British Columbia Institute Against Family Violence
Vancouver, British Columbia
and
Department of Psychology, Simon Fraser University
Burnaby, British Columbia

Spousal assault is a major public health concern due to its prevalence, its harmful impact on victims' physical and psychological well-being, and its associated economic costs (Koss et al., 1994). One

*This essay originally appeared in *Law and Human Behavior*, Vol. 24, No. 1, 2000. It has been reprinted with permission from Kluwer Academic/Plenum Publishers, New York.

response to the problem has been the development of criminal justice policies that encourage the arrest and conviction of perpetrators. This has led to a large increase in the volume of spousal assaults reported to police. In Canada, for example, spousal assaults now account for the vast majority (>80 percent) of simple assaults reported to police, which in turn constitute the majority (>80 percent) of all violent crimes reported to police (Statistics Canada, 1998). Possibly as a result of policy changes as well as improvements in information technology, it is becoming clear that a large proportion of correctional offenders—both probationers and prisoners—are known perpetrators of spousal assault. Focusing on Canada once again, surveys of correctional files indicate that at least 20 to 40 percent of all adult male offenders, regardless of the nature of their index offenses, have a documented history of spousal assault (Dutton and Hart, 1992; Hart, Kropp, Roesch, Ogloff, and Whittemore, 1994; Robinson, 1995). Official statistics from two Canadian provinces indicate that spousal assaulters now make up the single largest category of adult probationers, comprising about 25 percent of all offenders in British Columbia (personal communication, Information Systems, Corrections Branch, British Columbia Ministry of Attorney General, November 9, 1998) and 40 percent in Manitoba (Canadian Centre for Justice Statistics, 1994). Spousal assault is also a problem in United States correctional agencies (Healey and Smith, 1998).

The sheer number of spousal assault offenders in correctional facilities and on community release poses a major challenge to criminal justice agencies. The rational allocation of scarce supervisory and intervention resources is contingent on the accurate identification of those offenders who pose the highest risk of repeated violence and those who may be well suited to various management strategies, a process known as *violence risk assessment* or *violence prediction*. Although the assessment of risk for certain kinds of criminal behavior has a long and successful history in corrections (*see* discussions by Andrews and Bonta, 1998; Gottfredson and Gottfredson, 1988), there are as yet no widely accepted and well-validated procedures for assessing violence risk, including risk for spousal violence (Campbell, 1998).

The lack of a suitable tool led us to develop a set of professional guidelines that we called the *Spousal Assault Risk Assessment Guide (SARA)* (Kropp, Hart, Webster, and Eaves, 1994, 1995, 1998). Briefly, the *SARA* is a small book or manual that presents a series of recommendations concerning the assessment of risk for spousal violence. These recommendations include the training of evaluators, the nature and extent of information that should form the basis of evaluations, a set of twenty risk factors that should be considered (at a minimum) in every evaluation, and the manner in which judgments of risk should be documented and communicated. The twenty risk factors, presented in Table 1, were identified on the basis of a review of the relevant scientific literature as well as a consideration of relevant clinical and legal issues. Part 1 (factors 1-10) is related to violence risk in general, whereas part 2 (factors 11-20) is related specifically to risk of spousal violence. The *SARA* manual recommends that evaluators code the presence of each of the twenty risk factors; the presence of any additional case-specific risk factors; whether any of the risk factors is considered "critical" (that is, particularly relevant to decisions concerning the individual's risk); and the overall degree of risk posed by the individual, taking into account the nature, severity, likelihood, frequency, and imminence of any future violence.

The presence of individual *SARA* risk factors is coded numerically according to relatively detailed guidelines. Item codes can be combined arithmetically to yield several continuous scores, described in detail later, that may be of use in making descriptive judgments or in research. Because the scores are combined according to fixed and explicit algorithms, they can be considered actuarial in nature.[1] In contrast, critical

Table 1. Items in the *Spousal Assault Risk Assessment Guide (SARA)*

Part 1 (general violence risk factors)	Part 2 (spousal violence risk factors)
1. Past assault of family members	11. Past physical assault
2. Past assault of strangers or acquaintances	12. Past sexual assault/sexual jealousy
3. Past violation of conditional release or community supervision	13. Past use of weapons and/or credible threats of death
4. Recent relationship problems	14. Recent escalation in frequency or severity of assault
5. Recent employment problems	15. Past violation of "no contact" orders
6. Victim of and/or witness to family violence as a child or adolescent	16. Extreme minimization or denial of spousal assault history
7. Recent substance abuse/dependence	17. Attitudes that support or condone spousal assault
8. Recent suicidal or homicidal ideation/ intent	18. Severe and/or sexual assault (most recent incident)
9. Recent psychotic and/or manic symptoms	19. Use of weapons and/or credible threats of death (most recent incident)
10. Personality disorder with anger, impulsivity, or behavioral instability	20. Violation of "no contact" order (most recent incident)

item ratings and summary ratings of risk are not made according to fixed and explicit guidelines. The *SARA* manual recognizes there may exist no decision-making algorithm that is optimal across evaluation contexts, that any algorithms developed are likely to have complex and distinctly nonlinear rules, and that final decisions of risk may appropriately be influenced by external considerations such as the nature of the environment into which an individual is likely to be released. Because of their heavy reliance on professional judgment or discretion, then, critical item ratings and summary ratings of risk cannot be considered actuarial. We describe them as *structured professional judgment*.[2]

Due to its lack of a fixed and explicit information-gathering procedure, the *SARA* can be considered a test only if one defines that term broadly (American Psychological Association [APA], 1985). It is, however, possible and appropriate to evaluate scientifically the usefulness of assessment procedures, even procedures that were not developed on the basis of empirical studies or within the framework of psychometric theory (for example, APA, 1985; Milner and Campbell, 1995). In this paper, we evaluate the reliability and validity of judgments concerning violence risk made using the *SARA* in adult male offenders.

METHOD

Subjects

Subjects comprised two large groups of adult male offenders (N = 2,681). The probationers were 1,671 men from three different samples, designated Pl, P2, and P3. Pl included 1,424 men serving terms of probation of up to two years for index offenses related to spousal assault. They were consecutive admissions to the British Columbia provincial probation service during an eighteen-month time period (from January 1996 to July 1997). A minority (fewer than 10 percent) had served custodial sentences of less than two years before being released into the community. P2 included 145 men who were referred by criminal courts to a spousal assault treatment group in Vancouver, British Columbia, in 1996 and 1997. They were serving terms of probation of up to three years for index offenses related to spousal assault; none had served custodial sentences for their index offenses. P3 included 102 men convicted of offenses related to spousal violence and referred by criminal courts to attend a different group treatment program for spousal assaulters in Vancouver. They were part of a larger group of men who attended for assessment, and most were accepted into treatment and completed at least twelve of sixteen treatment sessions. Several years after the treatment terminated, the men were followed-up as part of a large treatment outcome study (Dutton, Bodnarchuk, Kropp, Hart, and and Ogloff, 1997). From the larger group, we randomly selected fifty men who were not charged with or convicted of spousal assault after treatment (nonrecidivists) and fifty-two men who were charged with or convicted of spousal assault (recidivists).

The inmates were 1,010 men from three samples, designated I1, I2, and I3. All were serving aggregate custodial sentences of at least two years in Canadian federal prisons, most (about 65 percent) for violent offenses other than spousal assault (for example, robbery, sexual assault). Sample I1 included 552 consecutive admissions to four regions of the prison service during a time period of about six months (September 1997 to March 1998) who had a documented history of spousal assault. (A documented history included past or current convictions for spousal assault offenses, a self-reported history of spousal assault, or credible reports of spousal assault from collateral informants.) Sample I2 included 86 consecutive admissions to a fifth region of the same prison service during the same time period, all of whom had a documented history of spousal assault and for whom additional assessment information was available (*see* later). Sample I3 included 372 men with no documented history of spousal assault who were admitted to federal prisons in the same time period as those in samples I1 and I2. They were referred for risk assessment because correctional staff had initially suspected a history of spousal violence because of factors such as history of nonspousal violence (for example, sexual assault of strangers, physical assault of family members) or expressions of misogynistic attitudes.

The median age of subjects was thirty-two years. About 80 percent were white, about 15 percent were Native Indian, and the remainder were other ethnocultural minorities, primarily Asian. Almost all the subjects with a history of spousal violence had been married or lived common-law in the past; a small number had committed acts of violence against a dating partner. More detailed information concerning the demographics of subjects was not available, due to privacy considerations and differences across samples in the way that such information was recorded.

Procedure

Evaluators

SARA ratings were made by correctional, mental health, and research staff. Evaluators were probation officers in sample P1; treatment staff (doctoral-level psychologists, counselors, and social workers) in P2; research assistants (doctoral level graduate students in clinical or counseling psychology) in P3; and correctional staff (case managers) in I1, I2, and I3. Only one set of ratings was available for each subject except in sample I2 in which a doctoral-level graduate student in clinical psychology coded the *SARA* on the basis of institutional files, blind to the original case managers' ratings.

There was considerable variability both within and across samples in the training and experience of evaluators. Also, all of the ratings, except those made by researchers in samples P3 and I2, were collected for use in routine decision making. The lack of confidentiality may have resulted in a tendency on the part of offenders to minimize or deny their spousal assault history. Our results are therefore likely to be a conservative or lower-bound estimate of the *SARA's* reliability and validity. However, the fact that our ratings were collected under conditions that parallel those in the real world increases the generalizability of our findings.

Assessment procedure

SARA ratings were based of an interview with the offender and a review of all relevant file information, as recommended in the manual. The exceptions were in samples P3 and I2, in which researchers made ratings on the basis of files only (although the files included summaries of previous interviews). Ratings in P3 were made blind to outcome status. Evaluators coded the presence of the twenty risk factors on a three-point scale (0 = absent, 1 = possibly or partially present, 2 = present). When items were omitted due to missing information, they were coded as absent. Evaluators also indicated whether they considered the risk factor to be a "critical item"—that is, present and strongly related to violence risk in the case at hand. Critical items ratings were made on a two-point scale (0 = not critical, 1 = critical), except in P1, in which the computerized record forms did not allow this option. Three continuous scores were calculated from the item ratings: Total scores reflected the sum of individual item ratings, ranging from 0 to 40; Number of factors present was an index of how many risk factors were rated present (that is, two vs. zero or one) in a given case, ranging from zero to twenty; and Number of Critical Items was an index of how many risk factors were rated critical, ranging from zero to twenty. Finally, evaluators coded Summary Risk Ratings, reflecting their judgments concerning offenders' risk for recidivistic spousal assault, on a three-point scale (0 = low risk, 1 = moderate risk, 2 = high risk).

Additional information

In sample P3, considerable additional information was available from the original treatment outcome study. The following demographic and criminal history variables were coded from the records of the initial assessment: age; education (0 = grade 10 or less, 1 = grade 11 or more); employment status (0 = unemployed, 1 = employed part- or full-time); marital status (0 = single, separated, or divorced; 1 = married or common-law); ethnicity (0 = minority, 1 = majority/white and English as a mother tongue); and number of convictions for spousal assault prior to instant offense(s). We also recorded a number of unstructured clinical ratings made by evaluators following the initial assessment: degree of motivation to participate in treatment (1 = low, 10 = high); acceptance of personal responsibility for role in past spousal assaults (1 = low, 10 = high); risk for recidivistic spousal assault (1 = low, 10 – high); and questionable suitability for treatment (0 = no, 1 = yes). Finally, we recorded two variables related to treatment participation: number of group treatment sessions attended, out of a possible sixteen, and time at risk, coded as the number of years at risk to recidivate following assessment. Finally, researchers rated the Screening Version of the Hare Psychopathy Checklist-Revised (PCL:SV) (Hart, Cox, and Hare, 1995), a test of psychopathic personality disorder, for each subject. The *SARA* ratings were made blind to all these variables, with the exception of the PCL:SV.

In sample I2, additional information that was available for some or all subjects included: PCL:SV ratings, made by the researcher; scores on the General Statistical Information on Recidivism Scale (GSIR) (Nuffield, 1982), an actuarial scale designed to assess risk of reincarceration in Canadian federal offenders; and scores on the Violence Risk Appraisal Guide (VRAG) (Quinsey, Harris, Rice, and Cormier, 1998), an actuarial scale developed in Canada to assess risk for violent recidivism. The *SARA* ratings of correctional staff were made blind to the researchers PCL:SV ratings, but not necessarily to scores on the GSIR or VRAG.

Overview of Analyses

The first set of analyses were aimed at providing descriptive information concerning the distribution of *SARA* ratings in probationers and inmates. Second, we examined the structural reliability—item homogeneity (mean interitem correlation, or MIC) and internal consistency (Cronbach's)—and interrater reliability of *SARA* ratings. Third, we examined the criterion- group or known-group validity of the *SARA* by comparing the ratings of federal offenders with and without a documented history of spousal assault—that is, by comparing ratings in samples I1 and I2 with those in sample I3. Fourth, we examined the concurrent validity of *SARA* ratings in sample I2 by calculating correlations with other risk-related scales, specifically the PCL:SV, the GSIR, and the VRAG. Finally, we examined the criterion-group validity of the *SARA* by comparing the ratings of recidivistic and nonrecidivistic spousal assaulters in sample P3. We were also able to examine the incremental validity of the *SARA* with respect to a number of other demographic, criminal history, and treatment-related variables. This type of design has also been described as "postdiction," "retrospective prediction," and "quasi-prediction" (for example, Quinsey et al., 1998), as it attempts to model events statistically on the basis of information available prior to their actual occurrence.

RESULTS

Descriptive Analyses

Table 2 presents the distribution (M, SD) of continuous *SARA* ratings—total score, number of factors present, and number of critical Items—in 2,309 probationers and inmates with a history of spousal assault (excluding sample I3). The results indicated that the offenders varied considerably with respect to the presence of individual risk factors and the perceived relevance of these factors to offenders' risk for spousal assault. This was true even for inmates, despite the fact that most of them were incarcerated for offenses unrelated to spousal assault, including robbery, drug, sex, and homicide offenses. Despite within-group variability, there was also a consistent pattern of between-group differences indicating that inmates had more risk factors on average than did probationers. The between group differences were particularly pronounced for part 1 of the *SARA*. This seems to have been the result of probationers frequently receiving ratings of 1 (possibly or partially present) on part 1 items. This is to be expected, given that Inmates were incarcerated primarily because of their history of general criminality and violence, rather than their history of spousal violence. Interestingly, there was no difference between groups on total scores for part 2 of the *SARA*.

A similar pattern of findings emerged when we analyzed the summary risk ratings. A small number of subjects—fewer than 3 percent in each group—did not receive a summary risk rating. The sample size of 2,242

TABLE 2. **Distribution of Total Scores, Number of Factors Present, and Number of Critical Items in Probationers and Inmates with a History of Spousal Assault**

SARA rating	Probationers		Inmates		Contrast		
	M	(SD)	M	(SD)	t	df	p
Total Score	12.98	(6.46)	16.39	(6.86)	10.86	1093.16	<0.001
Part 1	6.39	(3.60)	9.97	(3.68)	21.04	1130.41	<0.001
Part2	6.59	(3.80)	6.42	(4.46)	0.83	1009.35	0.410
Factors Present	4.27	(3.18)	6.51	(3.37)	14.51	1097.75	<0.001
Part 1	2.29	(1.82)	4.14	(1.90)	21.18	1112.75	<0.001
Part2	1.98	(1.85)	2.37	(2.16)	4.04	1011.42	<0.001
Critical Items	1.76	(1.43)	3.98	(3.80)	12.66	882.57	<0.001
Part 1	0.70	(0.90)	2.38	(2.08)	16.83	873.87	<0.001
Part2	1.06	(0.99)	1.60	(2.17)	5.07	860.24	<0.001

Note. N = 2,309 (1,671 probationers from samples P1, P2, and P3 and 648 Inmates from samples I1 and I2), except for critical items, in which N = 885 (247 probationers from samples P2 and P3 and 638inmates from samples I1 and I2). Items scored 0-2 for total score and 0-1 for number of factors present and critical items. Contrasts are t-tests, corrected for unequal variances.

for this analysis included 1,615 probationers and 627 inmates. Ratings of high risk were given to 28 percent of probationers and 37 percent of inmates; moderate risk ratings were given to 49 percent of probationers and 41 percent of inmates; and low risk ratings were given to 22 percent of both probationers and inmates. Overall, inmates were more likely to receive ratings of high risk than were probationers [$X^2(2, N = 2,242) = 14.35, p = 0.001$].

Not surprisingly, the associations among the various *SARA* ratings were strong. The correlation between total scores and number of risk factors present was very high [$r (2307) = .95, p < 0.001$]. Total scores and number of risk factors present were highly correlated with the number of critical items [$r(883) = .47$ and $.49$, respectively, both $p < 0.001$]. Finally, summary risk ratings were correlated highly with total scores and number of risk factors present [$r (2240) = .67$ and $.63$, respectively, both $p < 0.001$], and moderately with number of critical items [$r (872) = .34, p < 0.001$].

Reliability

Table 3 summarizes the results of reliability analyses. The correlations among ratings for the individual risk factors were all positive. Two things were evident in the pattern of MIC and results. First, correlations were higher among part 2 items than among part 1 items. This may be due to the fact that part 2 items reflect risk factors specific to spousal assault history, whereas part 1 items reflect general violence risk factors. Second, interitem correlations were higher for number of critical items than for total scores and number of risk factors present. This is probably because the former ratings represent the subjective judgments of evaluators (that is, the weight or importance they accord to risk factors) and therefore may be susceptible to a halo effect, whereas the latter represent more objective judgments (that is, the presence or absence of a risk factor).

TABLE 3. **Reliability of *SARA* Ratings: Item Homogeneity (Mean Interitem Correlation, or MIC) and Internal Consistency (Cronbach's Alpha), and Interrater Reliability (Intraclass Correlation Coefficient, or ICC)**

SARA rating	Item homogeneity	Internal consistency	Interrater reliability
Total Score	0.15	0.78	0.84
Part 1	0.16	0.66	0.68
Part2	0.21	0.73	0.87
Factors Present	0.14	0.75	0.83
Part 1	0.14	0.62	0.64
Part2	0.19	0.69	0.85
Critical Items	0.19	0.83	0.22
Part 1	0.18	0.70	0.18
Part2	0.27	0.77	0.38
Summary risk rating			
Low vs. moderate vs. high	———	———	0.63
Low/moderate vs. high	———	———	0.57

Note. For item homogeneity and internal consistency analyses, $N = 2,309$ (1671 probationers from samples PI, P2, and P3 and 638 Inmates from samples I1 and I2), except for critical items, in which $N = 885$ (247 probationers from samples P2 and P3 and 638 inmates from samples I1 and I2). For interrater reliability analyses, $N = 86$ (inmates from sample I2). Items scored 0-2 for total score and 0-1 for number offactors present and critical items. ICCs were calculated using a two-way mixed-effects model. All ICCs were significantly greater than 0 ($p < 0.05$).

Because the *SARA* is designed for use in risk assessment—that is, forecasting future behavior—rather than measuring the strength of a psychological disposition, item homogeneity and internal consistency are of limited use in evaluating the scale.[3] Much more important is interrater reliability: If raters cannot agree on the presence of individual risk factors or the implications that can be drawn from them, there is little point in conducting risk assessments. Recall that correctional staff made the original *SARA* ratings on the basis of an interview and a review of case history information. A doctoral-level graduate student in clinical psychology made the second ratings solely on the basis of case history information. Despite these differences in the information base used to make ratings—which may result in a conservative or lower-bound estimate—the interrater reliability of ratings was high. At the level of individual items, the interrater reliability of ratings made on a 3-point scale was good (*Mdn* $ICC_1 = 0.65$, range 0.45 to 0.86), as was that of ratings made on a 2-point scale (*Mdn* $ICC_1 = 0.60$, range = 0.24 to 0.83). It was difficult to assess the interrater reliability of critical item ratings, which were made infrequently. Only four items were rated critical by both raters in at least five cases; for these items, interrater reliability was low (*Mdn* $ICC_1 = 0.31$, range = 0.20 to 0.51).

Table 3 also summarizes the interrater reliability of *SARA* continuous scores and summary risk ratings from sample I2. Although the reliabilities generally were good, several aspects of the findings were noteworthy. First, interrater reliability was low for critical items. To some extent, this may have been artifactual, reflecting the restricted range of critical item scores in sample I2 (as discussed previously), but it also appeared to be due to real inconsistency across raters in their tendency to rate an item as critical. Second, reliabilities were higher for part 2 items than for part 1 items. This may be due in part to the fact that the researcher evaluated those part 1 items related to mental disorder (for example, items 8-10) more systematically than did correctional staff, who in many cases were forced to rely on existing mental health reports. Third, the reliability of summary risk ratings was good, even when they were dichotomized (high risk versus low or moderate risk).[4]

Criterion-Groups Validity, I: Comparison of Offenders with and without a History of Spousal Assault

We compared the *SARA* ratings of inmates with and without a documented history of spousal assault (that is, samples I1 and I2 versus I3).

As noted earlier, sample I3 men initially were suspected to have a history of spousal violence, but subsequent evaluation revealed no history of arrests for spousal assault, no self-reported history of spousal assault, and no history of spousal assault reported by third parties. Comparison of group means (t-tests, corrected for unequal variance) revealed significant differences for all twenty individual risk factors ($p < 0.05$).

Group means for the continuous *SARA* ratings are presented in Table 4. The between-group differences generally were large and statistically significant. There were two patterns evident in the means. First, the between-group differences were larger for part 2 items than for part 1 items, although even the latter differences were still moderate to large in magnitude. The magnitude of the differences is somewhat surprising, given that all the inmates were serious offenders and that many part 1 items (for example, items 8 and 9) were endorsed quite infrequently. Second, the differences were smaller for Critical Item scores than for the total scores or number of factors resent. This may be the result of the lower interrater reliability of critical item ratings.

A similar pattern of findings was observed for summary risk ratings. Of the 627 men with a history of spousal assault with valid data, 37 percent were rated high risk, 41 percent were rated moderate risk, and 22 percent were rated low risk. In contrast, of the 358 with no history of spousal assault who had valid data, 3 percent were rated high risk, 20 percent were rated moderate risk, and 77 percent were rated low risk. This difference was statistically significant [$X^2(2, N = 985) = 303.14, p < 0.001$].

Concurrent Validity: Correlations between *SARA* Ratings and Other Risk-Related Measures

We examined the concurrent validity of *SARA* ratings with respect to other measures related to risk for violence and criminality in sample I2. As discussed earlier, these other measures included the PCL:SV (Hart et al., 1995), a rating scale of psychopathic personality disorder that is predictive of violent reoffending; the GSIR (Nuffield, 1982), an actuarial scale related to risk for general criminality; and the VRAG (Quinsey et al., 1998), an actuarial scale related to risk for general violence. Recall that the PCL:SV ratings, but not the GSIR and VRAG ratings, were made blind to the *SARA* ratings. Also, note that high scores on the PCL-R and VRAG are associated with an increased risk for violence, whereas high scores on the GSIR are associated with a decreased risk for criminality.

TABLE 4. **Comparison of Inmates With and Without a History of Spousal Assault: Total Score, Numbers of Factors Present, and Number of Critical Items**

| | Spousal assault history | | | | | | |
| | No | | Yes | | Contrast | | |
SARA rating	*M*	*(SD)*	*M*	*(SD)*	*t*	*df*	*p*
Total Score	7.51	(3.56)	16.39	(6.86)	27.04	996.60	<0.001
Part 1	7.38	(3.50)	9.97	(3.68)	11.11	807.99	<0.001
Part2	0.12	(0.51)	6.42	(4.47)	35.24	665.54	<0.001
Factors Present	3.03	(1.84)	6.51	(3.37)	21.24	1004.26	<0.001
Part 1	3.01	(1.82)	4.14	(1.90)	9.39	800.90	<0.001
Part2	0.03	(0.21)	2.37	(2.16)	27.22	656.73	<0.001
Critical Items	1.93	(1.90)	3.98	(3.80)	11.44	988.33	<0.001
Part 1	1.90	(1.87)	2.38	(2.08)	3.82	843.54	<0.001
Part2	0.03	(0.20)	1.60	(2.17)	18.18	655.33	<0.001

Note. $N = 1,010$ (638 Inmates with a documented history of spousal assault from samples I1 and I2 and 372 with no such history from sample I3). Items scored 0-2 for total score and 0-1 for number of factors present and critical items. Contrasts are *t*-tests, corrected for unequal variances.

The concurrent validities are summarized in Table 5. Several things are apparent in the table. First, correlations with the number of critical items generally were small and not statistically significant, and so are not discussed here further. Second, PCL:SV generally had moderate correlations with the *SARA* ratings, and particularly with ratings for part 1 items (that is, general violence risk factors). Third, GSIR and VRAG scores had moderate to large correlations with ratings for *SARA* part 1 items, but the correlations with part 2 items and the summary risk rating generally were small and not statistically significant.

Criterion-Groups Validity, II: Comparison of Recidivistic and Nonrecidivistic Spousal Assaulters

We examined the ability of *SARA* ratings to discriminate between men who did or did not recidivate following referral to a group treatment program for spousal assaulters (all from sample P3). To reiterate, *SARA* ratings were made by trained research assistants on the basis of assessment and correctional files, blind to outcome status, and the validity of

TABLE 5. Correlation Between *SARA* Ratings and Other Risk-Related Measures

SARA rating	PCL:SV	GSIR	VRAG
Total Score	0.43***	-0.07	0.29
Part 1	0.45***	-0.40***	0.50***
Part 2	0.30**	0.15	0.08
Factors Present	0.38***	-0.07	0.25
Part 1	0.39***	-0.31**	0.53***
Part 2	0.26*	0.16	0.00
Critical Items	0.25*	0.06	0.10
Part 1	0.24*	-0.02	0.14
Part 2	0.19	0.13	0.05
Summary risk rating	0.34**	0.01	0.11

Note. $N = 86$ for analyses involving the PCL:SV and GSIR, $N = 39$ for analyses involving the VRAG (all inmates from sample I2). PCL:SV = Screening Version of the Hare Psychopathy Checklist-Revised (Hart et al., 1995); GSIR = General Statistical Information on Recidivism Scale (Nuffield, 1982); VRAG = Violence Risk Appraisal Guide (Quinsey et al., 1998). Items scored 0-2 for Total Score and 0-1 for Number of Factors Present and Critical Items. *$P < 0.05$; **$p < 0.01$; ***$p < 0.001$ (all two-tailed).

TABLE 6. Comparison of Recidivistic Spousal Assaulters: Background Variables at Time of Initial Assessment

	Recidivist				Contrast		
	No		Yes				
Variable	M	(SD)	M	(SD)	t	df	p
Age	33.71	(6.24)	33.02	(6.06)	-0.56	98.21	0.578
Education	0.59	(0.50)	0.64	(0.49)	0.44	75.21	0.665
Employment	0.57	(0.50)	0.69	(0.47)	1.20	84.59	0.233
Marital status	0.61	(0.49)	0.67	(0.48)	0.59	93.81	0.558
Ethnicity	0.69	(0.47)	0.69	(0.47)	0.04	86.76	0.972
Prior assaults	1.36	(1.31)	1.54	(0.85)	0.76	71.37	0.451

Note. $N = 102$ (50 nonrecidivistic and 52 recidivistic probationers from sample P3). Age = age at assessment; Education = years of education at assessment; Employment = employment status at assessment; Marital status = marital status at assessment; Ethnicity = ethnocultural minority status; Prior assaults = number of convictions for spousal assault prior to instant offense(s). *See* text for details regarding the coding of variables. Contrasts are *t*-tests, corrected for unequal variances. Sample sizes vary slightly for each contrast due to missing data.

SARA ratings was compared to that of demographic, criminal history, and clinical variables coded from institutional files, including PCL:SV scores.

As Tables 6 and 7 reveal, recidivistic and nonrecidivistic spousal assaulters did not differ with respect to demographic characteristics (age, education, employment, martial status at assessment, ethnicity) or assault history (number of prior assaults). Neither did they differ with respect to a number of clinical variables related to treatment, including degree of motivation to attend treatment, acceptance of personal responsibility for role in past spousal assaults, clinical (unstructured) assessments of risk for future violence, number of treatment sessions attended, time at risk after assessment, or PCL:SV scores. Indeed, the only treatment-related difference between the groups was that recidivistic spousal assaulters were more likely than nonrecidivists to have been deemed as possibly unsuitable for treatment at the time of their initial assessment.

Although the groups did not differ with respect to clinical or unstructured ratings of risk made at intake, there were significant between-groups differences with respect to several continuous *SARA* ratings, which can be

TABLE 7. Comparison of Recidivistic and Nonrecidivistic Spousal Assaulters: Assessment, Treatment and Follow-up Variables

Variable	Recidivist No		Recidivist Yes		Contrast		
	M	*(SD)*	*M*	*(SD)*	*t*	*df*	*p*
Motivation	5.89	(2.57)	6.61	(3.20)	1.02	61.20	0.310
Responsibility	5.83	(2.71)	5.61	(2.94)	-0.34	66.08	0.738
Clinical risk rating	4.15	(2.62)	4.53	(2.77)	0.59	64.76	0.561
Questionable suitability	0.00	(0.00)	0.12	(0.32)	2.58	51.00	0.013
Sessions attended	10.32	(5.44)	8.42	(6.59)	-1.59	97.78	0.116
Time at risk	3.13	(2.18)	3.88	(2.10)	1.77	99.40	0.080
PCL:SV	10.22	(5.75)	11.24	(5.03)	0.91	88.00	0.363

Note. N = 102 (50 nonrecidivistic and 52 recidivistic probationers from sample P3). Motivation = degree of motivation to participate in treatment; Responsibility = acceptance of personal responsibility for role in past spousal assaults; Risk = risk for recidivistic spousal assault; Questionable suitability = possibly unsuited for treatment; Sessions attended = number of group treatment sessions attended; Time at risk = number of years at risk to recidivate following assessment; PCL:SV = Screening Version of the Hare Psychopathy Checklist-Revised (Hart et al., 1995). *See* text for details regarding the coding of variables. Contrasts are *t*-tests corrected for unequal variances. Sample sizes vary slightly for each contrast due to missing data.

TABLE 8. Comparison of Recidivistic and Nonrecidivistic Spousal Assaulters: PCL:SV and *SARA* Ratings

| | Recidivist | | | | Contrast | | |
| | No | | Yes | | | | |
SARA rating	M	(SD)	M	(SD)	t	df	p
Total Score	15.68	(5.40)	17.69	(5.60)	1.85	100.00	0.068
Part 1	8.04	(3.63)	8.44	(3.74)	0.55	100.00	0.058
Part 2	7.64	(2.88)	9.25	(2.61)	2.96	98.19	0.004
Factors Present (no.)	5.76	(3.01)	6.98	(2.92)	2.08	99.53	0.040
Part 1	3.12	(1.98)	3.50	(1.95)	0.98	99.70	0.330
Part 2	2.64	(1.65)	3.48	(1.46)	2.72	97.50	0.008
Critical Items (no.)	1.00	(1.05)	1.83	(1.41)	3.37	94.17	0.001
Part 1	0.56	(0.76)	0.85	(0.94)	1.70	97.28	0.093
Part 2	0.44	(0.64)	0.98	(0.96)	3.35	89.51	0.001

Note. $N = 102$ (50 nonrecidivistic and 52 recidivistic probationers from sample P3). Items scored 0-2 for total score and 0-1 for number of factors present and critical items. Contrasts are *t*- tests corrected for unequal variances.

considered actuarial risk scores (as discussed earlier). These findings are summarized in Table 8. The biggest difference was on the number of critical items, followed by number of factors present. In general, differences were larger for part 2 (spousal violence) than for part 1 (general violence) ratings.

The between-groups difference was also significant for summary risk ratings, which can be considered structured professional judgments of risk. The findings are summarized in Table 9. There was a clear tendency for those rated high risk to be recidivists according to official records and for those rated low risk to be nonrecidivists [X^2, N = 102) = 13.69, $p = 0.001$]. The magnitude of the association was moderate.[5] This pattern also held after the summary risk ratings were dichotomized (high risk versus low or moderate risk) [X^2(1, N = 102) = 7.82, $p = 0.005$]. The magnitude of the association was slightly smaller, but still moderate.[6]

To compare the explanatory power of the actuarial ratings and structured professional judgments, we conducted multivariate analyses (hierarchical logistic regressions). The results of these analyses, summarized in Table 10, indicated that *SARA* summary risk ratings significantly differentiated between recidivists and nonrecidivists, even after controlling for treatment suitability, time at risk, and continuous (actuarial) scores on the

TABLE 9. Comparison of Recidivistic and Nonrecidivistic Spousal Assaulters: Summary Risk Rating

Summary risk rating	Recidivist	
	No	Yes
High risk	16 (32%)	31 (60%)
Moderate risk	16 (32%)	17 (33%)
Low risk	18 (36%)	4 (8%)

Note. N = 102 (50 nonrecidivistic and 52 recidivistic probationers from sample P3).

SARA. To the best of our knowledge, this is the first time in the violence literature that decisions made using a clinical method—in this case, structured professional judgment—have outperformed decisions made using an actuarial method when the two were compared directly.

DISCUSSION

Aside from Campbell's work on the more narrow issue of spousal homicide (Campbell, 1995), this is the first empirical report to evaluate the reliability and validity of a procedure for assessing the risk of spousal violence. Although the *SARA* was not constructed using empirical or psychometric methods, the research presented here supports its use in clinical and forensic decision making, as well as in research on perpetrators of spousal assault. Using the *SARA*, evaluators were able to differentiate offenders in terms of individual risk factors and overall perceived risk in a reliable manner. Furthermore, the *SARA* ratings made by evaluators were related to important external criteria in a systematic and logical manner.

Most of the analyses in this paper were based on data collected as part of field implementation of the *SARA*. There was more variability in the background and training of evaluators and in the assessment procedure than one would expect in controlled research settings. This is likely to increase the generalizability of our findings. We expect that other criminal justice agencies in North America using the *SARA* with adult male offenders will observe results similar to those reported here.[7] The generalizability to forensic psychiatric populations, female offenders, and agencies outside of North America is unclear at present. Also, our use of implementation data also likely resulted in a conservative or lower-bound

TABLE 10. Hierarchical Logistic Regression: Discrimination of Recidivistic and Nonrecidivistic Spousal Assaulters Using SARA Ratings, Controlling for Treatment Rejection and Time at Risk

Step/variable	B	(SE)	Wald
Step 1			
(Constant)	7.55	(24.62)	0.09
Rejected	-8.05	(24.62)	0.11
Time at risk	0.12	(0.10)	1.55
Step 2			
(Constant)	5.19	(24.08)	0.05
Questionable suitability	-7.48	(24.05)	0.10
Time at risk	0.18	(0.11)	2.84*
Total score, part 2	0.03	(0.23)	0.02
No factors present, part 2	-0.08	(0.40)	0.04
No. of critical items, part 2	0.56	(0.36)	2.33
Summary risk rating			
Moderate vs. low	1.28	(0.73)	3.06*
High vs. low	1.68	(0.85)	3.90**

Note. N = 102 (50 nonrecidivistic and 52 recidivistic Probationers from sample P3). Model fit: Step 1, $\chi^2(2, N = 102)$ = 10.04, p = 0.007; and Step 2, $\chi^2(5, N = 102)$ = 16.35, p = 0.006. *$p < 0.10$; **$p < 0.05$.

estimate of the reliability and validity of SARA ratings. Use of the SARA by raters with more specific expertise and training should result in improved reliability and validity.

The study design had a number of limitations, however. First, interrater reliability data were available only for a relatively small subsample of offenders. A larger sample might have resulted in increased variability and therefore higher reliability estimates; at the very least, it would have resulted in more stable estimates. A second problem was that we were not able to examine the test-retest reliability of *SARA* ratings. Given the historical or static nature of some *SARA* risk factors and the timeframe used to code some dynamic factors, we expect that *SARA* item scores and continuous scores (total, number of factors present) should be moderately to highly stable over periods of six to twelve months. However, critical item scores and summary risk ratings may be much more sensitive to evaluators' perceptions of changes in an individual's life circumstances, and we expect them to be less stable. Indeed, we hope that the *SARA* can be used to monitor changes in risk over time. If so, scores for at least some individuals should change over time, but the change scores should be reliable and associated with decreases in the likelihood of recidivistic spousal assault. A third problem was that we were unable to examine the usefulness of the *SARA* for making decisions about risk management. We hope in future research to evaluate whether implementation of the *SARA* results in improved report writing, treatment planning, and supervision decision making by agency personnel. Perhaps the ultimate test of validity would be whether implementation of the *SARA* in a given agency results in decreased rates of recidivistic violence due to improved case management.

Research on the *SARA* in progress or being planned examines many of the issues raised previously. First, other agencies in North America and Europe are evaluating the reliability and validity of *SARA* ratings. This includes research on adult male and female offenders in Colorado, funded in part by a grant from the National Institute of Justice, examination of the reliability and validity of *SARA* ratings following translation of the manual into different languages, including French and Swedish; and a "follow-back" study of Swedish spousal assault offenders who were the subject of comprehensive forensic psychiatric evaluations.

Second, we are planning prospective studies of the validity of *SARA* ratings. An important feature of this research is an attempt to monitor, measure, and control for postrelease interventions (for example, treatment, supervision). Most longitudinal research on violence ignores everything that occurs after offenders are released into the community after sentencing, up until the time their criminal records are inspected to determine whether they recidivated. The follow-up period is often as long as five years. Such a "passive" or "prediction-oriented" design is of limited use in evaluating the effectiveness of an assessment procedure whose primary purpose is to assist postrelease intervention (for example, Hart, 1998).

Third, we are evaluating the feasibility of alternative strategies for the actuarial interpretation of *SARA* ratings. Specifically, we are developing and testing nonlinear statistical models (for example, logistic regression, neural network models) and expert systems to aid professional judgment. The goal here is not to use these alternative strategies to make a decision, but rather to use them to guide report writing and intervention planning. The alternative strategies discussed previously may be particularly successful with the *SARA* because it provides a rich information base and because many risk factors included in the *SARA* are assumed to have a nonlinear association with violence risk.

Finally, we should discuss the implications of our findings for discussions concerning the relative superiority of clinical versus actuarial decision making in the area of violence risk assessment. There has been considerable debate in the forensic literature concerning the clinical and legal suitability of actuarial methods—those characterized by the use of a fixed and explicit decision-making algorithm, and generally (but not necessarily) constructed using an empirical approach (Grove and Meehl, 1996; Meehl, 1954/1996). At present, some authorities recommend against reliance on actuarial methods (for example, Melton, Petrila, Poythress, and Slobogin, 1997); some support the use of actuarial methods generally, but point out problems in their use and interpretation (for example, Janus and Meehl, 1997); and others argue that the use of nonactuarial (that is, discretion-based) procedures should be eliminated, as they are inherently unreliable and invalid (for example, Quinsey et al., 1998). Our findings cast doubt on the validity of the third argument. We found that the primary discretion-based rating on the *SARA*, the summary risk rating, had good reliability and validity. It may be that the format of the *SARA*, which requires explicit consideration and coding of a fixed set of risk factors, provides a sophisticated and flexible framework within which to exercise professional discretion. Alternatively, it may be that the *SARA* facilitates the reliable coding of professional judgment, which then can be subjected to appropriate statistical analysis.

ACKNOWLEDGMENTS

This paper summarizes data presented in the *Spousal Assault Risk Assessment Guide: User's Manual*, published by Multi-Health Systems, Inc., 65 Overlea Boulevard, Suite 210, Toronto, Ontario, Canada, M4H 1P1. Thanks to Christopher Webster, Derek Eaves, Karen Whittemore, Mark Bodnarchuk, and Don Dutton for their assistance and helpful comments. Thanks also to Angela Knoll and Judith Lawence of the Correctional Service of Canada, and to Tim Trytten of the British Columbia Ministry of the Attorney General for providing us with access to *SARA* data.

The research described herein was funded in part by the British Columbia Ministries of Health (Forensic Psychiatric Services Commission) and the Attorney General and by the Correctional Service of Canada. All opinions expressed are those of the authors and do not reflect official policies of the funding agencies or of the British Columbia Institute Against Family Violence.

Endnotes

[1] The defining feature of an actuarial risk scale is that items are weighted and combined according to a fixed and explicit algorithm; the manner in which the scale's content was determined—that is, empirically versus inductively—is irrelevant (*see* Grove and Meehl, 1996; Meehl, 1954/1996). This means that any decision-making procedure that relies at least in part on the use of the evaluator's discretion is considered to be clinical rather than actuarial in nature.

[2] We define *structured professional judgment* as a decision made without fixed and explicit rules but based at least in part on consideration of a standardized information base. Others have referred to this as the *guided clinical approach* (for example, Hanson, 1998; p. 52). We prefer the term *structured professional judgment* because a range of nonclinical professionals are responsible for conducting violence risk assessments (for example, corrections, law enforcement, security, and victim support workers). Regardless, note that according to Meehl's (1954/1996) definition, however, it is simply a form of clinical decision making.

[3] Indeed, assuming all the items in a risk scale are predictive of future behavior, the optimal situation would be to have an MIC around 0 (that is, maximal predictive validity with minimal redundancy).

[4] The raters agreed in 69 of 86 cases (80 percent): 19 were rated high risk, 31 were rated moderate risk, and 19 were rated low risk. There were no extreme disagreements in which one person gave a rating of high risk and another a rating of low risk. The other disagreements between the first and second raters were as follows: high versus moderate, 11; moderate versus high, 7; moderate versus low, 7; and low versus moderate, 11. Note that ICCs are mathematically equivalent to K_w with values greater than 0.50 to 0.60 generally considered to be good (Chicheti and Sparrow, 1981).

[5] Several indexes of effect size are commonly used in violence research. In this case, r_{pb} (100) = .36, $p < 0.001$; Cohen's d = 0.76; and the area under the curve (AUC) statistic of receiver operating characteristic (ROC) analysis = 0.70 (*SE* = 0.06).

[6] Different effect size indexes are appropriate, given that both variables are dichotomous. Here, (100) = .28, p = 0.005, and the odds ratio was 3.14, indicating that being rated high risk was associated with a three-fold increase in the odds of being a recidivist. An odds ratio of this magnitude is generally considered substantial or "strong," and is equivalent to a Cohen's d of 0.63 (*see* Haddock, Rindskopf, and Shadish, 1998; pp. 342, 349).

7 In general, U.S. offenders differ from Canadian offenders with respect to certain demographics—specifically, race. However, research using major forensic assessment instruments such as the Hare Psychopathy Checklist-Revised (PCL-R) (Hare, 1991) and the Level of Service Inventory-Revised (LSI-R) (Andrews and Bonta, 1996) indicate that offenders in the two countries appear to be similar with respect to important criminal history and psychological characteristics, despite superficial demographic differences.

References

American Psychological Association. 1985. *Standards for Educational and Psychological Testing.* Washington, D.C.: American Psychological Association.

Andrews, D. A. and J. Bonta. 1995. *The Level of Service Inventory-Revised* (LSI-R). Toronto: Multi-Health Systems, Inc.

————. 1998. *The Psychology of Criminal Conduct,* 2nd edition. Cincinnati, Ohio: Anderson.

Campbell, J. C. 1995. Prediction of Homicide of and by Battered Women. In J. C. Campbell, ed. *Assessing Dangerousness: Violence by Sexual Offenders, Batterers, and Child Abusers*, pp. 96-113. Thousand Oaks, California: Sage.

————. 1998, October. Commentary. In D. McGrogan (Chair), Lethality and Risk Assessment for Family Violence Cases. Symposium presented at the 4th International Conference on Children Exposed to Family Violence, San Diego, California.

Canadian Centre for Justice Statistics. 1994. The Winnipeg Family Violence Court. *Juristat Service Bulletin.* 14(12):1-22.

Chichetti, D. V. and S. S. Sparrow. 1981. Developing Criteria for Establishing Interrater Reliability of Specific Items: Applications to Assessment of Adaptive Behavior. *American Journal of Mental Deficiency.* 86:127-137.

Dutton, D. G., M. Bodnarchuk, R. Kropp, S. D. Hart, and J. R. P. Ogloff. 1997. Wife Assault Treatment and Criminal Recidivism: An 11-year Follow-up. *International Journal of Offender Therapy and Comparative Criminology.* 41:9-23.

Dutton, D. G. and S. D. Hart. 1992. Risk Markers for Family Violence in a Federally Incarcerated Population. *International Journal of Law and Psychiatry.* 15:101-112.

Gottfredson, M. R. and D. M. Gottfredson. 1988. *Decision-making in Criminal Justice: Toward the Rational Exercise of Discretion,* 2nd edition. New York: Plenum.

Grove, W. M. and P. E. Meehl. 1996. Comparative Efficiency of Informal (Subjective, Impressionistic) and Formal (Mechanical, Algorithmic) Prediction

Procedures: The Clinical-Statistical Controversy. *Psychology, Public Policy, and Law.* 2:293-323.

Haddock, C. K., Rindskopf, D., W. R. Shadish. 1998. Using Odds Ratios as Effect Sizes for Meta-analysis of Dichotomous Data: A Primer on Methods and Issues. *Psychological Methods.* 3:339-353.

Hanson, R. K. 1998. What Do We Know about Sex Offender Risk Assessment? *Psychology, Public Policy, and Law.* 4:50-72.

Hart, S. D. 1998. The Role of Psychopathy in Assessing Risk for Violence: Conceptual and Methodological Issues. *Legal and Criminological Psychology.* 3:123-140.

Hart, S. D., P. R. Kropp, R. Roesch, J. P. R. Ogloff, and K. Whittemore. 1994. Wife Assault in Community Resident Offenders. *Canadian Journal of Criminology.* 36: 435-446.

Healey, K. and C. Smith. 1998. *Batterer Intervention: Program Approaches and Criminal Justice Strategies* (NCJ Publication No. 168638). Washington, D.C.: National Institute of Justice.

Janus, E. S. and P. E. Meehl. 1997. Assessing the Legal Standard for the Prediction of Dangerousness in Sex Offender Commitment Proceedings. *Psychology, Public Policy, and Law.* 3:33-64.

Koss, M. P., L. A. Goodman, A. Brown, L. F. Fitzgerald, G. Keita, and N. F. Russo. 1994. *No Safe Haven: Male Violence Against Women at Home, at Work, and in the Community.* Washington, D.C.: American Psychological Association.

Kropp, P. R., S. D. Hart, C. W. Webster, and D. Eaves. 1994. *Manual for the Spousal Assault Risk Assessment Guide.* Vancouver, B.C.: British Columbia Institute on Family Violence.

————. 1995. *Manual for the Spousal Assault Risk Assessment Guide*, 2nd edition. Vancouver, B.C.: British Columbia Institute on Family Violence.

————. 1998. *Spousal Assault Risk Assessment: User's Guide.* Toronto: Multi-Health Systems, Inc.

Meehl, P. E. 1996. *Clinical Versus Statistical Prediction: A Theoretical Analysis and a Review of the Literature.* Northvale, New Jersey: Jason Aronson. (Original work published in 1954.)

Melton, G. B., J. Petrila, N. G. Poythress, and C. Slobogin. 1997. *Psychological Evaluations for the Courts: A Handbook for Mental Health Professionals and Lawyers,* 2nd edition. New York: Guilford.

Milner, J. S. and J. C. Campbell. 1995. Prediction Issues for Practitioners. In J. C. Campbell, ed. *Assessing Dangerousness: Violence by Sexual Offenders, Batterers, and Child Abusers*, pp. 20- 40. Thousand Oaks, California: Sage.

Nuffield, J. 1982. *Parole Decision-making in Canada: Research Towards Decision Guidelines*. Ottawa, Ontario: Ministry of Supplies and Services Canada.

Quinsey, V. L., G. T. Harris, M. E. Rice, and C. Cormier. 1998. *Violent Offenders: Appraising and Managing Risk*. Washington, D.C.: American Psychological Association.

Robinson, D. 1995. Federal Offender Family Violence: Estimates from a National File Review Study. *Forum on Corrections Research*. 7(2):15-18.

Statistics Canada. 1998. *Family Violence in Canada: A Statistical Profile*. Ottawa, Ontario: Ministry of Industry.

WHAT WORKS: EFFECTIVE INTERVENTION WITH SEX OFFENDERS

5

Pamela M. Yates, Ph.D. R. Psych
Manager, Sex Offender Programs
Correctional Services of Canada
Ottawa, Ontario, Canada

Sexual assault and sexual exploitation are serious and growing public concerns. The significant impact of sexual violence on victims, their families, and the community is undeniable. Consequently, the increased attention paid to the problem of sexual violence by the criminal justice system has resulted in substantial increases in the sexual offender population during the past decade in correctional systems in Canada (Gordon and Porporino, 1990; Motiuk and Belcourt, 1996), the United States (Becker, 1994; Becker and Murphy, 1998; Gordon and Porporino, 1990; McGrath, Hoke, and Vojtisek, 1998), and Britain (Fisher and Beech, 1999).

Given the impact of sexual violence on its victims and the number of sexual offenders within the criminal justice system, there is a growing need for interventions that are demonstrated to reduce the likelihood of sexual reoffending. Sex offender treatment is not a new endeavor. In fact, interventions for these offenders have been ongoing for many years

(Pithers, 1993), although the number and availability of programs for sex offenders has increased dramatically over the past decade. Yet, it is only relatively recently that empirical investigations of the efficacy of treatment have been conducted, and even more recently that a sufficient number of studies have been conducted to enable thorough reviews and the application of meta-analytic techniques to these data.

The literature currently available is fraught with theoretical, practical, and methodological limitations. Consequently, the efficacy of treatment for sex offenders, at first glance, appears equivocal at best. While many researchers conclude that treatment is effective in reducing the reoccurrence of sexual aggression (for example, Alexander, 1999; Becker and Murphy, 1998; Grossman, Martis, and Fichtner, 1999; Marshall, Jones, Ward, Johnson, and Barbaree, 1991; Nicholaichuk, Gordon, Gu, and Wong, 2000; Pithers and Cumming, 1989), others conclude that sex offenders do not benefit from treatment (Furby, Weinrott, and Blackshaw, 1989; Quinsey, Harris, Rice, and Lalumiere, 1993; Quinsey, Khanna, and Malcolm, 1998).

The purpose of this chapter is to evaluate the efficacy of interventions for sex offenders and to assess what works in the treatment and management of sex offenders. This is accomplished through a focus on qualitative and quantitative reviews of existing research and recent studies. While individual studies of especial note are described, the following does not purport to be a comprehensive review of the literature. Such reviews have been conducted elsewhere (for example, Alexander, 1999; Hall, 1995; Furby et al., 1989) and have been sufficiently informative that repeating the exercise herein is not warranted.

The following review and analysis concentrates primarily on adult male sexual offenders, as this has been the main focus of research. Interventions with juvenile sexual offenders are discussed in a separate section. Female sex offenders are beyond the scope of the chapter and therefore are not included.

The chapter is structured as follows. First, a description is provided of the major types of intervention approaches that have been undertaken in treatment with adult sex offenders. Next, a discussion of the methodological limitations associated with the research literature is provided as a framework for interpreting research and conclusions regarding the efficacy of treatment with sex offenders. Much of what is known about sex offender treatment has developed from research on risk assessment and recidivism prediction. Given the importance of this research and its implications for effective interventions with sex offenders, pertinent findings from this area are next reviewed. This is followed by a description of the principles of effective correctional treatment and their application to sex offenders. Finally, following a discussion of juvenile sex offenders, an analysis and synthesis of the research is offered, with a focus on what works with sex offenders and future directions for intervention, including community treatment and supervision.

Types of Sexual Offender Treatment

There are a variety of treatment interventions that have been implemented with adult sexual offenders, including general psychotherapeutic, organic, behavioral, cognitive-behavioral, and relapse prevention approaches. Earlier treatment approaches were based on the assumption that a single factor, such as difficulty in emotional expression or intimacy, motivated sexual offending (Becker and Murphy, 1998; Marshall, 1996). Over time, the multidimensional nature of sexual offending was recognized, and treatment incorporated a variety of components designed to address the multiple factors. Treatment now aims to increase some attributes of sex offenders, such as prosocial skills and empathy, and to decrease others, such as inappropriate or deviant sexual arousal. Interventions also aim to change cognitions associated with sexual offending (Abel and Rouleau, 1986) and the concept of relapse prevention has been introduced and applied (Laws, 1989; Pithers, Marques, Gibat, and Marlatt, 1983). These various types of treatment for sexual offenders are described below.

General Psychotherapy. Earlier interventions for sex offenders predominantly used general psychotherapeutic approaches. These interventions focused on understanding the intrapersonal dynamics underlying sexual offending and resolving such issues as developmental and intrapsychic conflicts that were hypothesized to result in sexual dysfunction or fixation (Becker and Murphy, 1998). These approaches have not tended to adopt a sex-offender specific orientation, but rather are general in their approach (Lockhart, Saunders, and Cleveland, 1988). These interventions have been found to be ineffective in reducing recidivism, are no longer commonly used with sex offenders (Quinsey, 1977) and, therefore, are not reviewed in greater detail.

Organic and Physical Treatments. Organic and physical treatments involve such procedures as surgical or chemical castration and neurosurgery to suppress sexual urges and behavior in an effort to decrease or eliminate deviant sexuality (Barbaree and Seto, 1997; Bradford, 1985,

1990; Marshall et al., 1991). It also has been suggested that antiandrogen treatments can alter the direction of sexual drives, in addition to reducing the drive (Bradford, 1985; 1990). The premise behind these interventions is that inhibiting gonadotropic pituitary function, blocking androgenic action, removing testosterone production centers, or damaging areas of the brain thought to influence sexual behavior will result in the reduction or elimination of sexual urges and/or behavior (Barbaree and Seto, 1997).

Physical castration has been widely used in Europe (Heim and Hursch, 1979; Marshall et al., 1991) and is based on the premise that removal of sexual glands will result in a reduction in testosterone, which will subsequently reduce sexual urges and drives (Lockhart et al., 1988). Surgical castration was used extensively in Denmark, particularly between 1935 and 1970. Many of these surgeries were performed on offenders who, by current standards, would not be regarded as high enough risk to warrant the procedure or those who had engaged in behaviors no longer regarded as illegal (Hansen and Lykke-Olesen, 1997), such as homosexuality. After disallowing the practice in 1970, Denmark reinstated it in 1989, due to the apparent success of the procedure in comparison to antiandrenergic interventions and psychotherapy (Hansen and Lykke-Olesen, 1997).

Although physical castration appears to reduce sexual reoffending over long follow-up periods (Bradford, 1990; Heim and Hursch, 1979; Marshall et al., 1991), the methodologies employed in many studies are questionable. In addition, more recent studies have found a higher incidence of sexual activity among castrated men than did earlier studies, as well as nonsexual reoffending. Given the considerable cost of the procedure to the offender, it is ethically questionable (Heim and Hursch, 1979) and is no longer commonly used (Marshall et al., 1991).

Surgical approaches involve such procedures as destroying portions of the brain thought to control sexual behavior (Barbaree and Seto, 1997; Marshall et al., 1991). Surgical procedures did not result in significant reductions in sexually deviant behaviors and have considerable negative side effects (Marshall et al., 1991). Neurosurgery is no longer used in the treatment of sex offenders (Barbaree and Seto, 1997).

Pharmacological Interventions. There are several specific pharmacological agents which have as their mechanism of action reducing sexual drive, urges, and fantasy, and, consequently, reducing sexually deviant behavior (Barbaree and Seto, 1997; Lockhart et al., 1990; Marshall et al., 1991). Agents such as estrogen, neuroleptics, and hormonal analogs such as CPA or MPA, which act as androgenic antagonists, have all been employed (Barbaree and Seto, 1997; Marshall et al., 1991). The latter class of pharmacological agents, the antiandrogens, are primarily used to bring sexual arousal to controllable levels in those offenders whose arousal is so high as to inhibit the effectiveness of any other psychological intervention (Bradford, 1990; Marshall et al., 1991; Robinson and Valcour, 1995).

Pharmacological interventions have been found to be effective in reducing sexual reoffending, compared to control groups of offenders not receiving this intervention (Meyer, Cole, and Emory, 1992). A review of pharmacological interventions supported the overall efficacy of these, at least among some types of sex offenders (Grossman, Martis, and Fichtner, 1999).

Side effects of pharmacological interventions can be considerable, and include dyskinetic and feminization effects, reduction in the size of the testes, increased blood pressure, and diabetes (Barbaree and Seto, 1997; Emory, Cole, and Meyer, 1992; Langevin, 1983; Marshall et al., 1991; Meyer et al., 1992) Another drawback associated with pharmacological therapy is the attrition rate, which can be as high as 100 percent (Barbaree and Seto, 1997). For those who do not complete pharmacological interventions, recidivism rates are very high, up to 91 percent (Marshall et al., 1991). Even among offenders who complete treatment, recidivism rates are as high as 30 percent. In addition, there is evidence to suggest that, although the pharmacological effects are achieved, for example, a reduction in testosterone levels, there may not be a corresponding reduction in sexual arousal or sexually deviant behavior (Marshall et al., 1991).

Research has found that posttreatment recidivism reductions associated with antiandrogeneric interventions are not significantly different from reductions following cognitive-behavioral treatment (Hall, 1995). Other research has found differential effects of pharmacological interventions. For example, progestogens have been found to have the greatest benefit among those sex offenders who are nonrecidivists, who are motivated to participate in treatment, and who have good social support (Cooper, 1986). These characteristics describe those sex offenders who would likely fare well with any intervention and who pose a lower risk of reoffending in comparison to other sex offenders.

Hormonal interventions demonstrating the greatest impact on recidivism are those that also make use of cognitive-behavioral or other interventions in addition to pharmacotherapy (Bradford, 1990; Cooper, 1986; Fedoroff, Wisner-Carlson, Dean, and Berlin, 1992; Marshall et al., 1991). Presently, pharmacological interventions are used primarily as adjunctive treatment with those sex offenders for whom sexual drive, urges, and fantasies are associated with sexually deviant behavior. Importantly, it has been estimated that such offenders comprise approximately 10 percent of the sex offender population (Marshall, 1996). Finally, it should be noted that the use of pharmacological agents with juvenile sex offenders is even more equivocal, given the potential negative effects on sexual development (Becker and Hunter, 1997).

Behavioral Interventions. Behavioral treatment focuses on changing sexual responses to inappropriate stimuli and reorienting sexual preference away from children to a preference for adults, or from a preference for violence to a preference for consensual sexual interactions. The rationale for these interventions arises from classical and operant conditioning theories and is based on the assumption that sexual arousal to violence, children, and other inappropriate targets is a result of learning through reinforcement, desensitization, generalization, and the pairing of inappropriate stimuli with sexual arousal (Abel, Becker, Cunningham-Rathner, Rouleau, Kaplan, and Reich, 1984). Behavioral techniques, therefore, involve extinguishing inappropriate and deviant responses and increasing sexual arousal to appropriate and legal stimuli (Lockhart et al., 1988).

Behavioral interventions involve the use of such techniques as masturbatory reconditioning, or satiation, covert sensitization, and aversion therapy. Satiation procedures involve repeated verbalization and/or masturbation to sexual fantasies until these become associated with boredom and a lack of sexual arousal (Abel and Blanchard, 1974; Lockhart et al., 1988).

Covert sensitization aims to reduce deviant sexual arousal by pairing sexually deviant fantasies with aversive mental images that produce negative emotions, such as fear and anxiety (Lockhart et al., 1990). Offenders engage in a sexually arousing deviant fantasy and, at the point at which the sexual arousal is achieved, the offender changes from the fantasy to an aversive image. Upon reaching the peak of anxiety, the offender again switches from the aversive image to an appropriate fantasy. Thus, through the use of imagery techniques, covert sensitization aims to pair deviant sexual arousal with anxiety, which is subsequently relieved by appropriate imagery. Note that such a procedure as covert sensitization is most appropriate for offenders possessing sufficient verbal and cognitive abilities to engage in the procedure (Abel et al., 1984).

Finally, aversion therapy aims to extinguish deviant sexual behavior or fantasy through the use of punishment and through the pairing of deviant sexual arousal with aversive experiences and, therefore, anxiety and unpleasantness. It is similar to covert sensitization, except that the aversive stimuli, such as chemical agents that induce nausea, mild electric shock, or unpleasant scents, are physically applied rather than imagined (Lockhart et al., 1988). Aversion therapy also can be self-administered by sex offenders outside of treatment settings, using such noxious agents as ammonia.

Although there are ethical and professional concerns (particularly associated with aversion therapy), covert sensitization and aversion therapy have been associated with positive posttreatment outcome, including reduced recidivism (Maletzky, 1980; Quinsey, Chaplin, and Carrigan, 1980). There is evidence that these methods have value in the treatment of sexual offenders (for example, Maletzky, 1991) and that they are more effective than psychotherapeutic methods (Laws and Marshall, 1990).

However, as with pharmacological interventions, behavioral treatments are not applicable to all sex offenders. As indicated above, it is estimated that only 10 percent of sex offenders show a strong association between sexually deviant thoughts and masturbation or strong urges to reoffend (Marshall, 1996). Thus, these interventions should be reserved for those offenders for whom deviant sexual arousal is associated with offending (Blanchette, 1996).

Finally, it has been suggested that such methods can function to alter sexual preference; however, that sexual preference can be changed through any therapy has not been demonstrated, and there is no reason to believe that treatment can effect such a change (Barbaree and Seto, 1997). It is suggested that the most appropriate goal of these interventions is behavioral control and management of sexual arousal, rather than the changing of sexual preference.

Cognitive-behavioral Treatment. Cognitive-behavioral interventions are based on social learning theory (Bandura, 1973, 1978, 1986) and are the most widely accepted type of intervention with offenders generally (Andrews and Bonta, 1998) and with sex offenders specifically (Becker and Murphy, 1998; Freeman-Longo and Knopp, 1992; Laws, 1989). Cognitive-behavioral interventions consistently demonstrate reductions in sexual and nonsexual recidivism following treatment (Barbaree and Seto, 1997; Marshall et al., 1991; Looman et al., 1999; Nicholaichuk et al., 2000).

Cognitive-behavioral interventions are based on the premise that cognitive processes and behavior are linked, and that cognitions influence behavior. Sexual offending is viewed as a pattern of behavior, which has developed and been maintained through the principles of learning and reinforcement and which results from maladaptive responses and coping mechanisms. Cognitive-behavioral interventions aim to replace maladaptive or deviant responses with adaptive, prosocial beliefs and behavior through targeting specific areas in which offenders are deficient. Cognitive-behavioral interventions therefore involve skills acquisition and rehearsal, development of effective problem-solving strategies, social and victim perspective taking, sexual and social relationships, and examination of the relationship between cognition, affect, and behavior.

One important component of cognitive-behavioral intervention involves addressing cognitive distortions. This has become an integral part of many treatment programs (for example, Becker and Murphy, 1998; Correctional Service of Canada, 1996, 2000). Cognitive distortions are those cognitive processes, attitudes, and beliefs which support sexual aggression and which allow sexual offending to occur by reducing cognitive dissonance associated with offending and providing justification for offending. Examples of cognitive distortions include blaming victims, minimizing harm caused, and rationalizing the occurrence of sexual aggression. Cognitive distortions are used by sex offenders against children (Abel et al., 1984) and adults (Yates, 1996) to provide justification for offending and to absolve themselves of responsibility for their actions. Cognitive behavioral treatment of cognitive distortions involves challenging and altering these beliefs and replacing them with ones that do not support sexual aggression.

Marshall et al. (1991) demonstrated the superiority of cognitive-behavioral interventions relative to behavioral treatment. In a study of treated exhibitionists, results indicated that behavioral techniques, such as electrical aversive therapy, desensitization, and orgasmic reconditioning, reduced reoffending, although recidivism rates remained substantial.

Examining both official and unofficial recidivism rates over a follow-up period of greater than eight years, researchers found that treated exhibitionists recidivated at a rate of 39 percent compared to a rate of 57 percent among untreated exhibitionists. Although recidivism was lower among the treated men, the rate of reoffending obviously remained unacceptably high. Marshall et al. (1991) later added cognitive and cognitive-behavioral elements to the behavioral treatment program, including cognitive restructuring, relationship skills, assertiveness training, stress management, and other similar methods. At follow-up (approximately four years), the recidivism rate of the group which received cognitive-behavioral intervention was 23.6 percent, which, when corrected for the difference in length of follow-up, was significantly lower than that of the treated men who had received only behavioral treatment.

Nicholaichuk et al. (2000) found that cognitive-behavioral treatment reduced sexual offending among high-risk rapists, pedophiles, mixed offenders, and incest offenders, compared to untreated sex offenders. Similarly, Marques, Day, Nelson, and West (1994) found a significant positive treatment effect for sex offenders treated within a comprehensive cognitive-behavioral treatment program (Marques, Day, Nelson, and Miner, 1989). These studies are reviewed in greater detail below. Currently, the majority of cognitive-behavioral interventions incorporate relapse prevention techniques (Grossman et al., 1999) as a strategy for risk management and offender self-management. Relapse prevention is reviewed below.

Relapse Prevention. Relapse prevention as a treatment approach for sex offenders was adapted from addictions research and is designed as a posttreatment intervention to assist in the maintenance of treatment and to prevent a return to sexual offending through the acquisition of self-management skills. Relapse prevention differs from many other approaches to treatment in that, while other approaches view sexual offending from the perspective of the medical model and, hence, attempt to "cure" or eliminate the problem, relapse prevention focuses on control of behavior, and conceptualizes treatment as a continuum or process rather than as an endpoint (Becker and Murphy, 1998; Pithers and Cumming, 1989). Sex offenders no longer are viewed as suffering from a disease, and it is recognized that they cannot be "cured." Thus, behavioral control is regarded as a more realistic goal of treatment (Pithers and Cumming, 1989).

Relapse prevention focuses on understanding and analyzing situations that place the offender at risk for reoffending sexually and on developing effective strategies to prevent reoffending in these situations. Relapse prevention assists the offender in identifying stimuli which trigger a progression of behaviors that previously were associated with sexual offending for that individual, and to manage responses and behavior throughout this progression of events. Offenders learn and rehearse responses to circumstances that will assist them in coping successfully and avoiding a return to sexual offending. Relapse prevention also examines lifestyle patterns and assists offenders in identifying and implementing lifestyle changes that are not conducive to sexual offending. Finally, relapse prevention identifies observable factors associated with risk for offending sexually, which assists service providers who are providing supervision for the offender.

It is difficult to evaluate the effectiveness of relapse prevention, since it is rarely implemented in isolation from other interventions, but is rather part of larger, more comprehensive cognitive-behavioral programs. Few studies evaluate the unique or incremental contributions of individual treatment components, including relapse prevention, but rather evaluate the intervention as a whole. In addition, as an intervention, relapse prevention is a relatively recent addition to the treatment of sex offenders.

Consequently, little research on the efficacy of relapse prevention is available. However, as indicated above, relapse prevention is a common component of cognitive-behavioral interventions that have demonstrated efficacy with sex offenders. Thus, the addition of this type of intervention is promising. Furthermore, with its focus on identifying and coping with high-risk circumstances, relapse prevention also shows promise as a supervision strategy for service providers working with sex offenders. The application of relapse prevention to the community supervision of sex offenders is discussed in a later section.

Other Treatment Approaches. Other treatment approaches frequently offered to sex offenders include such interventions as skills training and sex education (Lockhart et al., 1988). Although previously implemented as the sole method of treatment, these approaches currently are frequently incorporated into multifaceted cognitive-behavioral programs.

Social skills training is based on the assumption that deficits in social skills, such as communication, assertiveness, and interpersonal relationships, are contributing factors to sexual offending. Skills training approaches attempt to impart to offenders appropriate ways to interact with peers and sexual partners (Lockhart et al., 1988). Research on the utility of social skills training alone is equivocal with regard to effectiveness. Lockhart et al. (1988) suggest that such skills training may be required by only a subgroup of sex offenders for whom skills deficits are clearly associated with sexual offending. Similarly, sex education approaches are designed for use with those offenders for whom deficits in sexual knowledge are associated with avoidance of appropriate adult sexual and nonsexual relationships (Lockhart et al., 1988). As indicated above, cognitive-behavioral treatment tends to include such approaches as part of multifaceted, multicomponent interventions (for example, Correctional Service of Canada, 1996; Lockhart et al., 1988). Family-based approaches also have been used, predominantly with incest offenders

(Becker and Murphy, 1998; Lockhart et al., 1988) and juvenile sex offenders, although these interventions have tended to be adjunctive to other interventions and were only implemented among incest offenders. The majority of specialized sex offender treatment today uses a combination of behavioral, cognitive-behavioral, relapse prevention, and skills-based treatment using a combination of group and individual therapy and, when programming is offered in community settings, some degree of supervision (for example, McGrath, Hoke, and Vojtisek, 1998).

Community-based Intervention. As indicated above, the treatment of sexual offenders has consisted of numerous approaches of varying theoretical orientations and equivocal outcome. Community-based treatment of sexual offenders has received less empirical attention, although the existence of community-based programs has increased substantially during the past decade (Allam and Browne, 1998). These programs largely have been developed without the concomitant development of a rationale and intervention strategy or an evaluation framework (Allam and Browne, 1998). Nonetheless, community-based treatment and supervision are essential to the comprehensive treatment of sex offenders and have been in existence long enough to commence analysis of their effectiveness (Marshall and Eccles, 1991).

Methodological Limitations of Treatment Effectiveness Research

Research on sexual offender risk prediction and treatment outcome is hampered by a plethora of methodological limitations that affect the quality, validity, and generalizability of findings. Methodological issues that arise reflect problems with sample selection, study design, selection of comparison groups, length of follow-up periods, selection of outcome measures, and low base rates of reoffending. These are reviewed briefly below.

Sample selection has been a particular problem with outcome research, both with regard to bias in participant selection and in analysis of data. Many treatment programs select participants on the basis of some predetermined criterion, such as motivation for treatment, or exclude participants on the basis of some criterion, such as the existence of denial or previous sex offenses (Becker, 1994; Furby et al., 1989).

As a result, some programs exclude high-risk offenders and treat low-risk offenders, who do not tend to show treatment effects due to a floor effect (Nicholaichuk, 1996; Nicholaichuk et al., 2000). These biases result in "evidence" of a lack of a treatment effect or, alternatively, when aggregated with data for higher risk offenders, attenuate the magnitude of the treatment effect. Thus, treatment effects will vary as a function of offender risk.

For example, it is well-documented that recidivism among released offenders with more than one conviction for a sexual offense is considerably higher than among comparable offenders with only one conviction (for example, Marshall et al., 1991, Nicholaichuk et al., 2000). In their review, Marshall et al. (1991) found that studies have shown recidivism rates of 10 percent to 21 percent for first-time sexual offenders and rates of 33 percent to 71 percent for repeat offenders. Nicholaichuk et al. (2000) found similar differences among treated high-risk sexual offenders in the Canadian system, with first-time offenders reoffending at significantly lower rates than recidivist offenders.

Thus, depending on the selection criteria used in treatment or research, data analysis may yield an underestimate or an overestimate of recidivism rates according to the direction of the selection bias. It is important that treatment effects be assessed separately for offenders of different risk levels, although this is rarely done.

Similarly, although diversity among sex offenders is acknowledged, many outcome evaluation studies do not examine reoffending as a function of the type of sex offender. It consistently has been found that sex offenders against adults, against related versus unrelated children, and against male versus female children, against strangers versus acquaintances, differ significantly in their rates of recidivism (Marshall et al., 1991; Nicholaichuk et al., 2000). Data analyses that do not account for such variation will overestimate reoffending among those types of offenders who recidivate at the lowest rates (for example, incest offenders) and will underestimate reoffending among those offenders who recidivate at higher rates (for example, exhibitionists and pedophiles who offend against boys). Again, although this variation is acknowledged, data frequently are not analyzed differentially for different types of offenders.

Similarly, studies of specialized populations, such as mentally disordered or low functioning sex offenders, may not be generalizable to other, less specialized samples of sex offenders. For example, Rice, Quinsey, and colleagues (for example, Rice, Harris, and Cormier, 1992; Rice, Harris, and Quinsey, 1990; Rice, Quinsey, and Harris, 1991; Webster, Harris, Rice, and Quinsey, 1994) have assessed outcome among sex offenders treated within a maximum-security psychiatric institution, most of whom were referred for pretrial psychiatric assessment, were found not criminally responsible, or were certified mentally ill. Offenders treated within such programs may represent exceptionally high-risk and/or high-need offenders who are not comparable to incarcerated sex offenders or sex offenders under supervision in the community. Nonetheless, findings from research on these populations are frequently generalized to, or included in, studies with other samples of sex offenders, with the result that treatment effects are masked or attenuated.

In addition, many programs offer a single intervention to all offenders, ignoring variability in risk and treatment needs (Gordon and Nicholaichuk, 1996). This affects conclusions regarding the effectiveness of the intervention for various offenders, since it is reasonable to expect that specific interventions may be effective with some, but not all, sex offenders (Gordon and Nicholaichuk, 1996). Each of these problems in turn compromises the integrity of the treatment program, the evaluation, or both and, thus, affects conclusions made about the efficacy of treatment.

To assess the effects of treatment, it is important that a group of treated sex offenders be compared to a group of untreated sex offenders. Ideally, sex offenders would be randomly assigned to the treatment and no-treatment control conditions so that any differences in pretreatment characteristics do not systematically vary as a function of assignment to groups. However, such practice is ethically unacceptable (Becker, 1994), as treatment would be deliberately withheld from sex offenders requiring treatment, potentially resulting in additional victims.

Alternatively, samples of offenders may be matched at pretreatment on the basis of risk and offense characteristics, as has been done in several studies (for example, Hanson and Harris, 1998; Nicholaichuk et al., 2000). Most frequently, however, treated sex offenders are compared to convenience samples of untreated sex offenders, such as offenders who enter treatment but who do not complete the program. This procedure often results in substantial differences between the treated and untreated groups such that interpretation of any treatment effect found cannot be made, because the offenders differ on important characteristics other than having received intervention, such as risk levels.

One of the most prominent methodological limitations to sex offender treatment outcome research is the low baseline rate of recidivism among sex offenders. Examination of treatment outcome evaluation studies shows that authors consistently note that results are qualified by low rates of reoffending among offenders under study (for example, Hanson, 1997; Nicholaichuk et al, 2000). Low base rates of recidivism result in difficulty in detecting treatment effects and can result in the conclusion that treatment is ineffective.

A related concern regards the duration of follow-up posttreatment. Research has found that sexual reoffending can occur for extended periods following treatment (for example, Marques et al., 1989; Hanson, Steffy, and Gauthier, 1993). Therefore, the length of follow-up within a given study will affect conclusions regarding the efficacy of treatment. Generally, studies with shorter follow-up periods are more likely to find a treatment effect than those with longer follow-up periods. It is important to recognize the impact of the length of follow-up on conclusions about treatment efficacy and to take this into account when reviewing the research.

Another prominent methodological concern is the definition of recidivism used in the research. While some studies use only officially sanctioned recidivism, such as reconviction for a new sexual offense, other studies use officially detected (but not sanctioned) recidivism, such as rearrest or parole revocation, while still others use unofficial data, such as self-reported sexual reoffending or sexually deviant fantasy, or sexual arousal as measured using phallometry. A comparison of these various types of recidivism measures indicates that reconviction may be too conservative an outcome measure, and self-report measures and phallometric measures tend to be inaccurate (Grossman, 1985).

In addition, some studies assess the impact of treatment on sexual recidivism, while others assess the impact of treatment on any type of violent or nonviolent recidivism. Depending on the outcome measure selected, conclusions regarding the effectiveness of treatment will vary, often substantially.

Even with these limitations, it is possible to draw conclusions about the efficacy of sex offender treatment. The discussion that follows reviews the sexual offender treatment literature, with an emphasis on qualitative and quantitative reviews of the literature. A number of individual studies are reviewed; however, this review is not exhaustive. Numerous excellent reviews have been conducted (for example, Bradford, 1990; Furby et al., 1989; Hall, 1995; Marshall et al., 1991); that work is not repeated here.

Qualitative and Quantitative Reviews of Sex Offender Treatment Efficacy

As the above discussion indicates, it is apparent that there are numerous methodological limitations associated with sex-offender-treatment outcome research. It is also apparent from the preceding discussion that there are a wide variety of interventions available with which to treat sex offenders. This variety further complicates assessment of treatment outcome because studies frequently do not provide sufficient specificity of the methods and types of interventions employed, thereby inhibiting evaluation of a particular type of treatment. In addition, many interventions are multimodal, employing a variety of treatment and supervision methods. However, evaluations of these interventions frequently do not assess the impact of individual components. As a result, when a treatment effect is found, we are left with the conclusion simply that some aspect of treatment had an impact on the offender, without an understanding of the specific components contributing to the effect (Pithers, 1993).

That general psychotherapeutic approaches do not impact recidivism either within the general correctional population (Andrews and Bonta, 1998) or with sex offenders (Barbaree and Seto, 1997) is generally a widely accepted conclusion. However, what we do know about the efficacy of treatment vis a vis what works with sex offenders is considerably less definitive. The following review evaluates the efficacy of treatment with sex offenders, with a focus primarily on the work of previous reviewers and a number of pertinent recent treatment outcome evaluation studies.

One of the first comprehensive reviews of sex offender treatment was conducted by Furby and colleagues (1989). Studies selected for review were limited to those in which official criminal record data were available, various types of sex offenders and treatment approaches were included, data were available for both treated and untreated sex offenders, and there was a minimum sample size of ten subjects per study. Due to methodological limitations, the authors did not conduct a meta-analysis. However, they conducted a qualitative analysis of forty-two studies, examining patterns evident across the studies, with a focus on recidivism, treatment effectiveness in reducing recidivism, and variation in rates of recidivism as a function of sex offender type.

With regard to recidivism, Furby et al. (1989) found that, in those studies for which multiple follow-up periods of the same subjects were conducted, there was a tendency for general recidivism (such as any reoffense) to increase over time, although there was no corresponding tendency evidenced for sexual reoffending. However, this finding was associated with three studies with samples of apparently particularly high-risk or persistent sex offenders (exhibitionists, pedophiles, "criminal sexual psychopaths," and hospitalized offenders), and may have been an artifact of methodological variability among the studies.

With regard to treatment effectiveness, eight of nine studies of untreated sexual offenders revealed low rates of sexual recidivism (less than 12 percent), with follow-up periods of up to ten years. However, examination of the numbers of subjects within these studies revealed that greater than two-thirds of treated sex offenders recidivated sexually at a rate in excess of 12 percent. In addition, in six of seven studies, treated sexual offenders recidivated at a greater rate than did untreated sexual offenders, although the treated and untreated offenders differed considerably at pretest. The only study employing random assignment of offenders to the treatment and no-treatment conditions yielded non-significant differences between these two groups. Furby et al. (1989) noted as well that these studies were dated and suggested that the treatment techniques employed may have been outdated at the time of their review and, therefore, may have used less effective methods.

Finally, Furby et al. (1989) attempted to compare recidivism rates for different types of offenders. Again, the number of studies analyzed was small, but these indicated a lower recidivism rate for pedophiles than for exhibitionists and rapists, as well as a higher recidivism rate for homosexual pedophiles than for heterosexual pedophiles, a finding which held only among untreated sex offenders, and not among treated offenders.

Furby et al. (1989) concluded that there was no evidence that treatment for sexual offenders reduced recidivism, either generally or differentially, for different groups of offenders. This conclusion is regarded by most subsequent reviewers as overly pessimistic (for example, Marshall et al., 1991; Marshall and Pithers, 1994). Among the problems associated with the Furby et al. (1989) review were the tendency to hold the studies reviewed to overly rigorous, unrealistic methodological standards (Marshall et al., 1991), the finding that many of the interventions applied in the treatment programs were out of date by the time of publication, and the finding that a number of the samples of offenders overlapped between the studies included in the review (Pithers, 1993). However, the Furby et al. (1989) review was a valuable contribution to the sex offender research literature as it highlighted the methodological limitations associated with treatment outcome research and stimulated additional research pertaining to treatment efficacy with sex offenders.

In one of these subsequent reviews, Hall (1995), using meta-analytic techniques, examined twelve studies including approximately 1,300 offenders which were published subsequent to the Furby et al. (1989) review and which examined recidivism of treated sex offenders in comparison to sex offenders who had not been treated or who had completed a comparison treatment program. Recidivism was broadly defined as additional sexually aggressive behavior that resulted in official legal charges.

Hall (1995) found that, in comparison to untreated sexual offenders, there was a stronger effect size for treated sexual offenders. The overall effect size for treatment, at $r = .12$, was small but robust. The overall recidivism rate for the treated sexual offenders was 19 percent, compared to an overall recidivism rate of 27 percent for the untreated or comparison treated sexual offenders. However, treatment effect sizes varied considerably across studies, likely as a function of stronger effect sizes associated with higher base rates of recidivism in some studies. The range of treatment effect sizes was from $r = -.07$ to $r = .55$, with studies with longer follow- up periods demonstrating the strongest effect sizes. Hall (1995) concluded that treatment was effective, but that the low base rates of recidivism among sex offenders may preclude finding statistically significant treatment effects.

Other potential sources of heterogeneity of effect sizes identified by Hall (1995) included methodological differences between studies and participant risk or pathology. Specifically, effect sizes were significantly greater for studies in which participants were treated on an outpatient basis (r = approximately .30) than those in which participants received treatment as inpatients (r = approximately .10). This finding suggests that either outpatient treatment has a greater impact on the reduction of recidivism or that offenders who are treated on an outpatient basis are at lower risk to re-offend than are offenders treated on an inpatient basis. Conversely, inpatient treatment may be more generalized and less specific to sexual offending, resulting in a weaker treatment effect.

Hall (1995) also examined differential treatment as a potential source of variability in effect size. Studies in which either cognitive-behavioral (r = approximately .28) or hormonal treatments (r = approximately .32) were administered yielded significantly greater effect sizes than studies in which behavioral treatment alone was employed (r = approximately -.10). Effect sizes for cognitive-behavioral and hormonal treatments were not significantly different from each other. These data suggest differential treatment effects on recidivism as a function of treatment type, and the superiority of cognitive-behavioral and hormonal treatments relative to behavioral treatments. Cognitive-behavioral treatments may be the treatment of choice, given that the refusal and attrition rates for hormonal treatments are considerably greater than those for cognitive-behavioral interventions (Hall, 1995).

Thus, unlike Furby et al. (1989), Hall presented a much more optimistic view of sex offender treatment, and identified the potential for differential treatment effects as a function of such factors as type of treatment, location of treatment, and risk or pathology of offenders. Differential treatment effects are viewed as an important source of variability in treatment outcome, and have implications for pretreatment assessment, treatment assignment, and posttreatment management of sexual offenders, as will be discussed in greater detail in later sections.

In an recent review, Alexander (1999) conducted a quantitative analysis of 79 sex offender treatment outcome studies, encompassing almost 11,000 treated and untreated sex offenders. Although meta-analytic techniques were not employed in this study, Alexander (1999) examined rearrest rates for both treated and untreated sexual offenders, including adults and juveniles, and compared treatment effectiveness as a function of type of offender, type of intervention, location of intervention, date of publication of the research, and length of follow-up. Excluded from the analyses were female sex offenders and developmentally disabled sex offenders, studies involving fewer than ten subjects, studies in which outcome data were not provided or were not clear, and evaluations of biomedical and physical castration treatments.

Alexander (1999) found that, overall, treated adult sex offenders recidivated at a lower rate than did untreated sex offenders (13 percent versus 18 percent). This was true for the various subtypes of sex offenders, including treated and untreated rapists (20.1 percent versus 23.7 percent), child molesters (14.4 percent versus 25.8 percent), and exhibitionists (19.7 percent versus 57.1 percent), but not when the subtype of sex offender was not specified in the original study (13.1 percent versus 12 percent). This finding highlights the importance of specifying and examining posttreatment outcome according to the type of sex offender, and suggests that treatment effects may be masked when overall recidivism rates are examined.

For treated juvenile sex offenders, the overall recidivism rate was 7.1 percent. There were no data available for untreated juvenile sex offenders. When examined by subtype, the data indicated that treated juvenile rapists recidivated at a rate of 5.8 percent, treated juvenile child molesters at a rate of 2.5 percent, and unspecified treated juvenile sex offenders at a rate of 7.5 percent. As compared to adult offenders, treated juvenile rapists recidivated at a much lower rate (20.1 percent versus 5.8 percent). Finally, among both adult and juvenile offenders, Alexander (1999) found differences in recidivism rates supporting the use of relapse prevention as an intervention; however, due to a lack of specification of types of treatment in these studies, the findings are not reviewed in detail here.

With regard to treatment effectiveness as a function of location of treatment, both juveniles and adults tended to fare better, in terms of reduced recidivism, in outpatient, prison, or in unspecified or mixed settings rather than in hospital settings. When examined by type of offender, however, it was found that child molesters fared considerably better in terms of reduced recidivism when treatment was offered in outpatient rather than prison settings (13.9 percent versus 21.4 percent). Unfortunately, interactions were not examined by Alexander (1999), so the interaction between treatment type and location, which would be expected to be significant, was not established. The findings supporting prison settings over hospital settings, for example, may be a result of a greater availability of cognitive-behavioral treatment in prison settings, whereas hospital settings may not provide either cognitive-behavioral or sex-offender-specific treatment. Thus, these findings should be interpreted with caution.

Alexander (1999) also examined treatment efficacy as a function of type of sex offender. This analysis revealed little difference in posttreatment recidivism between treated and untreated adult rapists (20.1 percent versus 23.7 percent) and between treated and untreated child molesters with female victims (15.6 percent versus 15.7 percent). However, treated child molesters whose victims were male recidivated at a significantly lower rate (18.2 percent) than those who were untreated (34.1 percent). Unfortunately, Alexander did not include in this analysis offenders who offended against both male and female child victims, who may represent a distinct, higher-risk group of offenders (Nicholaichuk et al., 2000). Similarly, treated incest offenders recidivated at a substantially lower rate (4.0 percent) than untreated incest offenders (12.5 percent).

In examining recidivism rates in relation to the date of publication of individual studies, Alexander (1999) found that recidivism rates declined for research published in the 1990s as compared to the 1980s for treated adult rapists (21.9 percent versus 13.6 percent), adult child molesters of female victims (17.2 percent versus 10.7 percent), incest offenders (6.4 percent versus 3.1 percent), and nonincest offenders (17.7 percent versus 6.1 percent). Conversely, recidivism increased from the 1980s to the 1990s among adult offenders against male children (17.6 percent versus 21.3 percent) and among juvenile sex offenders (2.9 percent versus 10.6 percent).

Finally, Alexander (1999) found that, as the length of follow-up period increased, recidivism rates rose for juvenile sex offenders, adult rapists, and adult offenders against female victims. Conversely, over time, recidivism rates fell for adult sex offenders against male victims and exhibitionists. Unfortunately, however, these data were not analyzed using methods accounting for time at risk.

Alexander's (1999) research provides a valuable contribution to an understanding of the efficacy of treatment with both adult and juvenile sex offenders. Importantly, this research also demonstrated that treatment effects may be masked when sexual offenders are considered as a homogeneous group, but may become evident when offenders are considered according to a typology which reflects the heterogeneity of this group of offenders. Furthermore, Alexander's (1999) and Hall's (1995) research both highlight the importance of considering additional factors, such as treatment location and offender risk, in evaluating the effectiveness of sex offender treatment.

One recent study conducted to assess a specialized cognitive-behavioral intervention (McGrath et al., 1998) illustrates yet another important principle in sex offender treatment. In this study, McGrath et al. (1998) compared the effectiveness of specialized sex offender treatment to nonspecialized treatment and to an untreated control group. Results indicated a very low overall recidivism rate of 6.6 percent for all offenders (treated and untreated). In addition, the data indicated that posttreatment sexual recidivism was lowest among offenders receiving specialized sex offender treatment (1.4 percent), followed by those receiving no treatment (10.5 percent), and those receiving nonspecialized treatment (15.6 percent). Although the untreated comparison group was higher risk at pretreatment, as reflected by significantly more previous convictions for nonsexual violent and nonviolent offenses and a significantly longer period of incarceration, these data illustrate that treatment, in some cases, may be associated with higher rates of recidivism than not providing treatment at all, particularly if the treatment provided is nonspecific or inappropriate.

Marques et al. (1989) provided an evaluation of an intensive treatment program for sex offenders, employing a range of cognitive-behavioral, skills-based, behavioral, educational, and relapse prevention techniques, and follow-up care. This project, at Atascadero State Hospital, provides the only study of random assignment to treatment and control groups in the assessment of sex offender treatment. Marques et al. (1989) examined both in-treatment changes on target measures and posttreatment recidivism. At a mean seven-year follow-up period, it was found that treated sex offenders recidivated at a lower rate (8.2 percent) as compared to two control groups, who reoffended sexually at a rate of approximately 13 percent, and to offenders who left treatment before completion (37.5 percent; Marques et al., 1994).

In a study of treated high-risk Canadian sex offenders, Nicholaichuk and colleagues (2000) have demonstrated the importance of differential effects of treatment on outcome. Consistent with other findings described thus far, this study found that treated sex offenders recidivated sexually at a lower rate (14.5 percent) than a matched control group of untreated sex offenders, 33.2 percent of whom recidivated sexually. Similar to other research findings, the rate of recidivism for nonsexual offenses was higher than that for sexual offenses. Treated sex offenders reoffended at significantly lower rates and showed a greater reduction in severity of criminal offending when they did reoffend than did untreated sex offenders. In addition, first-time sex offenders reoffended sexually at a significantly lower rate (8.8 percent) than repeat offenders (23.5 percent). Among treated offenders, different types of offenders recidivated at different rates, with the lowest rate of reoffending among incest offenders (3.0 percent), followed by rapists (14.0 percent), pedophiles (18.3 percent), and men who offended against both adults and children (19.6 percent).

Using a sample of provincially incarcerated offenders, Nicholaichuk (1996) found that treated and untreated sex offenders did not differ in their recidivism rates. While emotional and social functioning improved, treatment did not impact on recidivism among this low-risk group of sex offenders incarcerated at the provincial level. Conversely, a treatment effect was found for the high-risk group of sex offenders, as described in the preceding study (Nicholaichuk et al., 2000). Such findings are consistent with the principles of effective correctional treatment, described below.

The treatment effects described above represent both statistically and clinically significant findings. In the medical literature, treatments obtaining correlations as low as $r = .15$ are effective treatments for disease, while correlations of $r = .25$ are considered to represent effective psychological treatment generally (Gendreau, 1998). Thus, the magnitude of effects associated with sex offender treatment would be considered substantial and clinically relevant within these fields, and suggest that sex offender treatment is effective in reducing the occurrence of sexual reoffending.

The most effective interventions are those which are applied differentially to different types of offenders. The construct of differential risk

and treatment has been well established in the general offender literature; however, its application to sex offender treatment has not been as
frequently encountered. Many programs incorporate these principles
into treatment (for example, Correctional Service of Canada, 2000); however, research pertaining to sex offenders rarely evaluates these
principles for their application to sex offender intervention and its effectiveness in light of these principles. These principles of effective
correctional treatment are reviewed below, followed by a review of their
application to sex offender risk assessment.

Principles of Effective Correctional Treatment

It is well documented in the criminological literature that effective
interventions are those which are matched to offender risk, need, and
responsivity (Andrews and Bonta, 1998). *Risk factors* refer to those characteristics of the offender and his or her circumstances that are
associated with likelihood of engaging in criminal behavior and which,
when changed, are associated with concurrent changes in the likelihood
of reoffending (Andrews and Bonta, 1998). A distinction is made between
static and dynamic risk factors. *Static risk factors* are those which are not
amenable to influence, and include such factors as previous offense history, family of origin, and age. *Dynamic risk factors* are also associated
with likelihood of reoffending, but are amenable to influence or change
through intervention and, when changed, are associated with a change in
likelihood of reoffending. These include factors such as attitudes, values,
and beliefs, criminogenic peers, and instability in employment. Dynamic
risk factors predict general recidivism at least as well as, or better than,
static predictors.

Risk varies according to the circumstances of individual offenders,
and variations in risk are associated with variation in recidivism. The risk
principle states that risk is predictable and can be influenced, and that
the most intensive levels of intervention should be reserved for higher-
risk offenders, while lower levels of intervention, or no intervention,
should be applied to lower-risk offenders. Treatment of offenders, including sex offenders, is most effective for higher risk offenders (Andrews and
Bonta, 1998; Gendreau and Goggin, 1996; 1997; Gendreau, Little, and
Goggin, 1996; Gordon and Nicholaichuk, 1996), while treatment of lower-
risk offenders is not warranted, has a lesser likelihood of demonstrating
a treatment effect due to a floor effect (Nicholaichuk, 1996), and is not the
best use of limited resources (Prentky and Burgess, 1990). As indicated in

the preceding review, treatment for sex offenders is rarely applied differentially as a function of offender risk.

Effective correctional treatment also targets the criminogenic needs of offenders (Andrews and Bonta, 1998; Gendreau and Goggin, 1996; 1997; Gendreau et al., 1996). *Criminogenic needs* refer to those characteristics of offenders and their circumstances that are amenable to influence through intervention and which, when changed, are associated with changes in risk and recidivism (Andrews and Bonta, 1998). For sex offenders, these include such factors as attitudes, cognitive distortions, and deviant sexual arousal. The need principle of effective correctional intervention states that the most effective interventions are those which target the criminogenic needs of offenders (Andrews and Bonta, 1998).

A distinction is made between criminogenic and noncriminogenic needs. Criminogenic needs are factors that are associated with risk for reoffending, while noncriminogenic needs are factors that are not associated with risk for reoffending. Criminogenic needs are those factors which, when changed through intervention, are associated with changes in the risk of reoffending. While noncriminogenic needs are dynamic and changeable, they are not associated with risk and, therefore, are not appropriate targets of treatment. The need principle also specifies that evaluations of correctional interventions should be conducted such that changes in criminogenic dynamic need factors are measured, and these changes are related to treatment outcome measures (such as recidivism) at some future point in time (Andrews and Bonta, 1998; Hanson and Harris, 1998). However, as the preceding review indicates, this is rarely done in sex offender treatment outcome research.

Finally, effective correctional intervention is that which is applied according to the responsivity principle, which states that interventions should be based on cognitive, behavioral, and social learning principles and methods and should be delivered in a manner which is consistent with offenders' learning styles and abilities (Andrews and Bonta, 1998; Gendreau and Goggin, 1996; 1997; Gendreau et al., 1996). In treatment with offenders, individual responsivity factors, such as language, culture, personality style, intelligence, anxiety levels, and cognitive abilities, affect the manner in which the offender interacts with the treatment process which, in turn, influences the effectiveness of the intervention for that offender. According to the responsivity principle, treatment should be varied and adapted according to these learning styles to maximize the potential effectiveness of the intervention.

Again, as indicated in the preceding discussion, such adaptation rarely occurs in treatment with sex offenders, although some attempts are made through the addition of adjunctive individual therapy and specialized groups to address different learning styles (for example, Correctional Service of Canada, 1996, 1998). The adoption of group therapy as the most cost-efficient method of delivering intervention to sex offenders also has contributed to a lack of attention paid to the individual needs of sex offenders and to a lack of tailoring of treatment (Maletzky, 1999).

Sex Offender Risk and Prediction of Recidivism

As the preceding discussion exemplifies, risk and criminogenic need are integral components of assessment and intervention in the criminal justice system. Although this has been well established in the general criminal behavioral research, the application of the principles of effective correctional treatment to sex offender intervention has been less forthcoming, perhaps as a result of the relative infancy of sex offender risk assessment research or as a result of a lack of understanding of the risk that sex offenders pose. Sex offenders are a political and public concern (Schwartz and Cellini, 1995), and the abhorrent nature of their offending behavior tends to be confounded with perceptions of risk. As a result, a tendency to regard most sex offenders as high risk has developed and has been perpetuated; however, research clearly indicates that sex offenders vary in the risk they pose to reoffend.

Numerous excellent reviews and analyses of sex offender risk and prediction of recidivism have been conducted. A review of this literature is beyond the scope of the present paper. However, this research, in providing information about predictors of recidivism, is relevant to treatment efficacy in that the most effective treatments are those which are matched to offender risk and which target intermediate criminogenic factors known to be associated with recidivism. Therefore, to the extent that this body of research informs intervention planning and evaluation, relevant research is reviewed. Again, the emphasis in the following discussion is on qualitative and quantitative reviews and recent findings.

One problem with risk prediction is that it is typically conducted post hoc (Grubin and Wingate, 1996). That is, when variables are identified as having a relationship to sexual reoffending, they are offered as explanations after the fact, without a full understanding of the nature of their influence. If the predictor is a static or historical predictor, its value lies predominantly in predicting recidivism in the long-term more so than in predicting imminent recidivism while the offender is under supervision (Hanson and Harris, 1998). In addition, much of the work has relied on single variables, and has not taken the multivariate approach needed to establish meaning and to understand the manner in which these variables impact on behavior in individual cases (Grubin and Wingate, 1996). Furthermore, assessment and evaluation of dynamic risk factors are notably absent in recidivism research (Furby et al., 1989; Hanson and Bussière, 1996).

Motiuk and Brown (1996), using file review methodology, examined the recidivism rates of various subtypes of sex offenders and the factors that differentiated between offenders who recidivated and those who did not, using a sample of Canadian sex offenders followed up for an average of 3.5 years. As with treatment effectiveness research, prediction of sexual recidivism was limited due to a low base rate of reoffending. Specifically, Motiuk and Brown (1996) found a low rate of sexual reoffending overall (7.0 percent). Recidivism rates for violent nonsexual and general (nonviolent) reoffending were higher, at 19.5 percent and 33.5 percent, respectively. Of those offenders who had been supervised in the community over a longer period of time, sexual recidivism was lowest for incest offenders (4.4 percent), similar for rapists (5.9 percent), and highest for pedophiles (9.7 percent), although these differences were not statistically significant. While rates for general and violent reoffending were lowest among incest offenders (8.7 percent and 8.7 percent, respectively), rapists demonstrated higher recidivism rates for violent (21.2 percent) and general (42.2 percent) offenses than did pedophiles (18.4 percent and 27.2 percent), although only the latter difference was statistically significant.

Finally, Motiuk and Brown (1996) examined predictors of recidivism using information obtained from offender files. This analysis indicated that the only predictors of sexual reoffending among newly released sex offenders were a pattern of increasing severity (a composite measure of previous sex offense history and escalation in sex offending), and scores on the General Statistical Information on Recidivism Scale (GSIR; Nuffield, 1982). General and violent recidivism were predicted by a variety of static and dynamic factors, such as previous sex offenses, age at release, unemployment, unstable living arrangements, GSIR score, and substance abuse.

Hanson and Bussière (1996) conducted a meta-analysis of predictors of sexual offender recidivism with 87 articles representing 61 independent data sets from six countries and nearly 29,000 sexual offenders. To be included in the review, studies were required to include a follow-up period, to identify a group of sexual offenders, to compute the relationship between some initial characteristic and subsequent recidivism, to report sufficient statistical information, and to record sexual, nonsexual violent, or any recidivism as the outcome measure (Hanson and Bussière, 1996). For those studies in which the information was provided, treatment outcome was explicitly excluded from the meta-analysis as a potential predictor variable.

Findings indicated that, generally, different variables predicted sexual reoffending as compared to other (nonsexual) reoffending. The strongest predictors of sexual recidivism included those associated specifically with sexual deviance, including phallometric assessment of sexual preference for children (r = .32), prior sexual offenses (r = .19), and early onset of sexual offending (r = .12). To a lesser extent, general criminological variables were also predictive of sexual recidivism, including age (r = -.13), any previous offenses (r = .13), and never having been married (r = .11).

Conversely, nonsexual reoffending by sexual offenders was predicted by more general criminological variables, similar to those which predict recidivism among nonsexual offenders. These included age, marital status, personality disorder, ethnicity, and previous violent and nonviolent offense history. Reoffending among both these groups tended to occur among recidivists who were younger, single, evidenced an antisocial and/or psychopathic personality disorder, and had a more extensive violent and nonviolent offense history.

Risk assessment and prediction among sexual offenders has focused predominantly on static predictors of reoffending behavior. Yet, clinicians, therapists, parole officers, probation officers, and others working with sex offenders need to know those factors, be they affective, behavioral, or situational in nature, that are dynamic (in other words, changeable) to effectively treat and supervise sex offenders. Service providers in the community, in particular, need to know those dynamic, observable factors, which are associated with variations in risk for sexual reoffending (Hanson and Harris, 1998).

In the only analysis thus far to do so, Hanson and Harris (1998) examined the relationships between static, stable dynamic, and acute dynamic factors and recidivism among sex offenders. Static factors, such as age and offense history, and the more stable dynamic factors, such as personality disorders or sexual preference for children, assist in the long-term prediction of risk (Hanson and Harris, 1998). However, those dynamic factors which are more acute in nature (such as those which have a stronger temporal association with reoffending or those which may change rapidly), such as negative mood or intoxication, may be more amenable to observation by supervising officers and service providers and may indicate that risk has increased such that reoffending is more imminent than it was previously (Hanson and Harris, 1998).

Using a retrospective design, Hanson and Harris (1998) examined static, stable dynamic, and acute dynamic factors among sex offenders who recidivated and those who did not recidivate while on community supervision. Data were collected at six months and again at one month prior to recidivism, and at an equivalent time period for the nonrecidivists. Recidivists and nonrecidivists were matched on victim type, geographic region, and other relevant characteristics such as mental health status and risk. However, even after matching, the two groups remained significantly different on several static factors, including age, sexual deviance, rates of treatment failure, family background and history, personality disorder, and criminal risk. Taken together, these differences indicated higher risk and greater dysfunction on the part of the recidivists than the nonrecidivists.

There were several significant differences between recidivists and nonrecidivists on the more stable dynamic characteristics (Hanson and Harris, 1998). Specifically, recidivists tended to be more recently unemployed, to have substance abuse problems during supervision, to have fewer positive and more negative social influences, to have intimacy problems, to hold attitudes supportive of sexual offending, to view themselves as being at low risk to reoffend, and to engage in socially deviant behaviors, such as sexual fantasy, excessive masturbation, and the use of prostitutes. As compared to nonrecidivists, recidivists tended to have a more chaotic and antisocial lifestyle, to use leisure time aimlessly, to be more disengaged from treatment and supervision, to attempt to deceive and manipulate supervising officers, and to miss appointments. Recidivists and nonrecidivists were not significantly different on measures of psychological symptoms, such as negative mood, anger, psychiatric symptoms, and life stress, and demonstrated few differences on social adjustment factors, such as social problems and association with other sex offenders.

With regard to acute dynamic risk factors, Hanson and Harris (1998) examined changes during the course of community supervision. Most of the stable dynamic risk factors which were significantly different for recidivists and nonrecidivists were also significantly different as acute dynamic risk factors, in that the recidivists either failed to improve or deteriorated in these areas, as compared to nonrecidivists. That is, the ongoing stable difficulties tended to worsen just prior to recidivism (Hanson and Harris, 1998).

Recidivists were found to have increased their substance use just prior to reoffending. In addition, the majority of offenders who were taking antiandrogen medications were likely to recidivate, particularly those who started taking the medication later in their period of supervision. Just prior to reoffending, as compared to nonrecidivists, recidivists' social isolation also tended to increase, and their psychological functioning decreased. Recidivists also showed little change in attitudes supportive of sexual offending, as compared to nonrecidivists, who became more empathic. Recidivists minimized their risk of reoffending and exposed themselves to high-risk situations and, immediately prior to reoffending, their cooperation with supervision decreased and they missed more appointments than nonrecidivists. Immediately prior to reoffending, supervising officers noted that recidivists demonstrated increased evidence of sexual preoccupation and deviance, viewed themselves as not being at risk, had access to potential victims, and demonstrated increased anger (Hanson and Harris, 1998).

In summary, as compared to nonrecidivists, offenders under supervision who recidivated sexually tended to have poor social supports, attitudes supportive of sexual aggression, antisocial lifestyles, poor self-management strategies, and were rated by supervising officers as demonstrating poorer cooperation with supervision (Hanson and Harris, 1998). Immediately prior to reoffending, recidivists tended to exhibit an increase in anger and subjective distress. Thus, psychological symptoms were associated with sexual offending more so as acute, rather than stable, dynamic risk factors (Hanson and Harris, 1998).

These differences between recidivists and nonrecidivists remained statistically significant when preexisting differences on static factors between the two groups were controlled, suggesting that recidivists tended to have more problems generally, as well as a deterioration in behavior immediately prior to reoffending (Hanson and Harris, 1998). Note that these differences pertain predominantly to adult rapists and sexual offenders against boys, and less so to sexual offenders against girls, suggesting that the latter may follow a different offense pattern (Hanson and Harris, 1998). In another study, it was similarly found that while static factors, including previous sex offending, never having been married, and having male victims were predictive of sexual reoffending;

in-treatment changes in personality and anxiety measures were not (Hanson et al., 1993).

A history of sexual offending has been associated with future sexual recidivism. It has been stated that the best predictor of future behavior is previous behavior (Grubin and Wingate, 1996), although, in some instances, this is not the case (Yates and Nicholaichuk, 1998). Nonetheless, it has been found, with reasonable consistency, that recidivism is higher among sex offenders with histories of previous sexual offenses than for first-time sexual offenders (Marshall, 1994; Marshall et al., 1991; Nicholaichuk et al., 2000). In short, among sex offenders, a comparatively large number of offenders recidivate at a low rate, while a relatively small number recidivate at a high rate (Grubin and Wingate, 1996), which is also true for offenders generally (Broadhurst and Maller, 1992).

Another factor resulting in differential rates of recidivism is the type of sex offender. Hanson et al. (1993) found that incest offenders recidivated at the lowest rate, followed by offenders against female children, while offenders against male children offended at the highest rate among offenders against children. As indicated above, sex offenders against female children may follow a different offense pattern than sex offenders against male children or against adults (Hanson and Harris, 1998). Among sex offenders against children, incest offenders have been found to recidivate at a lower rate than do nonincest offenders (Hanson et al., 1993; McGrath, 1991; Nicholaichuk et al., 2000; Quinsey, Lalumiere, Rice, and Harris, 1995). Among pedophiles, offenders against male victims recidivate at a higher rate than offenders against female victims (Hanson et al., 1993; McGrath, 1991).

Quinsey, Rice, and Harris (1995), in a study of sexual offenders at a maximum-security psychiatric facility, found that sex offenders against children tended to be less antisocial, had lower psychopathy scores, had fewer previous convictions, and had inflicted less physical injury on their victims than had rapists. As compared to nonrecidivists, sexual recidivists had a more extensive history of sexual and general criminal offending, were less likely to have been married, had a higher rating of psychopathy, and evidenced greater sexual deviance as measured phallometrically. Conversely, other research (Yates and Nicholaichuk, 1998) found that psychopathy was unrelated to either a history of sexual offending or to severity of reoffending behavior following treatment. Note that the sample of sex offenders employed by Quinsey, Rice, and Harris (1995) is highly selective in that it is comprised of men who had not been convicted for sexual offenses, but rather, men who had been remanded for pretrial psychiatric assessment, were certified as mentally ill, or had been found not guilty by reason of insanity. Thus, it is unlikely that findings from this sample of sex offenders are generalizable to other samples of sex offenders.

This selected risk prediction review indicates that, not only are sex offenders a heterogeneous group, but that this heterogeneity is differentially associated with recidivism among both treated and untreated sex offenders. In addition, studies have identified characteristics of offenders and their circumstances which are associated with a higher or lower risk of reoffending, and which are differentially associated with risk of reoffending sexually or nonsexually. Furthermore, research on risk prediction demonstrates that there are dynamic risk factors which are predictive of sexual recidivism, and that a reliance solely on actuarial measures (for example Barbaree, Seto, and Maric, 1995; Hanson, 1997; Webster et al., 1994), which are not amenable to change through intervention, is not a comprehensive enough strategy.

That dynamic factors are associated with reoffending is important in that it is these factors which will provide the most appropriate targets for treatment with sexual offenders. While actuarial assessment will assist in assessing recidivism over the long term (Hanson and Harris, 1998), reliance solely on this type of assessment will not provide targets for intervention, will preclude assessment of change as a result of intervention and, in fact, implies that sexual offenders, as a group, cannot be treated, either through intervention or maturation (Grubin and Wingate, 1996).

Juvenile Sexual Offenders

Compared to that for adult sexual offenders, considerably less information pertaining to juvenile sexual offenders is available. Researchers and clinicians have tended to focus on adult offenders and to neglect adolescent sex offenders (Becker, Harris, and Sales, 1993; Becker and Hunter, 1997; Camp and Thyer, 1993; Epps, 1997). In addition, many of the sexual offenses committed by youth historically have been regarded as normal adolescent experimentation (Camp and Thyer, 1993; Ryan, 1997) and, therefore, the behaviors were not viewed as problematic or as requiring intervention.

However, more recent information indicates that the incidence of adolescent sexual offending is greater than was previously believed. In fact, as many as 80 percent of adult sex offenders report that their sexual offending behavior began in adolescence (Abel, Mittelman, and Becker,

1985; Groth, 1979; Groth, Longo, and McFadin, 1982; Knight and Prentky, 1993). As a result, research has tended to focus on delineating the characteristics of sexually aggressive youth, frequently without comparison to other offenders or to nonoffenders (Becker and Hunter, 1997), and on comparing the characteristics of young sexual recidivists to juvenile sex offenders who do not reoffend. In addition, these data are often descriptive, with few articles applying statistical analyses to these characteristics or to treatment outcome (Becker and Hunter, 1997).

Regardless of the lack of research into its effectiveness, the treatment of juvenile sex offenders has increased substantially, with greater than 600 programs, more than 80 percent of which are community-based, operating in the United States (Becker et al., 1993). These programs may vary somewhat, but the majority focus on the development of social and assertiveness skills, victim empathy, sexual interests, and sex education, taking a cognitive-behavioral and multisystemic approach to treatment (Becker et al., 1993; Camp and Thyer, 1993). A multisystemic approach focuses on a variety of areas, which may be associated with sexual offending behavior, including cognitive processes, family relationships, peer relations, and school performance (Becker et al., 1993).

Perhaps more so than treatment for adult sex offenders, there appears to be considerable consensus regarding targets of treatment among juvenile sex offenders (Worling and Curwen, 1999). These targets include increasing responsibility and accountability for behavior, addressing cognitive, affective, and behavioral factors which support sexual offending, reducing deviant sexual arousal, improving relationships among family members, enhancing victim empathy, improving social skills, developing healthy attitudes toward relationships and sex, reducing the effects of personal trauma (Worling and Curwen, 1999), and targeting cognitive distortions (Richardson, Bhate, and Graham, 1997).

The etiology, dynamics, and motivations for juvenile sexual offending are not well established in the literature (Becker et al., 1993; Becker and Hunter, 1997). Although there is agreement on treatment approaches (Worling and Curwen, 1999), there is no generally accepted theory of the etiology of juvenile sex offending (Becker and Hunter, 1997). Treatment for juvenile sex offenders has been developed using models of treatment for adult sex offenders, and typically involves cognitive-behavioral therapy, relapse prevention, family systems therapy and, occasionally, pharmacological interventions as adjunctive therapy (Becker and Hunter, 1997).

Given the above, the brief discussion which follows describes research pertaining to both the characteristics of juvenile sex offenders and available treatment outcome findings. The focus of this discussion is again on pertinent reviews and recent research.

Characteristics of Juvenile Sexual Offenders. In their reviews of the literature, Becker and colleagues (Becker, 1994; Becker et al., 1993) found several trends evident among juvenile offenders, including a lack of social and assertiveness skills, a history of nonsexual deviancy, low academic performance frequently associated with learning disabilities and difficulties, a tendency to act impulsively, below average skills in anger control, depression, and a lack of sex education provided by parental figures. These characteristics, however, are not exclusive to juvenile sexual offenders, and several studies have found no significant differences between juvenile sexual offenders and other nonsexual juvenile offenders on these characteristics (Becker et al., 1993).

In addition, examination of the family and social environments of juvenile sexual offenders revealed that they were characterized by distal or nonexistent relationships with siblings and parents, an unhealthy home situation, for example, viewing sexual interactions between parental figures, and prior abuse history (Becker, 1994; Becker et al., 1993). Social isolation was a commonly assessed factor, including an inability to establish or maintain close relationships with peers. Finally, depression appears to be more common among juvenile sex offenders than among adolescents in the general population (Becker and Hunter, 1997).

Schram, Milloy, and Rowe (1991) examined the characteristics and treatment outcome among juvenile sexual offenders. The profile derived of these youth indicated that they were young males (with a median age of 14.5 years), who had experienced physical and sexual abuse in their families of origin and who had committed at least one previous offense, typically a nonsexual offense. Their victims tended to be very young girls with whom they were acquainted, primarily through a shared residence and/or a care-taking or supervisory relationship. The majority of their sexual offenses involved penetration and also frequently involved the use of verbal and/or physical coercion to obtain compliance from victims.

As with adult sexual offenders, research suggests that juvenile sexual offenders are a heterogeneous group (Becker and Hunter, 1997) and that, therefore, comprehensive assessment and multisystem treatment which is tailored to meet the needs of individual youth is the treatment approach of choice. However, it has been found that treatment generally is ill-defined and eclectic, and well-formulated community supervision plans tend to be absent (Schram et al., 1991). Nonetheless, recidivism rates, particularly for sexual recidivism, tended to be low for juvenile offenders.

Using rearrests as the criterion, the sexual recidivism rate was 12 percent after approximately a seven-year follow-up period (Schram et al., 1991). Few juveniles continued on to reoffend sexually, suggesting that past behavior may not be a strong predictor of future behavior with regard to sexual offending among youth. Furthermore, community intervention appeared to be effective in suppressing posttreatment recidivism, although these findings should be viewed with caution as offenders treated within institutional settings were at significantly higher risk at pretreatment than were offenders treated within community settings (Schram et al., 1991).

Among those who recidivated sexually, their offenses were committed against children and involved penetration. Among the juveniles generally, sexual offending appeared to be part of a pattern of generalized delinquent behavior —sexual and nonsexual recidivists were indistinguishable from one another. In addition, sexual recidivists, as compared to nonsexual recidivists and nonrecidivists, had a tendency to engage in cognitive distortions and to report deviant sexual fantasy, suggesting that these two areas may be promising targets of treatment for juvenile sexual offenders (Schram et al., 1991). Additionally, as risk factors, these are dynamic in that they are amenable to influence through intervention, suggesting that targeting these through treatment may decrease risk to reoffend both sexually and nonsexually.

In addition, research on juvenile sex offenders suffers from similar methodological limitations as studies of adult sexual offenders, most notably, a low baseline rate of reoffending among juvenile sexual offenders, and a lack of an untreated control or comparison groups against which to assess treatment effectiveness.

Treatment Outcome and Efficacy. Like treatment for adult sex offenders, treatment for juveniles should be specialized sex offender treatment, although little is known about the efficacy of treatment programs for adolescent sex offenders. Reviews of recidivism following treatment (for example, Worling and Curwen, 1999) indicate that the few studies which exist, all conducted in the United States, indicate low rates of sexual recidivism among treated juvenile sex offenders (less than 15 percent). However, assessment of the efficacy of treatment programs and the generalizability of such findings are fraught with the same methodological limitations described above, including short follow-up periods, biased sample selection, and lack of comparison groups of untreated juvenile sex offenders.

In one of the few controlled studies of treatment effectiveness among juvenile sex offenders, Worling and Curwen (1999) followed up adolescents ($\underline{N}$ = 90; 86 males, 4 females) for an average of greater than six years following a comprehensive, cognitive-behavioral, relapse prevention sexual offender program in Canada (Worling, 1998). Recidivism of treated adolescent sex offenders was compared to that of three comparison groups, from whom the treated offenders were not significantly different at pretreatment. Offenders in the comparison group were either adolescent sex offenders who received assessment only ($\underline{N}$ = 46), who refused treatment ($\underline{N}$ = 17), or who dropped out of treatment within one year ($\underline{N}$ = 27). Overall recidivism rates were relatively low. Specifically, among the treated adolescents, 5.2 percent recidivated sexually, 18.9 percent recidivated violently but nonsexually, and 20.7 percent recidivated nonviolently. By contrast, the comparison group recidivated at significantly higher rates: sexually (17.8 percent), violent nonsexually (32.2 percent), and nonviolent (50.0 percent) reoffending (Worling and Curwen, 1999). Thus, the rate of reoffending was two to three times greater for the untreated juvenile sex offenders than for treated offenders on all measures of recidivism.

Worling and Curwen (1999) also examined predictors of recidivism. Predictors of sexual recidivism included self-reported sexual interest in children, a composite measure comprised of sexual fantasies involving children, higher levels of grooming victims, more intrusive sexual activity with children, and lower rates of nonsexual delinquent behavior. Predictors of nonsexual recidivism were similar to those commonly found to be predictive of general criminality, including a history of prior offending, prior nonsexual offending, an antisocial personality, financial instability in the family, a history of sexual victimization, and low self-esteem (Worling and Curwen, 1999). Thus, similar to findings for adult offenders, predictors of sexual recidivism among juveniles included factors specific to sexual deviancy, while more general criminological factors were predictive of nonsexual reoffending.

There is a substantial attrition rate among juvenile sexual offenders in treatment, between 50 percent and 70 percent in some treatment programs (Kraemer, Salisbury, and Spielman, 1998). Kraemer et al. (1998) found that approximately 50 percent of juvenile sex offenders did not complete their program, a residential treatment program consisting of some combination of behavioral and insight-oriented therapy. In examining differences between those who completed treatment and those who did not, it was found that the two groups did not differ on IQ, ethnicity, or grade level. Regression analysis indicated that age and impulsivity resulted in a correct classification rate of almost 77 percent, with non-completers being significantly older and significantly more impulsive than completers. The two groups were not significantly different on self-reported measures of psychological maladjustment, defensiveness, knowledge of sexuality, or sexual obsessions (Kraemer et al., 1998). Although there are some methodological problems associated with this study (for example, self-report measures, biased sample selection), these findings suggest that, similar to adult offenders, treatment for juvenile sexual offenders needs to be individualized, and efforts need to be made to tailor treatment so as to increase treatment completion rates.

In summary, comparatively little is known about juvenile sex offenders. They tend to reoffend sexually at relatively low rates, and their pattern of reoffending is similar to adults in that recidivism is greater for nonsexual violent and nonviolent offenses than for sexual offenses. A number of factors have been identified as characteristics of adolescent sex offenders; however, these do not tend to be significantly different from adolescent nonsexual offenders and nonoffenders. Treatment has been shown to reduce sexual reoffending among these young sex offenders, although the attrition rate appears exceptionally high, suggesting that motivation to participate in treatment needs to be addressed in interventions with this population of sex offenders.

So, What Works with Sex Offenders?

As the preceding review demonstrates, research suggests that treatment is effective in reducing recidivism among both adult and juvenile sex offenders. Future work should not focus on debating whether treatment works, but on understanding what works for which types of sex offenders, based on knowledge of the predictors of recidivism and the principles of effective correctional treatment and supervision. Of course, research also should focus on delineating additional factors associated with the risk for sexual offending which accounts for incremental variance in the prediction of recidivism so that these factors may be incorporated into interventions as well.

We also must bear in mind, as demonstrated in the preceding review, that not all sex offenders are at a high risk to reoffend, as is commonly perceived (Grubin and Wingate, 1996). The preceding discussion indicates that treated adult and juvenile sex offenders tend to recidivate sexually at relatively low levels. In fact, many treated and untreated sexual offenders are more likely to recidivate nonsexually than sexually. Even given these low rates of recidivism, however, when sex offenders do reoffend, the potential for harm to victims is great. Therefore, intervention strategies need to balance risk and public safety in a manner which is responsible and which provides for the greatest protection for society.

It is evident that the majority of sex offenders do not require indefinite or lengthy incarceration, which is expensive (Freeman-Longo and Knopp, 1992). Interventions can be offered in a variety of settings based on risk to reoffend. Risk can be effectively managed through individualized interventions tailored to meet the criminogenic needs of individual offenders. Offenders who receive intervention in correctional institutions should be reassessed to determine if their risk has decreased to a level at which it can be safely managed under supervision in the community (Alexander, 1999). Treating lower-risk offenders and applying interventions and supervision which are more intensive than necessary is not cost effective, particularly given the limited resources available for intervention (Prentky and Burgess, 1990; Nicholaichuk, 1996). Reliance on incarceration as a stand-alone intervention is not an appropriate solution to the problem of sexual offending, especially considering the low risk that some sex offenders present for reoffending (McGrath et al., 1998) and given the economic, practical, ethical, and humanitarian concerns associated with such a strategy (Hanson and Harris, 1998; Prentky and Burgess, 1990), as well as its lack of effectiveness in changing behavior (Andrews and Bonta, 1998; Lockhart et al., 1988).

As has been stated, sexual offenders are a heterogeneous group (Gordon and Porporino, 1990; Knight, Prentky, and Cerce, 1994). Research indicates that different types of offenders recidivate at different rates and that they differ on many personal, criminological, developmental, psychological, circumstantial, and risk variables (Gordon and Porporino, 1990; Nicholaichuk, 1996; Hanson, 1997). For example, recidivist sex offenders generally reoffend at higher rates following treatment than do first-time sex offenders. This suggests that recidivist sex offenders are higher risk and, therefore, require more intensive intervention, while first-time sex offenders may benefit from lower levels of interventions. Similarly, the consistently low rates of recidivism found among incest offenders suggests that these lower risk offenders, as a group, will benefit from less intense levels of intervention (Nicholaichuk, Hyanes, and Yates, 1998). These offenders are unlikely to benefit from intensive service, the application of which would also be cost-inefficient as well as potentially ineffective. Their risk can likely be safely managed in community settings.

Sex offenders also differ in terms of their motivations for offending and the nature and dynamics of their offenses. Knight and his colleagues (for example Knight and Prentky, 1990; Knight, Prentky, and Cerce, 1994) have developed taxonomic classification systems for adult sex offenders and offenders against children. These systems categorize sex offenders according to such factors as degree of pervasive anger, social competence, fixation on children, degree of contact with victims, sadism, and impulsivity. In their typology, rapists' motivation may be opportunistic, angry, sexual, or vindictive, with various subdivisions among these types.

Hall and Hirschman (1991, 1992) have also proposed a typology, based on whether the primary motivation for sexual offending is physiological, cognitive, affective, or developmental. These typologies necessarily prescribe different treatment approaches (Cooper, 1994; Hall and Hirschman, 1992; Hall, Shondrick, and Hirschman, 1993). For example, offenders whose motivation for sexual offending is physiological may be treated for deviant sexual arousal, while those for whom the motivation is affective-based may be treated for anger or depression. Such classification systems emphasize the considerable variation in the motivation, dynamics, and expressions of sexual offending behavior and support the application of differential interventions.

It is obvious, then, given these substantial differences, that not all sex offenders should receive treatment of equal intensity, duration, and content (Gordon and Porporino, 1990; Nicholaichuk et al., 2000). For example, as indicated previously, it is estimated that only 10 percent of sex offenders demonstrate sexual arousal or fantasy which is deviant and which is associated with their sexual offending behavior (Marshall, 1996). It therefore follows that a comparable number of sex offenders should receive intervention for deviant sexuality, while the remainder who do not demonstrate problematic arousal or fantasy should not receive this intervention. Similarly, pharmacological interventions are best reserved for those offenders whose sexual arousal is so great as to preclude participation in other interventions. Such interventions should therefore not be routinely applied to all sex offenders, but only with those who demonstrate criminogenic needs in these areas.

That differential levels of intervention are applied to sex offenders is evident in that these offenders receive a variety of sanctions and dispositions upon initial contact with the criminal justice system. For example, offenders may be sentenced to lengthier terms of incarceration, or to community supervision rather than incarceration, in part due to the nature and intrusiveness of their index sexual offenses. Differential sentencing and disposition are consistent with the principles of effective correctional intervention (Andrews and Bonta, 1998).

However, as seen in the preceding review, once detained within the correctional system, differential treatment is rarely applied to sex offenders. Much of the research reviewed indicated that single treatments of equal intensity and duration were provided to all sexual offenders. Furthermore, some offenders were denied access to treatment programming as a result of motivational, learning, or disability factors. It is not known whether these offenders were offered other, more specialized intervention, although this would have been an appropriate strategy. Within Canada, specialized sex offender programs in some jurisdictions are offered to mentally disordered or low functioning sex offenders; however, this may not be standard procedure in all jurisdictions or correctional systems. Furthermore, examination of treatment programs generally indicates that sex offenders are routinely excluded from treatment programs as a result of motivational issues. Thus, lower risk offenders receive treatment while higher-risk, more difficult clients, are excluded (Andrews and Bonta, 1998). This is not consistent with the principles of effective correctional treatment delineated above.

Treatment of sex offenders is based on the assumption that targeting factors thought to be associated with sexual offending will result in some within-treatment effects, which will be associated in some manner with posttreatment outcome, in particular, reduced sexual offending (Barbaree and Seto, 1997). Unfortunately, as reviewed above, many treatment programs do not specify the goals or targets of treatment and, when this is done, these targets are rarely analyzed for their relationship to treatment outcome. As suggested above, research suggests that treatment can be effective; however, the intermediary variables mediating the effect of treatment are frequently not specified in treatment outcome research (Barbaree and Seto, 1997). Research on the assessment of risk and the prediction of recidivism, however, suggests a number of mediating factors, such as attitudes supportive of sexual aggression, cognitive distortions, substance abuse, and deviant sexual arousal, which are associated with future reoffending and which, therefore, are appropriate targets for the treatment of sex offenders.

Sexual offenders, therefore, should be treated and managed as follows. Prior to receiving a disposition, a comprehensive assessment should be conducted to determine an offender's risk for reoffending, which should inform disposition, decision-making, and management. Applying the principles of effective correctional treatment, higher-intensity interventions, including security, treatment, and supervision, should be reserved for higher-risk offenders. It is suggested here that a substantial number of sex offenders can be safely managed within community settings, with appropriate treatment and supervision. Treatment should be cognitive-behavioral in orientation, should include relapse prevention, should focus on skills acquisition, and should explicitly target those criminogenic need factors identified during initial assessment, as well as any other criminogenic need factors identified later, for example, during treatment. The relapse-prevention plan should identify precursors to sexual offending behavior, as well as observable cognitive, attitudinal, affective, and behavioral indicators of changes in risk, so that service providers conducting supervision of sex offenders in the community can assess and reassess risk as required. Adjunctive interventions, such as behavioral reconditioning or pharmacological interventions, should be applied as necessary in individual cases, again based on assessment findings.

Treatment of juvenile sex offenders should target clarification of sexual values and the promotion of healthy, age-appropriate sexuality, cognitive restructuring, development of empathy, human sexuality education, anger management, impulse control, understanding the nature and process of sexually abusive behavior, academic, vocational, and living skills, and family therapy (Becker and Hunter, 1997). Individual, group, and family therapies should each be used, again based on individual needs and circumstances. Additionally, supervision of adolescent (Epps, 1997) and adult sex offenders also should vary as a function of degree of internal versus external control of behavior (Prentky, Knight, Lee, and Cerce, 1995). Sex offenders with a greater degree of internal behavioral control should require less intensive supervision, while those with a lesser degree of internal control will require the external behavioral control that is provided by more intensive supervision. Similarly, offenders who tend to be impulsive may reoffend more quickly than offenders who are not impulsive and, consequently, the former may require treatment which focuses on developing control of responding and behavior.

Gordon and Porporino (1990) have recommended specific differential intervention strategies for various subtypes of adult sexual offenders, based on variation in characteristics among these groups. Pedophiles, particularly those whose victims are boys, tend to recidivate at a higher rate than rapists. However, upon reoffending, rapists tend use greater violence and to commit nonsexual offenses. This suggests that pedophiles should receive predominantly sex offender specific programming, whereas rapists should receive programming which targets general criminological factors associated with nonsexual offending in addition to sexual offending. Rapists who tend not to be considerably different from nonsexual offenders also should be treated and supervised with attention paid to indicators of a return to a general criminal lifestyle and/or nonsexual violence, in addition to indicators of risk to reoffend sexually.

In addition, it is suggested that effective treatment of sexual offenders also depends on effective risk management, including, but not limited to, community supervision. Relatively low recidivism rates for treated sex offenders suggest that, ethically and responsibly, sex offenders ought to be released to the community at the earliest possible opportunity when they can be monitored and community-safety maximized. With such low baseline rates of sexual recidivism, continued incarceration of offenders with a low likelihood of reoffending is ethically questionable and cost ineffective. However, research also suggests that risk for sexual recidivism increases over time, thus suggesting that supervision may need to be adjusted as a function of time at risk for a given individual offender. When assessing and supervising sex offenders, reliance on multiple sources of information about behavior is recommended (Pithers and Cumming, 1989). Thus, supervision in the community also should include contacts with significant and collateral others.

Relapse prevention is gaining in popularity for the treatment of sexual offenders, although it is accepted that this technique alone is insufficient (Pithers, Martin, and Cumming, 1989). Many sex offender treatment programs use relapse prevention as a component of treatment and/or as follow-up or a maintenance element of sex offender treatment. Relapse prevention is an important component of both institutional and community maintenance programs. Within institutions, maintenance programming assists in maintaining gains made during treatment, continuing skill development, and refining relapse prevention plans. In the community, maintenance programming also performs these functions and additionally provides a framework for supervision (Correctional Service of Canada, 2000). It is therefore recommended that community interventions make use of a relapse prevention model in the supervision of sex offenders. The relapse prevention plan also can be used to assist in the assessment of changes in risk levels. When risk is seen to increase and changes are observed which are associated with increased risk, a reassessment of likelihood of reoffending can be conducted and, where necessary, changes in the risk management strategy may be implemented.

There is a need for the development of more community-based treatment programs for sex offenders who have been released from institutions, many of whom may not have received treatment (Hall, 1995). Community-based programs also must reassess sex offenders upon release from institutions (Marshall and Eccles, 1991), including those who have received treatment. Since treatment does not "cure" sex offenders, and relapse prevention teaches control of behavior (Pithers and Cumming, 1989), exposure to high-risk situations or changes in coping ability can increase risk in the community (Marshall and Eccles, 1991). Thus, risk should be continually reassessed while offenders are under supervision in the community. Although risk prediction and evaluation of sex offender treatment are still relatively recent and information is still lacking about precisely what works with sex offenders (Freeman-Longo and Knopp, 1992), the research suggests that specialized sex offender treatment is effective in reducing sexual reoffending. Thus, through the application of the principles of effective correctional intervention, known predictors of sexual reoffending, and attention to individualized risk and needs, sex offenders may be reintegrated in the community in a manner which is responsible and timely and which provides the necessary degree of public safety and reduces the harm caused to victims of sexual violence.

References

Abel, G. G., J. V. Becker, J. Cunningham-Rathner, J. Rouleau, M. Kaplan, and J. Reich. 1984. *The Treatment of Child Molesters*. Atlanta, Georgia: Behavioral Medicine Laboratory, Emory University.

Abel, G. G., and E. B. Blanchard. 1974. The Role of Fantasy Treatment of Deviation. *Archives of General Psychiatry*. 30(4):467-475.

Abel, G. G., M. S. Mittleman, and J. V. Becker. 1985. Sexual Offenders: Results of Assessment and Recommendations for Treatment. In M. H. Ben-Aron, S. J. Hucker, and C. D. Webster, eds. *Clinical Criminology: The Assessment and Treatment of Criminal Behaviour*, pp. 191-205. Toronto, Ontario: Clarke Institute of Psychiatry.

Abel, G. G. and J. L. Rouleau. 1986. Sexual Disorders. In G. Winokur and P. Clayton, eds. *The Medical Basis of Psychiatry*, pp. 246-267. Philadelphia: W. B. Saunders.

Alexander, M. A. 1999. Sexual Offender Treatment Efficacy Revisited. *Sexual Abuse: A Journal of Research and Treatment*. 11(2):101-116.

Allam, J. M. and K. D. Browne. 1998. Evaluating Community-based Treatment Programmes for Men Who Sexually Abuse Children. *Child Abuse Review*. 7:13-29.

Andrews, D. A. and J. Bonta. 1998. *The Psychology of Criminal Conduct*. Cincinnati, Ohio: Anderson Publishing Co.

Bandura, A. 1973. *Aggression: A Social Learning Analysis*. Englewood Cliffs, New Jersey: Prentice-Hall, Inc.

————. 1978. Social Learning Theory of Aggression. *Journal of Communication*. 28(3):12-29.

————. 1986. *Social Foundations of Thought and Action: A Social Cognitive Theory*. Englewood Cliffs, New Jersey: Prentice-Hall, Inc.

Barbaree, H. E. and M. C. Seto. 1997. Pedophilia: Assessment and Treatment. In D. R. Laws and W. T. O'Donoghue, eds. *Sexual Deviance: Theory, Assessment, and Treatment*, pp.175-193. New York: Guilford Press.

Barbaree, H. E., M. C. Seto, and A. Maric. 1995. *Working Papers in Impulsivity Research: Sex Offenders' Characteristics, Response to Treatment, and Correctional Decisions at the Warkworth Sexual Behaviour Clinic*. Toronto, Ontario: Forensic Division, Clarke Institute of Psychiatry, University of Toronto.

Becker, J. V. 1994. Offenders: Characteristics and Treatment. *The Future of Children*. 4(2):176-197.

Becker, J. V., C. D. Harris, and B. D. Sales. 1993. Juveniles Who Commit Sexual Offenses: A Critical Review of Research. In G. C. N. Hall and R. Hirschman, eds. *Sexual Aggression: Issues in Etiology, Assessment, and Treatment*, pp. 215-228. Washington, D.C.: Taylor and Francis Group.

Becker, J.V. and J. A. Hunter. 1997. Understanding and Treating Child and Adolescent Sexual Offenders. *Advances in Clinical Child Psychology*. 19:177-197.

Becker, J. V. and W. D. Murphy. 1998. What We Know and Do Not Know About Assessing and Treating Sex Offenders. *Psychology, Public Policy, and Law*. 4(1-2):116-137.

Blanchette, K. 1996. *Sex Offender Assessment, Treatment and Recidivism: A Literature Review*. Ottawa, Ontario: Correctional Service of Canada.

Bradford, J. M. W. 1985. Organic Treatments for the Male Sexual Offender. *Behavioural Sciences and the Law*. 3(4):355-375.

————. 1990. The Antiandrogen and Hormonal Treatment of Sex Offenders. In W. L. Marshall and H. E. Barbaree, eds. *Handbook of Sexual Assault: Issues, Theories, and Treatment of the Offenders*, pp. 297-310. New York: Plenum Press.

Broadhurst, R. G. and R. A. Maller. 1992. The Recidivism of Sex Offenders in the Western Australian Prison Population. *British Journal of Criminology.* 32(1):54-80.

Camp, H. H. and B. A. Thyer. 1993. Treatment of Adolescent Sex Offenders: A Review of Empirical Research. *The Journal of Applied Sciences.* 17(2):191-206.

Cooper, A. J. 1986. Progesterones in the Treatment of Male Sex Offenders: A Review. *Canadian Journal of Psychiatry.* 31(1):73-79.

Cooper, M. 1994. *Setting Standards and Guiding Principles for the Assessment, Treatment and Management of Sex Offenders in British Columbia.* Vancouver, British Columbia: Institute on Family Violence.

Correctional Service of Canada. 2000. *National Sex Offender Treatment.* Ottawa, Ontario: Correctional Service of Canada.

————. 1996. *Standards and Guidelines for the Provision of Services to Sex Offenders.* Ottawa, Ontario: Correctional Service of Canada.

Emory, L. E., C. M. Cole, and W. J. Meyer. 1992. The Texas Experience with Depo Provera: 1980-1990. *Journal of Offender Rehabilitation.* 18(3/4):125-139.

Epps, K. J. 1997. Managing Risk. In M. S. Hoghughi, S. R. Bhate, and F. Graham, eds. *Working with Sexually Abusive Adolescents*, pp. 35-51. London: Sage Publications.

Fedoroff, J. P., R. Wisner-Carlson, S. Dean, and F. S. Berlin. 1992. Medroxy-progesterone Acetate in the Treatment of Paraphilic Sexual Disorders: Rate of Relapse in Paraphilic Men Treated in Long-term Group Psychotherapy with or without Medroxy-progesterone Acetate. *Journal of Offender Rehabilitation.* 18 (3/4):109-123.

Fisher, D. and A. R. Beech. 1999. Current Practice in Britain with Sexual Offenders. *Journal of Interpersonal Violence.* 14(3):240-256.

Freeman-Longo, R. E. and H. F. Knopp. 1992. State-of-the-art Sex Offender Treatment: Outcome and Issues. *Annals of Sex Research.* 5(3):141-160.

Furby, L., M. R. Weinrott, and L. Blackshaw. 1989. Sex Offender Recidivism: A Review. *Psychological Bulletin.* 105(1):3-30.

Gendreau, P. 1998. Making Corrections Work. Presented at the 17th Annual Association for the Treatment of Sexual Offenders, Vancouver, British Columbia.

Gendreau, P. and C. Goggin. 1996. Principles of Effective Correctional Programming. *Forum on Corrections Research.* 8(3):38-41.

————. 1997. Correctional Treatment: Accomplishments and Realities. In P. Van Voorhis et al., eds. *Correctional Counselling and Rehabilitation,* pp. 271-279. Cincinnati, Ohio: Anderson.

Gendreau, P., T. Little, and C. Goggin. 1996. A Meta-analysis of the Predictors of Adult Offender Recidivism: What Works! *Criminology.* 34(4):3-17.

Gordon, A. and T. Nicholaichuk. 1996. Applying the Risk Principle to Sex Offender Treatment. *Forum on Corrections Research.* 8(2):36-38.

Gordon, A. and F. J. Porporino. 1990. *Managing the Treatment of Sexual Offenders: A Canadian Perspective* (Research Report No. B-05). Ottawa, Ontario: Correctional Service of Canada.

Grossman, L. S. 1985. Research Directions in the Evaluation and Treatment of Sexual Offenders: An Analysis. *Behavioural Sciences and the Law.* 3(4):421-440.

Grossman, L. S., B. Martis, and C. G. Fichtner. 1999. Are Sex Offenders Treatable? A Research Review. *Psychiatric Services.* 50(3):349-361.

Groth, A. N. 1979. The Adolescent Sexual Offender and His Prey. *International Journal of Offender Therapy and Comparative Criminology.* 21(3):249-254.

Groth, A. N., R. E. Longo, and J. B. McFadin. 1982. Undetected Recidivism Among Rapists and Child Molesters. *Crime and Delinquency.* 28(3):450-458.

Grubin, D. and S. Wingate. 1996. Sexual Offence Recidivism: Prediction Versus Understanding. *Criminal Behaviour and Mental Health.* 6:349-359.

Hall, G. C. N. 1995. Sexual Offender Recidivism Revisited: A Meta-analysis of Recent Treatment Studies. *Journal of Consulting and Clinical Psychology.* 63(5):802-809.

Hall, G. C. N. and R. Hirschman. 1991. Toward a Theory of Sexual Aggression: A Quadripartite Model. *Journal of Consulting and Clinical Psychology.* 59(5):662-669.

————. 1992. Sexual Aggression Against Children: A Conceptual Perspective of Etiology. *Criminal Justice and Behaviour.* 19(1):8-23.

Hall, G. C. N., D. D. Shondrick, and R. Hirschman. 1993. Conceptually-derived Treatments for Sexual Aggressors. *Professional Psychology: Research and Practice.* 24:62-69.

Hanson, H. and L. Lykke-Olsen. 1997. Treatment of Dangerous Sexual Offenders in Denmark. *Journal of Forensic Psychiatry.* 8(1):195-199.

Hanson, R. K. 1997. How to Know What Works with Sexual Offenders. *Sexual Abuse: A Journal of Research and Treatment.* 9(2):129-145.

Hanson, R. K. and M. Bussière. 1996. Predictors of Sex Offender Recidivism: A Meta-analysis. Ottawa, Ontario: Department of the Solicitor General of Canada.

Hanson, R. K. and A. Harris. 1998. *Dynamic Predictors of Sexual Recidivism.* Ottawa, Ontario: Department of the Solicitor General of Canada.

Hanson, R. K., R. A. Steffy, and R. Gauthier. 1993. Long-term Recidivism of Child Molesters. *Journal of Consulting and Clinical Psychology.* 61(4):646-652.

Heim, N. and C. J. Hursch. 1979. Castration for Sex Offenders: Treatment or Punishment? A Review and Critique of Recent European Literature. *Archives of Sexual Behaviour.* 8(3):281-304.

Knight, R. A. and R. A. Prentky. 1990. Classifying Sexual Offenders: The Development and Corroboration of Taxonomic Models. In W. L. Marshall and D. R. Laws, eds. *Handbook of Sexual Assault: Issues, Theories, and Treatment of the Offender,* pp. 23-52. New York: Plenum Press.

———. 1993. Exploring Characteristics for Classifying Juvenile Sex Offenders. In H. E. Barbaree, W. L. Marshall, and S. M. Hudson, eds. *The Juvenile Sex Offender,* pp. 45-83. New York: Guilford Press.

Knight, R. A., R. A. Prentky, and D. D. Cerce. 1994. The Development, Reliability, and Validity of An Inventory for the Multidimensional Assessment of Sex and Aggression. *Criminal Justice and Behaviour.* 21(1):72-94.

Kraemer, B. D., S. B. Salisbury, and C. R. Spielman. 1998. Pretreatment Variables Associated with Treatment Failure in a Residential Juvenile Sex-offender Program. *Criminal Justice and Behaviour.* 25(2):190-202.

Langevin, R. 1983. *Sexual Strands.* Hillsdale, New Jersey: Earlbaum.

Laws D. R. 1989. *Relapse Prevention with Sex Offenders.* New York: Guilford Press.

Laws, D. R. and W. L. Marshall. 1990. A Conditioning Theory of the Etiology and Maintenance of Deviant Sexual Preference and Behaviour. In W. L. Marshall and H. E. Barbaree, eds. *Handbook of Sexual Assault: Issues, Theories, and Treatment of Offenders,* pp. 103-113. New York: Plenum Press.

Lockhart, L. L., B. E. Saunders, and P. Cleveland. 1988. Adult Male Sexual Offenders: An Overview of Treatment Techniques. *Journal of Social Work and Human Sexuality.* 7(2):1-32.

Looman, J., J. Abracen, and T. P. Nicholaichuk. 1999. Recidivism Among Treated Sexual Offenders and Matched Controls: Data from the Regional Treatment Centre (Ontario). *Journal of Interpersonal Violence.* 15(3):279-320.

Maletzky, B. M. 1980. Self-referred Versus Court-referred Sexually Deviant Patients: Success with Assisted Covert Sensitization. *Behaviour Therapy.* 11(3):306-314.

———. 1991. *Treating the Sexual Offender.* Newbury Park, California: Sage Publications.

———. 1999. Organizing Sexual Abuse. *Sexual Abuse: A Journal of Research and Treatment.* 11(2):97-100.

Marques, J. K., D. M. Day, C. Nelson, and M. H. Miner. 1989. The Sex Offender Treatment and Evaluation Project: California's Relapse Prevention Program. In D. R. Laws, ed. *Relapse Prevention with Sex Offenders*, pp. 247-267. New York: Guilford Press.

Marques, J. K., D. M. Day, C. Nelson, and M. West. 1994. Effects of Cognitive-behavioural Treatment on Sex Offender Recidivism: Preliminary Results of a Longitudinal Study. *Criminal Justice and Behaviour.* 21(1):28-54.

Marshall, W. L. 1994. Treatment Effects on Denial and Minimization in Incarcerated Sex Offenders. *Behaviour Research and Therapy.* 32(4): 559-564.

———. 1996. Assessment, Treatment and Theorizing about Sex Offenders: Developments During the Past Twenty Years and Future Directions. *Criminal Justice and Behaviour.* 23(1):162-199.

Marshall, W. L. and A. Eccles. 1991. The Value of Community Treatment of Sex Offender Programs for Released Sex Offenders. *Forum on Corrections Research.* 3(4):12-15.

Marshall, W. L, R. Jones, T. Ward, P. Johnson, and H. E. Barbaree. 1991. Treatment Outcome with Sex Offenders. *Clinical Psychology Review.* 11(4):465-485.

Marshall, W. L. and W. D. Pithers. 1994. A Reconsideration of Treatment Outcome with Sex Offenders. *Criminal Justice and Behaviour.* 21(1):10-27.

McGrath, R. J. 1991. Sex-offender Risk Assessment and Disposition Planning: A Review of Empirical and Clinical Findings. *International Journal of Offender Therapy and Comparative Criminology.* 35(4):328-350.

McGrath, R. J., S. E. Hoke, and J. E. Vojtisek. 1998. Cognitive-behavioural Treatment of Sex Offenders. *Criminal Justice and Behaviour.* 25(2):203-225.

Meyer, W. J., C. Cole, and E. Emory. 1992. Depo Provera Treatment for Sex Offending Behaviour: An Evaluation of Outcome. *Bulletin of the American Academy of Psychiatry and Law*. 20(3):249-259.

Motiuk, L. and R. Belcourt. 1996. Profiling the Canadian Federal Sex Offender Population. Research in Brief. *Forum on Corrections Research*. 8(2):3-7.

Motiuk, L. and S. L. Brown. 1996. Factors Related to Recidivism among Released Federal Sex Offenders. Paper presented at the 26th International Congress of Psychology. Montreal, Canada.

Nicholaichuk, T. P. 1996. Sex Offender Treatment Priority: An Illustration of the Risk/Need Principle. *Forum on Corrections Research*. 8(2):30-32.

Nicholaichuk, T. P., A. Gordon, D. Gu, and S. Wong. 2000. Outcome of an Institutional Sexual Offender Treatment Program: A Comparison between Treated and Matched Untreated Offenders. *Sexual Abuse: A Journal of Research and Treatment*. 12(2):139-153.

Nicholaichuk, T. P., A. K. Haynes, and P. M. Yates. 1999. Incest Offenders: An Examination of Risk and Need. Presented at the 17th Annual Research and Treatment Conference of the Association for the Treatment of Sexual Abusers. Vancouver, British Columbia.

Nuffield, J. 1982. *Parole Decision-making in Canada: Research Towards Decision Guidelines*. Ottawa, Ontario: Communication Division, Correctional Service of Canada.

Pithers, W. D. 1993. Treatment of Rapists: Reinterpretation of Early Outcome Data and Exploratory Constructs to Enhance Therapeutic Efficacy. In G. C. Nagayama Hall and R. Hirschman, et al., eds. *Sexual Aggression: Issues in Etiology, Assessment, and Treatment. Series in Applied Psychology: Social Issues and Questions*, pp. 167-196. Washington, D.C.: Taylor and Francis Group.

Pithers, W. D. and G. F. Cumming. 1989. Can Relapse Be Prevented? Initial Outcome Data from the Vermont Treatment Program for Sexual Aggressors. In D. R. Laws, ed. *Relapse Prevention with Sex Offenders*, pp. 313-325. New York: Guilford Press.

Pithers, W. D., J. K. Marques, C. C. Gibat, and G. A. Marlatt. 1983. Relapse Prevention with Sexual Aggressives: A Self-control Model of Treatment and Maintenance of Change. In J. G. Greer and I. R. Stuart, eds. *The Sexual Aggressor: Current Perspectives on Treatment*, pp. 214-239. New York: Van Nostrand Reinhold Company.

Pithers, W. D., G. R. Martin, and G. F. Cumming. 1989. Vermont Treatment Program for Sexual Aggressors. In D. R. Laws, ed. *Relapse Prevention with Sex Offenders*, pp. 292-310. New York: Guilford Press.

Prentky, R. A. and A. W. Burgess. 1990. Rehabilitation of Child Molesters: A Cost-benefit Analysis. *American Journal of Orthopsychiatry*. 60(1):108-117.

Prentky, R. A., R. A. Knight, A. F. S. Lee, and D. D. Cerce. 1995. Predictive Validity of Lifestyle Impulsivity for Rapists. *Criminal Justice and Behaviour*. 22(2):106-128.

Quinsey, V. L. 1977. The Assessment and Treatment of Child Molesters: A Review. *Canadian Psychological Review*. 18:204-220.

Quinsey, V. L., T. C. Chaplin, and W. F. Carrigan. 1980. Biofeedback and Signalled Punishment in the Modification of Inappropriate Sexual Age Preferences. *Behaviour Therapy*. 11(4):567-576.

Quinsey, V. L., G. T. Harris, M. E. Rice, and M. Lalumiere. 1993. Assessing the Treatment Efficacy in Outcome Studies of Sex Offenders. *Journal of Interpersonal Violence*. 8(4):512-523.

Quinsey, V. L., A. Khanna, and P. B. Malcolm. 1998. A Retrospective Evaluation of the Regional Treatment Centre Sex Offender Treatment Program. *Journal of Interpersonal Violence*. 13(5):621-644.

Quinsey, V. L., M. L. Lalumiere, M. E. Rice, and G. T. Harris. 1995. Predicting Sexual Offenses. In J. C. Campbell, eds. *Assessing Dangerousness: Violence by Sexual Offenders, Batterers, and Child Abusers*, pp. 114-137. Thousand Oaks, California: Sage Publications.

Quinsey, V. L., M. E. Rice, and G. T. Harris. 1995. Actuarial Prediction of Sexual Recidivism. *Journal of Interpersonal Violence*. 10(1):85-105.

Rice, M.E., G. T. Harris, C. A. Cormier. 1992. An Evaluation of A Maximum Security Therapeutic Community for Psychopaths and Other Mentally Disordered Offenders. *Law and Human Behaviour*. 16(4):399-412.

Rice, M. E., G. T. Harris, V. L. Quinsey. 1990. A Follow-up of Rapists Assessed in a Maximum-security Psychiatric Facility. *Journal of Interpersonal Violence*. 5(4):435-448.

Rice, M. E., V. L. Quinsey, and G. T. Harris. 1991. Sexual Recidivism Among Child Molesters Released From A Maximum Security Psychiatric Institution. *Journal of Consulting and Clinical Psychology*. 59(3):381-386.

Richardson, G., S. Bhate, and F. Graham. 1997. Cognitive-based Practice with Sexually Abusive Adolescents. In M. S. Hoghughi, S. R. Bhate, and F. Graham, eds. *Working with Sexually Abusive Adolescents*, pp. 128-143. London: Sage Publications.

Robinson, T. and F. Valcour. 1995. The Use of Depo-provera in the Treatment of Child Molesters and Sexually Compulsive Males. *Sexual Addictions and Compulsivity*. 2(4):277-294.

Ryan, G. 1997. Incidence and Prevalence of Sexual Offenses Committed by Juveniles. In G. Ryan and S. Lane, eds. *Juvenile Sexual Offending: Causes, Consequences, and Correction*, pp. 9-15. San Francisco: Jossey-Bass Inc.

Schram, D. D., C. D. Milloy, and W. E. Rowe. 1991. *Juvenile Sex Offenders: A Follow-up Study of Reoffense Behaviour*. Olympia, Washington: Washington State Institute for Public Policy.

Schwartz, B. K. and H. R. Cellini. 1995. *The Sex Offender*. Kingston, New Jersey: Civic Research Institute, Inc.

Webster, C. D., G. T. Harris, M. E. Rice, and V. L. Quinsey. 1994. *The Violence Prediction Scheme: Assessing Dangerousness in High Risk Men*. Toronto, Ontario: Centre of Criminology, University of Toronto.

Worling J. R. 1998. Adolescent Sexual Offender Treatment at the SAFE-T Program. In W. L. Marshall and H. E. Barbaree, eds. *Sourcebook of Treatment Programs for Sexual Offenders*, pp. 353-365. New York: Plenum Press.

Worling, J. R. and T. Curwon. 1999. Adolescent Sexual Offender Recidivism: Success of Specialized Treatment and Implications for Risk Prediction. Unpublished manuscript.

Yates, P. M. 1996. An Investigation of Factors Associated with Definitions and Perceptions of Rape, Propensity to Commit Rape, and Rape Prevention. Unpublished doctoral dissertation, Carleton University, Ontario.

Yates, P. M. and T. Nicholaichuk. 1998. The Relationship between Criminal Career Profile, Psychopathy, and Treatment Outcome in the Clearwater Sex Offender Program. Presented at the Annual Conference of the Canadian Psychological Association. Edmonton, Alberta.

PSYCHOPATHY AS A RISK FACTOR FOR VIOLENCE*

6

Robert D. Hare, Ph.D.
Professor of Psychology
University of British Columbia
Vancouver, British Columbia

Introduction

In its landmark decision, *Kansas v. Hendricks* (June, 1997), the U.S. Supreme Court held that the Kansas Sexually Violent Predator Act ". . . comports with due process requirements and neither runs afoul of double jeopardy principles nor constitutes an exercise in impermissible ex post facto lawmaking." The Kansas Act established procedures for the involuntary civil confinement of sexually violent predators, defined as "any person who has been convicted of or charged with a sexually violent

* This chapter is a revised and expanded version of a paper presented in the symposium "Dealing with Psychopathy: The United States Supreme Court's *Kansas v. Hendricks* Decision and Beyond." Annual meeting of the American Psychiatric Association, Toronto, Canada, May 30-June 4, 1998. The original paper was published in *Psychiatric Quarterly 70/3* (1999): 181-197 and is published with their permission.

offense and who suffers from a mental abnormality or personality disorder which makes the person likely to engage in the predatory acts of sexual violence."

The decision upheld the right of government to detain a specific class of sane but dangerous individuals following completion of their prison sentences. Many, if not most, of these sexually violent predators would qualify for a diagnosis of antisocial personality disorder or, more particularly, psychopathy. The latter has emerged as one of the most potent risk factors for violence in general, and for sexual violence in particular, and is the topic of this paper. The author will discuss both types of violence, on the grounds that the arguments underlying *Kansas v. Hendricks* may be—and indeed, have been in many jurisdictions—extended to nonsexual forms of violence.

Before proceeding, note that the introduction of sexually violent predator (SVP) legislation probably will involve construction of many new correctional facilities. William Tucker (1999) has described New York State's efforts along these lines. Not long ago, an architectural firm charged with the design of a facility for sexually violent predators in a mid-Western state contacted the author. Our discussions revolved around the problems faced in attempting to meet the often conflicting needs of custody and treatment. Although one of the stated goals of most sexually violent predator legislation will be treatment and rehabilitation, it is likely that few facilities actually will be designed and built with this goal firmly in mind. Rather, because of the nature of the offenders to be housed in these facilities, and because of the difficulty in successfully treating sex offenders, particularly psychopathic ones, the focus understandably will be on secure custody, with little more than lip service being paid to treatment.

This would be unfortunate, for several reasons. First, the long-term warehousing of violent offenders who have little or no hope of ever being released from prison is a prescription for trouble. Second, because something is difficult to do does not mean that it cannot be done. With respect to psychopathic offenders, for example, the traditional view that "nothing works" typically results in psychopaths being excluded from institutional treatment and management programs. A more prudent strategy would be to introduce new programs specifically aimed at the institutional treatment of offenders typically deemed untreatable (*see* Losel, 1998; Wong and Hare, in press). The proposal that architects might consult with behavioral scientists and program providers prior to the design and construction of a sexually violent predator facility is, in this author's opinion, an excellent one.

Note that civil commitment *after* an offender has completed his prison sentence is different from detention procedures used in many other countries. For example, in Canada a violent offender can be sentenced to an indefinite term as a *dangerous offender*, but the term is served in a federal correctional facility, with a variety of treatment options being available during the entire period of incarceration. Moreover, custodial and treatment plans are facilitated by psychological and other assessments (including the PCL-R; see below) made at the beginning of the sentence. In many respects, the Canadian procedures are consistent with the dissenting opinion written by Supreme Court Justice Breyer in *Kansas v. Hendricks*. He wrote:

> . . . the Kansas statute insofar as it applies to previously convicted offenders, such as Hendricks, commits, confines, and treats those offenders after they have served virtually their entire criminal sentence. . . . The Act explicitly defers diagnosis, evaluation, and commitment proceedings until a few weeks prior to the "anticipated release" of a previously convicted offender from prison. . . . But why, one might ask, does the Act not commit and require treatment of sex offenders sooner, say soon after they begin to serve their sentences?

The Construct of Psychopathy

Psychopathy is a clinical construct traditionally defined by a constellation of interpersonal, affective, and lifestyle characteristics (*see* Cleckley, 1976; Hare, 1991, 1998a). On the interpersonal level, psychopaths are grandiose, arrogant, callous, dominant, superficial, and manipulative. Affectively, they are short-tempered, unable to form strong emotional bonds with others, and lacking in guilt or anxiety. These interpersonal and affective features are associated with a socially deviant lifestyle that includes irresponsible and impulsive behavior and a tendency to ignore or violate social conventions and mores (Hare, 1991). Although not all psychopaths come into formal contact with the criminal justice system (*see* Babiak, 1995; Hare, 1998b), their defining features clearly place them at high risk for aggression and violence (Hart and Hare, 1997). The problem, of course, is to identify these individuals as accurately as possible. This is particularly crucial in situations where a diagnosis of psychopathy has enormous implications for both the individual and society.

The Assessment of Psychopathy

Two major approaches to the assessment of psychopathy have influenced clinical practice and empirical research. One is reflected in the DSM-III, -III-R, and -IV criteria for antisocial personality disorder (ASPD), and is based in part on the assumptions that it is difficult for clinicians to assess personality traits reliably, and that early-onset delinquency is a cardinal symptom of the disorder. These assumptions account for the heavy emphasis on delinquent and antisocial behavior in the criteria set for antisocial personality disorder (see Hare and Hart, 1995; Robins 1978; Widiger et al., 1996).

The other approach stems naturally from rich European and North American clinical traditions, and is reflected in the writings of Cleckley (1976) and in the Hare Psychopathy Checklist-Revised (PCL-R; Hare, 1991) and its derivatives, including the Screening Version (PCL: SV; Hart, Cox, and Hare, 1995) and the Youth Version (PCL:YV; Forth, Kosson, and Hare, in press). The rationale for the PCL-R is that assessment must be based on the full range of psychopathic symptomatology. A focus on antisocial behaviors, to the exclusion of interpersonal and affective symptoms (for example, callousness, grandiosity, deceitfulness, lack of empathy), leads to the overdiagnosis of psychopathy in criminal populations and to underdiagnosis in noncriminals (Hare, Hart, and Harpur, 1991; Lilienfeld, 1994).

To ensure accurate diagnosis, the PCL-R uses expert observer (in other words, clinical) ratings, based on a semistructured interview, a review of case history materials such as criminal or psychiatric records, interviews with family members and employers, and so forth, and supplemented with behavioral observations, whenever possible (Hare, 1991). Specific scoring criteria are used to rate each of 20 items on a 3-point scale (0, 1, 2) according to the extent to which it applies to a given individual. Total scores can range from 0 to 40 and reflect the degree to which the individual matches the prototypical psychopath. A score of 30 typically is used as a diagnostic cutoff for psychopathy.

PCL-R assessments are highly reliable and valid when made by qualified clinicians and researchers. Indeed, Fulero (1995) described the PCL-R as the "state of the art . . . both clinically and in research use" (p. 454). Although developed primarily with data from male offenders and forensic patients, the psychometric properties of the PCL-R now are well established in a variety of other offender and patient populations, including females, adolescents, substance abusers, and sex offenders (for example, see Brandt, Kennedy, Patrick, and Curtin, 1997; Cooke, Forth, and Hare, 1998; Hare, 1998a; Cooke and Michie, 1997; Loucks and Zamble, 2000; Salekin, Rogers, and Sewell, 1997). The PCL-R also has good cross-cultural generalizability (Cooke, 1998; Cooke, Kosson, and Michie, in press).

The twelve-item PVL: SV was developed for use in the MacArthur Risk Assessment study (Steadman et al., 1994). It is conceptually and empirically related to the PCL-R (Hart et al., 1995; Cooke, Michie, Hart, and Hare, 1999) and is used as a screen for psychopathy in forensic populations or as a stand-alone instrument for research with noncriminals, including civil psychiatric patients (as in the MacArthur study). There is rapidly accumulating evidence for the construct validity of PCL: SV, including its ability to predict aggression and violence in offenders and in both forensic and civil psychiatric patients (see below).

Psychopathy and Crime

In the past few years, there has been a dramatic change in the role played by psychopathy in the criminal justice system. Formerly, a prevailing view was that clinical diagnoses of psychopathy were of little value in understanding and predicting criminal behaviors. However, even a cursory inspection of the features that define the disorder—callousness, impulsivity, egocentricity, grandiosity, irresponsibility, lack of empathy, guilt, or remorse, and so forth—indicates that psychopaths should be much more likely than other members of the general public to bend and break the rules and laws of society. Because they are emotionally unconnected to the rest of humanity, and because they callously view others as little more than objects, it should be relatively easy for psychopaths to victimize the vulnerable and to use violence as a tool to obtain what they want.

Although there never has been a shortage of anecdotal reports and clinical speculations about the association between psychopathy and crime, the introduction and widespread adoption of the PCL-R provided empirical evidence on the association between psychopathy and crime. There now is an extensive and robust research literature on this association (see Dolan and Doyle, 2000; Hemphill, Hare, and Wong, 1998; Salekin, Rogers, and Sewell, 1996). One of the interesting findings to emerge from this research is that in spite of their small numbers—perhaps 1 percent of the general population—psychopaths make up a significant proportion of our prison populations and are responsible for a markedly disproportionate amount of serious crime and social distress.

Although psychopathy is closely associated with antisocial and criminal behavior, it should not be confused with criminality in general. Psychopaths are qualitatively different from others who routinely engage in criminal behavior, different even from those whose criminal conduct is extremely serious and persistent. They have distinctive "criminal careers" with respect to the number and type of antisocial behaviors they commit, as well as the ages at which they commit them. Furthermore, it appears that the antisocial behavior of psychopaths is motivated by different factors than is that of nonpsychopaths, with the result that the behavioral topography of their criminal conduct (in other words, their victimology or modus operandi) also is different. The personality and social psychological factors that explain antisocial behavior in general may be less applicable to psychopaths than they are to other criminals.

The typical criminal career is relatively short, but there are individuals who devote most of their adolescent and adult life to delinquent and criminal activities. Among these persistent offenders are psychopaths who begin their antisocial and criminal activities at a relatively early age, and continue to engage in these activities throughout much of the lifespan (Forth and Burke, 1998). Many of these "career" criminals become less grossly antisocial in middle age. About half of the criminal psychopaths we have studied show a relatively sharp reduction in criminality around age thirty-five or forty, primarily with respect to nonviolent offenses (Hare, McPherson, and Forth, 1988). This does not mean that they have given up crime completely, only that their level of general criminal activity has decreased to that of the average persistent offender.

Psychopathy and Violence

The rate of community and institutional violence is much higher among psychopathic offenders and forensic patients than among other offenders and forensic patients (for example, Douglas, Ogloff, and Nicholls, 1997; Hart and Hare, 1997; Heilbrun et al., 1998; Hill, Rogers, and Bickford, 1996). In addition, the violence of psychopaths tends to be more instrumental, dispassionate, and predatory than that of other offenders (for example, Cornell et al., 1996; Hart and Dempster, 1997). Psychopathic violence and aggression seem remorseless and typically motivated by what others would describe as greed, vengeance, anger, retribution, or money. The victims of psychopaths are often strangers. A study by the Federal Bureau of Investigation (1992) found that almost half of the law enforcement officers who died in the line of duty were killed by individuals who closely matched the personality profile of the psychopath.

It appears that the propensity for psychopaths to engage in instrumental violence and aggression decreases very little with age (Hare et al., 1988; Harris, Rice, and Cormier, 1991). One explanation of the persistence of the psychopath's potential for violence may lie in the finding that age-related decreases in antisocial behavior, and in the features associated with such behavior (impulsivity, sensation-seeking, and so forth), are not necessarily paralleled by decreases in the egocentric, manipulative, and callous traits fundamental to psychopathy (Harpur and Hare, 1994).

Psychopathy and the Prediction of Violence

The significance of psychopathy as a risk factor for recidivism in general, and for violence in particular, is now well established. In their meta-analytic review, Salekin, Rogers, and Sewell (1996) concluded that the ability of the PCL-R to predict violence was "unparalleled" and "unprecedented" in the literature on the assessment of dangerousness. In a more recent meta-analysis, Hemphill et al., (1998) found that in the first year following release from prison, psychopaths are three times more likely to reoffend, and four times more likely to violently reoffend, than are other offenders.

Although the prevalence of psychopathy is lower in forensic psychiatric populations than in offender populations, the presence of psychopathic attributes in forensic patients is as much a risk factor for recidivism and violence as it is in prison populations. For example, Rice and Harris (1992) found that scores on the PCL-R were as predictive of recidivism in a sample of male not-guilty-by-reason-of-insanity schizophrenics as in a sample of nonpsychotic offenders. Hart and Hare (1989) found that only a small minority of consecutive admissions to a forensic psychiatric hospital were psychopaths, but that many patients exhibited a significant number of PCL-R symptoms. Further, the PCL-R predicted recidivism rates in a five-year follow-up period (Wintrup, Coles, Hart, and Webster, 1994). A recent study of a large sample of violent forensic patients in Sweden, most of whom were schizophrenics, found that those with a score above twenty-five on the PCL-R were four times more likely to violently recidivate in the postrelease follow-up period (which averaged fifty-one months) than were those with a PCL-R score of twenty-five or below (Tengstrom, Grann, Lanfstrom, and Kullgren, 2000).

Several studies have found that the PCL: SV is predictive of institutional aggression and violence in forensic psychiatric hospitals (Hill, Rogers, and Bickford, 1996; Heilbrun et al., 1998). The PCL: SV also predicts violence following release from a psychiatric institution. Douglas, Ogloff, and Nicholls (1997) assessed postrelease community violence in a large sample of male and female patients who had been involuntarily committed to a civil psychiatric facility. Although very few of the patients had a score high enough to warrant a diagnosis of psychopathy, the PCL: SV nevertheless was highly predictive of violent behaviors and arrests for violent crimes. When the distribution of PCL: SV scores was split at the median, the odds ratio for an arrest for violent crime was about ten times higher for patients above the median than it was for those below the median.

In the MacArthur Foundation's Violence Risk Assessment Study, the most extensive and thorough study of its sort ever conducted, 134 potential predictors of violence in 939 patients were evaluated over a twenty-week period following discharge from a civil psychiatric facility (Steadman et al., 2000). The single best predictor was the PCL: SV. The prevalence of postdischarge violence was 35.7 percent for patients with a PCL: SV score of 13 or more (out of a maximum of 24), but only 12.6 percent for patients with a PCL: SV score of less than 13. In presenting their results, the authors used a "classification tree" approach in which a hierarchy of decisions is made about the risk posed by a given patient. In this scheme, the first decision is whether the patient has a PCL: SV score of 13 or more. Silver, Mulvey, and Monahan (1999) used a subsample of 293 of these patients to investigate the impact that neighborhood factors have on individual risk factors for violence in discharged patients. Again, the single best predictor of violence was the PCL: SV; the odds that a patient with a PCL: SV score of 13 or more would commit a violent act were 5.3 times higher than were the odds that a patient with a score below 13 would commit such an act. Although patients discharged into neighborhoods with "concentrated poverty" generally were at higher risk for violence than were those discharged into neighborhoods with less poverty, the odds ratio for psychopathy associated with violence changed very little (from 5.3 to 4.8) when concentrated poverty was added to the equation.

Relatively little research has been conducted on psychopathy in female and adolescent offenders. However, the available data are consistent with those from the adult male literature. Thus, the recidivism rates of female psychopathic offenders (as defined by the PCL-R) are higher than are those of other female offenders (Loucks and Zamble, 2000; Hare, 1998; Salekin, Rogers, Ustad, and Sewell, 1998). Adolescent psychopaths are at much higher risk for recidivism and violence than are other adolescent offenders (Brandt et al., 1997; Forth and Burke, 1998; Gretton, McBride, Hare, O'Shaughnessy, and Kumka, 2001; Gretton, McBride, O'Shaughnessy, and Hare, 2001; Toupin, Mercier, Déry, Côté, and Hodgins, 1996; *see also* Forth et al., in press).

Sexual Violence

Perhaps the findings most relevant to the SVP designation are those that stem from research on the association between psychopathy and sexual violence. Of course, not all sex offenders are psychopaths, but those who are pose special problems for the entire criminal justice system.

Several studies have determined the prevalence of psychopathy among various types of sex offenders (for example, Brown and Forth, 1997; Miller, Geddings, Levenston, and Patrick, 1994; Quinsey, Rice, and Harris, 1995). In general, the prevalence of psychopathy, as measured by the PCL-R, is much lower in child molesters (around 10 to 15 percent) than in rapists or "mixed" offenders (around 40 to 50 percent). The offenses of psychopathic sex offenders are likely to be more violent or sadistic than are those of other sex offenders (Barbaree, Seto, Serin, Amos, and Preston, 1994; Brown and Forth, 1997; Gretton et al., 2001; Miller et al., 1994).

A Deadly Combination

Sex offenders generally are resistant to treatment (Quinsey, 1990), but it is the psychopaths among them who are most likely to recidivate early and often. For example, Quinsey et al. (1995), in a follow-up of treated rapists and child molesters, concluded that psychopathy functions as a general predictor of sexual and violent recidivism. They found that within six years of release from prison, more than 80 percent of the psychopaths, but only about 20 percent of the nonpsychopaths, had violently recidivated. Many, but not all, of their offenses were sexual in nature.

But it is psychopathy, coupled with evidence of deviant sexual arousal, that is one of the most deadly combinations to emerge from the recent research on sex offenders (Gretton et al., 2001; Harris and Hanson, 1998; Rice and Harris, 1997). Anecdotally, the point is illustrated by a former criminal with a record for instrumental violence. He once told the author that robbing a bank at gunpoint was a thrill for him, and that the enterprise always produced an erection. As he put it, "The excitement, the fear in her eyes; what a turn on." For him, and for many others like him, violence and sexual arousal are intertwined. In extreme cases—for example, among serial killers—comorbidity of psychopathy and sadistic personality is very high (Stone, 1998). Even in less extreme cases, psychopathy may be associated with elements of sexual sadism (Dempster and Hart, 1996; Quinsey et al., 1995; Serin, Malcolm, Khanna, and Barbaree, 1994).

In a follow-up of a large sample of sex offenders, Rice and Harris (1997) reported that the PCL-R was highly predictive of violent recidivism in general. In addition, however, they found that sexual recidivism (as opposed to violent recidivism in general) was strongly predicted by a combination of a high PCL-R score and phallometric evidence of deviant sexual arousal, defined as any phallometric test that indicated a preference for deviant stimuli (children, rape cues, or nonsexual violence cues). Similarly, Harris and Hanson (1998) reported that offenders with a high PCL-R score and behavioral (file) evidence of sexual deviance had committed more pre-index sexual offenses, more kidnapping and forcible confinements, and more general (nonsexual) offenses and were more likely to violently recidivate than were other offenders.

The implications of psychopathy and deviant sexual arousal are just as serious among adolescent sex offenders as among their adult counterparts. Gretton et al., (2001) found that the reconviction rate for sexual offenses in the first five years following release was low (about 15 percent) and only moderately related to psychopathy (PCL-R). However, the pattern for other types of offenses was quite different. Thus, in the follow-up period, half of the offenders committed another crime; the rate of offending was more than three times as high in psychopaths as in nonpsychopaths. Further, psychopaths who exhibited phallometric evidence of deviant sexual arousal—the deadly combination—posed by far the highest risk of reoffending; about 80 percent of these individuals committed at least one offense in the follow-up period. The difference between these results and those obtained with adult sex offenders (Rice and Harris, 1997) is that the deadly combination was predictive of sexual violence in adults, whereas it was predictive of general offending, including violence, in adolescents. It is possible that as adolescent offenders age, the combination of psychopathy and deviant sexual arousal will become less predictive of offending in general, and more predictive of sexual offending in particular.

In any case, it is likely that many sex offenders, and most psychopathic ones, are more likely to be convicted of a nonsexual than a sexual offense. Many of these individuals are not so much specialized sex offenders as they are general, versatile offenders, and their misbehavior—sexual and otherwise—presumably is a reflection of a factors not specifically related to sexual behavior. For the psychopaths, these factors no doubt include a propensity to violate social and legal expectations. It may be as important to target the antisocial tendencies and behaviors of so-called sex offenders as it is to treat their sexual deviancy.

Response to Treatment

Most clinicians and researchers are pessimistic about the treatability of psychopaths, with good reason. Unlike most other offenders, psychopaths suffer little personal distress, see little wrong with their attitudes and behavior, and seek treatment only when it is in their best interests to do so, such as when applying for probation or parole. It is therefore not surprising that they derive little benefit from traditional treatment programs, particularly those aimed at the development of empathy, conscience, and interpersonal skills (Hare, 1998b; Losel, 1998). For example, Ogloff, Wong, and Greenwood (1990) reported that offenders with a high score on the PCL-R derived little benefit from an intensive therapeutic community program designed to treat personality-disordered offenders. The psychopaths stayed in the program for a shorter time, were less motivated, and showed less clinical improvement than did other offenders. Hemphill and Wong (1991) reported that once released from prison, the reconviction rate in the first year was twice as high for the psychopaths as for the other offenders.

Rice, Harris, and Cormier (1992) retrospectively scored the PCL-R from the institutional files of patients of a maximum-security psychiatric facility. Psychopaths were defined by a PCL-R score of twenty-five or more, and nonpsychopaths by a score below twenty-five. The violent recidivism rate of nonpsychopaths who had been treated in an intensive and lengthy therapeutic community program was lower than that of a matched group of untreated patients. However, the violent recidivism rate of treated psychopaths was *higher* than that of untreated psychopaths.

The finding that a treatment program increased the risk for violence by psychopaths makes sense if we accept that group therapy and insight-oriented programs may help them to develop better ways of manipulating, deceiving, and using people, but do little to help them to understand themselves. As a consequence, following release into the community they may be more likely than untreated psychopaths to continue to place themselves in situations where the potential for violence is high. However, before we spend too much effort in trying to determine why therapy makes psychopaths worse, we need more evidence that it, in fact, does so. The findings by Rice et al. (1992), though intriguing and suggestive, were based on retrospective research with a particular population of mentally disordered offenders, and with an unusual, complex, and controversial treatment program that included "nude encounter" sessions and ingestion of LSD.

These problems notwithstanding, there is recent evidence that psychopaths are not good candidates for traditional forms of prison treatment. Hobson, Shine, and Roberts (2000) administered the PCL-R to patients when they entered an English prison hospital for treatment in a well-developed therapeutic community program. Their behavior during treatment sessions and while on the wards was evaluated with specially designed checklists. High scores on the PCL-R were strongly predictive of disruptive behaviors during treatment sessions and on the wards three months and six months following admission to the prison. The effect was entirely due to the interpersonal and affective features of psychopathy (PCL-R Factor 1). The results clearly indicated that the psychopaths manipulated the system to satisfy their own need for power, control, and prestige. They played "head games" with other inmates and staff, continually tested the boundaries, and looked for people and things to exploit, and showed no genuine interest in changing their own attitudes and behavior. Nevertheless, they managed to manipulate and fool some staff into thinking their efforts were sincere and that they were making good progress.

A recent prospective analysis of reoffending in the English Prison Service (Hare, Clark, Grann, and Thornton, 2000) indicated that the various short-term treatment programs, including educational upgrading and the development of social skills, had little effect on the postrelease recidivism rates of offenders with low or moderate PCL-R scores.

However, these same programs appear to *increase* the postrelease recidivism rates of offenders with high PCL-R scores. The effect was particularly strong when offenders were divided on the basis of their score on the interpersonal/affective items (Factor 1) of the PCL-R. Thus, the two-year postrecidivism rate for those with a low Factor 1 score was 31 percent for those who had participated in a prison treatment program and 32 percent if they had not done so. In sharp contrast, the recidivism rate for offenders with a high Factor 1 score was 58 percent if they had not taken part in a prison treatment program, but 85 percent if they had not.

At best, the results of these and other studies are discouraging. But we should emphasize that there is no conclusive evidence that psychopaths are completely untreatable or that their behavior cannot be modified. Major methodological weaknesses in the relevant literature, including inadequate assessment procedures, poorly defined treatments, lack of posttreatment follow-ups, and lack of adequate control or comparison groups, make it difficult to be certain that "nothing works." We need to mount a concerted effort to develop innovative procedures designed specifically for psychopathic offenders (Losel, 1998).

Guidelines for development of such a program have been provided by Wong and Hare (in press). In brief, we propose that relapse-prevention techniques be integrated with elements of the best available cognitive-behavioral correctional programs. The program would be less concerned with developing empathy and conscience or effecting changes in personality than with convincing participants that they alone are responsible for their behavior and that they can learn more prosocial ways of using their strengths and abilities to satisfy their needs and wants.

It would involve tight control and supervision, both in the institution and following release into the community, as well as comparisons with carefully selected groups of offenders treated in standard correctional programs. The experimental design would permit empirical evaluation of its treatment and intervention modules (what works and what does not work for particular individuals). That is, some modules or components might be effective with psychopaths but not with other offenders, and vice versa. We recognize that correctional programs are constantly in danger of erosion because of changing institutional priorities, community concerns, and political pressures. To prevent this from happening, we propose stringent safeguards for maintaining the integrity of the program.

Whether sexually violent predator facilities and programs will consider it worthwhile to develop programs for the treatment of their inmates remains to be seen. However, if steps are not taken to reduce the likelihood of violence by these individuals and to prepare at least some of them for eventual conditional release, the designers of sexually violent predator institutions should give serious thought to the provision of special geriatric wings to house and care for a population of offenders who will spend the rest of their days in custody.

Psychopathy and Risk Assessment

Although the PCL-R is a potent predictor of violence, it should be used in conjunction with information about other established risk factors (Hart, 1998). For example, a high PCL-R score may imply high risk, but a low score does not necessarily imply low risk. Pedophiles often will receive a low PCL-R score but nevertheless may be at high risk for sexual reoffending. The PCL-R (or the PCL: SV) is a key component of modern risk instruments, including actuarial scales (for example, Webster, Harris, Rice, Cormier, and Quinsey, 1994) and scales based on structured clinical judgments about recognized risk factors (for example, the HCR-20; Webster, Douglas, Eaves, and Hart, 1997).

Uses and Misuses

In spite of their strong psychometric properties, there is no guarantee that a given clinician will use the PCL-R or PCL: SV properly or in a professional manner. Because of their increasingly important role in the criminal justice and mental health systems, the potential misuse of these instruments poses a serious problem for society, as well as for the individual offender or patient. The issues are discussed in detail elsewhere (Hare, 1998c). For present purposes, perhaps the most important issues have to do with the use of the PCL-R by clinicians or other individuals who (1) lack the professional and legal qualifications to conduct psychological assessments; (2) have inadequate training and experience in the use of the PCL-R; and (3) fail to adhere to accepted professional standards for test administration and interpretation. Although the author and his colleagues address these and related issues in formal PCL-R workshops and in the PCL-R certification program, users of the PCL-R and PCL: SV must be held accountable to the professional associations and regulatory bodies responsible for ensuring the integrity of their clinical practice. In addition, judicial awareness of the issues involved in the use of risk assessment instruments will help to ensure that the rights and concerns of both society and the individual are respected.

References

Babiak, P. 1995. When Psychopath Go To Work. *International Journal of Applied Psychology.* 44:171-188.

Barbaree, H., M. Seto, R. Serin, N. Amos, and D. Preston. 1994. Comparisons between Sexual and Nonsexual Rapist Subtypes. *Criminal Justice and Behavior.* 21:95-114.

Brandt, J. R., W. A. Kennedy, C. J. Patrick, and J. J. Curtin. 1997. Assessment of Psychopathy in a Population of Incarcerated Adolescent Offenders. *Psychological Assessment.* 9:429-435.

Brown, S. L. and A. E. Forth.1997. Psychopathy and Sexual Assault: Static Risk Factors, Emotional Precursors, and Rapist Subtypes. *Journal of Consulting and Clinical Psychology.* 65:848-857.

Cleckley, H. 1976. *The Mask of Sanity,* 5th ed. St. Louis, Missouri: Mosby.

Cooke, D. J. 1998. Psychopathy Across Cultures. In D. J. Cooke, A. E. Forth, and R. D. Hare, eds. *Psychopathy: Theory, Research, and Implications for Society.* Dordrecht, The Netherlands: Kluwer.

Cooke, D. J., A. E. Forth, and R. D. Hare, eds. 1998. *Psychopathy: Theory, Research, and Implications for Society.* Dordrecht, The Netherlands: Kluwer.

Cooke, D. J., D. Kosson, and C. Michie (in press). Structural Item and Test Generalizability of the Psychopathy Checklist Revised (PCL-R) in Caucasian and African-American Offenders. *Psychological Assessment.*

Cooke, D. J. and C. Michie. 1997. An Item Response Theory Evaluation of Hare's Psychopathy Checklist. *Psychological Assessment.* 9:2-13.

Cooke, D. J., C. Michie, S. D. Hart, and R. D. Hare. 1999. Evaluation of the Screening Version of the Hare Psychopathy Checklist-Revised (PCL: SV): An Item Response Theory Analysis. *Psychological Assessment.* 11:3-13.

Cornell, D., J. Warren, G. Hawk, E. Stafford, G. Oram, and D. Pine. 1996. Psychopathy in Instrumental and Reactive Violent Offenders. *Journal of Consulting and Clinical Psychology.* 64:783-790.

Dempster, R. J. and S. D. Hart. 1996, March. Utility of the FBI's Crime Classification Manual: Coverage, Reliability, and Validity for Adolescent Murderers. Paper presented at the Biennial Meeting of the American Psychology-Law Society (APA Div. 41), Hilton Head, South Carolina.

Dolan, M. and M. Doyle. 2000. Violence Risk Prediction: Clinical and Structural Measures and the Role of the Psychopathy Checklist. *British Journal of Psychiatry.* 177:303-311.

Douglas, K. S., J. R. Ogloff, and T. L. Nicholls. 1997, June. Personality Disorders and Violence in Civil Psychiatric Patients. In C. D. Webster (Chair), Personality

Disorders and Violence. Symposium conducted at the meeting of the Fifth International Congress on the Disorders of Personality. Vancouver, Canada.

Federal Bureau of Investigation. 1992. *Killed in the Line of Duty.* Washington, D.C.: U.S. Department of Justice.

Forth, A. E. and H. C. Burke. 1998. Psychopathy in Adolescence: Assessment, Violence, and Developmental Precursors. In D. J. Cooke, A. E. Forth, and R. D. Hare, eds. *Psychopathy: Theory, Research, and Implications for Society*, pp. 205-229. Dordrecht, The Netherlands: Kluwer.

Forth, A. E., D. Kosson, and R. D. Hare (in press). *The Hare Psychopathy Checklist: Youth Version.* Toronto: Multi-health Systems.

Fulero, S. M. 1995. Review of the Hare Psychopathy Checklist-Revised. In J. C. Conoley and J. C. Impara, eds. *Twelfth Mental Measurements Yearbook*, pp. 453-454. Lincoln, Nebraska: Buros Institute.

Gretton, H., M. McBride, R. O'Shaughnessy, and R. D. Hare. 2001. *A Retrospective Longitudinal Study of Recidivism in Adolescent Offenders.* Manuscript in preparation.

Gretton, H., M. McBride, R. D. Hare, R. O'Shaughnessy, and G. Kumka. 2001. Psychopathy and Recidivism in Adolescent Sex Offenders. *Criminal Justice Behavior.* 28:427-449.

Hare, R. D. 1991. *The Hare Psychopathy Checklist-Revised.* Toronto, Ontario: Multi-Health Systems.

———. 1998a. Psychopaths and their Nature: Implications for the Mental Health and Criminal Justice Systems. In T. Millon, E. Simonson, M. Burket-Smith, and R. Davis, eds. *Psychopathy: Antisocial, Criminal, and Violent Behavior*, pp. 188-212. New York: Guilford Press.

———. 1998b. Without Conscience: *The Disturbing World of the Psychopaths among Us.* New York: Guilford Press.

———. 1998c. The Hare PCL-R: Some Issues Concerning its Use and Misuse. *Legal and Criminological Psychology.* 3:101-122.

Hare, R. D., D. Clark, M. Grann, and D. Thornton. 2000. Psychopathy and the Predictive Validity of the PCL-R: An International Perspective. *Behavioral Sciences and the Law.* 18:623-645.

Hare, R. D. and S. D. Hart. 1995. Commentary on Antisocial Personality Disorder: The DSM-IV Field Trial. In W. J. Livesley, ed. *The DSM-IV Personality Disorders*, pp. 127-134. New York: Guilford Press.

Hare, R. D., S. D. Hart, and T. J. Harpur. 1991. Psychopathy and the DSM-IV Criteria for Antisocial Personality Disorder. *Journal of Abnormal Psychology.* 100:391-398.

Hare, R. D., L. E. McPherson, and A. E. Forth. 1988. Male Psychopaths and Their Criminal Careers. *Journal of Consulting and Clinical Psychology.* 56:710-714.

Harpur, T. J. and R. D. Hare. 1994. The Assessment of Psychopathy as a Function of Age. *Journal of Abnormal Psychology.* 103:604-609.

Harris, A. J. R. and R. K. Hanson. 1998. Supervising the Psychopathic Sex Deviant in the Community. Paper presented at 17th Annual Research and Treatment Conference, the Association for the Treatment of Sexual Abusers, Vancouver, Canada, October 14-17, 1998.

Harris, G. T., M. E. Rice, and C. A. Cormier. 1991. Psychopathy and Violent Recidivism. *Law and Human Behavior.* 15:625-637.

Hart, S. D. 1998. The Role of Psychopathy in Assessing Risk for Violence: Conceptual and Methodological Issues. *Legal and Criminological Psychology.* 3:121-137.

Hart, S. D., D. N. Cox, and R. D. Hare. 1995. *Manual for the Hare Psychopathy Checklist— Revised: Screening Version (PCL: SV).* Toronto: Multi-Health Systems, Inc.

Hart, S. D. and R. J. Dempster. 1997. Impulsivity and Psychopathy. In C. D. Webster and M. A. Jackson, eds. *Impulsivity: New Directions in Research and Clinical Practice,* pp. 212-232. New York: Guilford Press.

Hart, S. D. and R. D. Hare. 1989. Discriminant Validity of the Psychopathy Checklist in a Forensic Psychiatric Population. *Psychological Assessment: A Journal of Consulting and Clinical Psychology.* 1:211-218.

————. 1997. Psychopathy: Assessment and Association with Criminal Conduct. In D. M. Stoff, J. Maser, and J. Brieling, eds. *Handbook of Antisocial Behavior,* pp. 22-35. New York: Wiley.

Heilbrun, K., S. D. Hart, R. D. Hare, D. Gustafson, C. Nunez, and A. White. 1998. Inpatient and Post-discharge Aggression in Mentally Disordered Offenders: The Role of Psychopathy. *Journal of Interpersonal Violence.* 13:514-527.

Hemphill, J. F., R. D. Hare, and S. Wong. 1998. Psychopathy and Recidivism: A Review. *Legal and Criminological Psychology.* 3:141-172.

Hemphill, J., C. Strachan, and R. D. Hare. 1998. *Psychopathy in Female Offenders.* Manuscript in preparation.

Hemphill, J. F., and S. Wong. 1991. Efficacy of the Therapeutic Community for Treating Criminal Psychopaths [Abstract]. *Canadian Psychology.* 32:206.

Hill, C. D., R. Rogers, and M. E. Bickford. 1996. Predicting Aggressive and Socially Disruptive Behavior in a Maximum Security Forensic Psychiatric Hospital. *Journal of Forensic Sciences.* 41:56-59.

Hobson, J., J. Shine, R. Roberts. 2000. How Do Psychopaths Behave in a Prison Therapeutic Community? *Crime, Law and Psychology.* 6:139-154.

Kansas v. Hendricks, 521 US 346 (1997).

Lilienfeld, S. O. 1994. Conceptual Problems in the Assessment of Psychopathy. *Clinical Psychology Review.* 14:17-38.

Losel, F. 1998. Treatment and Management of Psychopaths. In D. J. Cooke, A. E. Forth, and R. D. Hare, eds. *Psychopathy: Theory, Research, and Implications for Society*, pp. 303-354. Dordrecht, The Netherlands: Kluwer.

Loucks, A. D. and E. Zamble. 2000. Predictors of Criminal Behavior and Prison Misconduct in Serious Female Offenders. *Empirical and Applied Criminal Justice Review.* 1:1-47.

Miller, M. W., V. J. Geddings, G. K. Levenston, and C. J. Patrick. 1994, March. The Personality Characteristics of Psychopathic and Nonpsychopathic Sex Offenders. Paper presented at the Biennial Meeting of the American Psychology-Law Society (Div. 41 of the American Psychological Association), Santa Fe, New Mexico.

Ogloff, J. R. P., S. Wong, and A. Greenwood. 1990. Treating Criminal Psychopaths in a Therapeutic Community Program. *Behavioral Sciences and the Law.* 8:81-90.

Porter, S., D. Fairweather, J. Drugge, H. Herve, A. Birt, and D. P. Boer. 2000. Profiles of Psychopathy in Incarcerated Sexual Offenders. *Criminal Justice and Behavior.* 27:216-233.

Quinsey, V. L. 1990. Sexual Violence. In P. Bowden and R. Bluglass, eds. *Principles and Practice of Forensic Psychiatry*, pp. 563-570. Edinburgh: Churchill Livingstone.

Quinsey, V. L., M. E. Rice, and G. T. Harris. 1995. Actuarial Prediction of Sexual Recidivism. *Journal of Interpersonal Violence.* 10:85-105.

Rice, M. E. and G. T. Harris. 1992. A Comparison of Criminal Recidivism among Schizophrenic and Nonschizophrenic Offenders. *International Journal of Law and Psychiatry.* 15:397-408.

Rice, M. E. and G. T. Harris. 1997. Cross-validation and extension of the Violence Risk Appraisal Guide for Child Molesters and Rapists. *Law and Human Behavior.* 21:231-241.

Rice, M. E., G. T. Harris, and C. A. Cormier. 1992. An Evaluation of a Maximum Security Therapeutic Community for Psychopaths and Other Mentally Disordered Offenders. *Law and Human Behavior*. 16:399-412.

Robins, L. N. 1978. Etiological Implications in Studies of Childhood Histories Relating to Antisocial Personality. In R. D. Hare and D. Schalling, eds. *Psychopathic Behavior: Approaches to Research*, pp. 255-271. Chichester, England: Wiley.

Salekin, R. T., R. Rogers, and K. W. Sewell. 1996. A Review and Meta-analysis of the Psychopathy Checklist and Psychopathy Checklist-Revised: Predictive Validity of Dangerousness. *Clinical Psychology: Science and Practice*. 3:203-215.

————. 1997. Construct Validity of Psychopathy in a Female Offender Sample: A Multitrait- Multimethod Evaluation. *Journal of Abnormal Psychology*. 106:576-585.

Salekin, R W., R. Rogers, K. L. Ustad, and K. W. Sewell. 1998. Psychopathy and Recidivism among Female Inmates. *Law and Human Behavior*. 22:109-128.

Serin, R. C., P. B. Malcolm, A. Khanna, and H. E. Barbaree. 1994. Psychopathy and Deviant Sexual Arousal in Incarcerated Sexual Offenders. *Journal of Interpersonal Violence*. 9:3-11.

Silver, E., E. P. Mulvey, and J. Monahan. 1999. Assessing Violence Risk among Discharged Psychiatric Patients: Toward an Ecological Approach. *Law and Human Behavior*. 23:237-255.

Steadman, H., J. Monahan, P. Applelbaum, T. Grisso, E. Mulvey, L. Roth, P. Robbins, and D. Klassen. 1994. Designing a New Generation of Risk Assessment Research. In J. Monahan and H. Steadman, eds. *Violence and Mental Disorder: Developments in Risk Assessment*, pp. 287-318. Chicago: University of Chicago Press.

Steadman, H., E. Silver, J. Monahan, P. S. Appelbaum, P. M. Robbins, E. P. Mulvey, T. Grisso, L. H. Roth, and S. Banks. 2000. A Classification Tree Approach to the Development of Actuarial Violence Risk Assessment Tools. *Law and Human Behavior*. 24:83-100.

Stone, M. H. 1998. Sadistic Personality in Murderers. In T. Millon, E. Simonson, M. Burket-Smith, and R. Davis, eds. *Psychopathy: Antisocial, Criminal, and Violent Behavior*, pp. 346- 358). New York: Guilford Press.

Tengstrom, A., M. Grann, N. Langstrum, and G. Kullgren. 2000. Psychopathy (PCL-R) as a Predictor of Violent Recidivism among Criminal Offenders with Schizophrenia. *Law and Human Behavior*. 24:45-58.

Toupin, J., H. Mercier, M. Déry, G. Côté, and S. Hodgins. 1996. Validity of the PCL-R for Adolescents. In D. J. Cooke, A. E. Forth, J. P. Newman, and R. D. Hare, eds. *Issues in Criminological and Legal Psychology: No. 24, International Perspectives on Psychopathy*, pp. 143-145. Leicester, England: British Psychological Society.

Tucker, W. 1999. The "Mad" vs. the "Bad" Revisited: Managing Predatory Behavior. *Psychiatric Quarterly*. 70:221-230.

Webster, C. D., K. S. Douglas, D. Eaves, and S. D. Hart. 1997. *HCR-20: Assessing Risk for Violence—Version 2*. Burnaby, British Columbia: Mental Health, Law, and Policy Institute, Simon Fraser University.

Webster, C. D., G. T. Harris, M. E. Rice, C. A. Cormier, and V. A. Quinsey. 1994. *The Violence Prediction Scheme: Assessing Dangerousness in High Risk Men*. Toronto, Ontario: Center for Criminology, University of Toronto.

Widiger, T. A., R. Cadoret, R. D. Hare, L. Robins, M. Rutherford, M. Zanarini, A. Alterman, M. Apple, E. Corbitt, A. E. Forth, S. D. Hart, J. Kultermann, G. Woody, and A. Frances. 1996. DSM-IV Antisocial Personality Disorder Field Trial. *Journal of Abnormal Psychology*. 105:3-16.

Wintrup, A., M. Coles, S. Hart, and C. D. Webster. 1994. The Predictive Validity of the PCL-R in High-risk Mentally Disordered Offenders [Abstract]. *Canadian Psychology*. 35:47.

Wong, S. and R. D. Hare (in press). *Program Guidelines for the Institutional Treatment of Violent Psychopaths*. Multi-Health Systems: Toronto, Ontario.

WHAT WORKS: ASSESSING PSYCHOPATHY IN JUVENILES

7

Adelle E. Forth, Ph.D.
Associate Professor, Department of Psychology
Carleton University
Ottawa, Ontario, Canada

Donna L. Mailloux
Research Officer
Correctional Service of Canada
Ottawa, Ontario, Canada

Psychopathy is a personality disorder that is associated with a constellation of affective, interpersonal, and behavioral characteristics, central to which are a profound lack of guilt and a callous disregard for the feelings, rights, and welfare of others (Cleckley, 1976; Hare, 1991). Psychopaths are impulsive, deceitful, selfish, sensation-seeking and irresponsible.

---

* This report is an updated version of the following chapter: A. E. Forth and D. L. Mailloux. 2000. Psychopathy in Youth: What Do We Know? In C. Gacono, ed. *Clinical and Forensic Applications of Psychopathy*. New Jersey: Erlbaum and is published with their permission.

Among adults, psychopathy has been linked to serious repetitive crime, violent behavior, and poor treatment prognosis (for reviews *see* Hare, 1998a; Hart and Hare, 1997).

Although a considerable amount of research has focused on psychopathy in adults, substantially less research has been conducted among children and adolescents. However, interest in the developmental aspects of this disorder has intensified (Forth and Burke, 1998; Frick, 1998; Frick, O'Brien, Wootton, and McBurnett, 1994; Lynam, 1996).

Given the psychopaths' resistance to treatment as adults (Ogloff, Wong, and Greenwood, 1990; Rice, Harrris, and Cormier, 1992), the optimal strategy to attenuate psychopathic behavior may be to identify and intervene early in development. Early intervention strategies may modify the pathway to persistent, diverse, and serious antisocial behaviors that are associated with psychopathy. It is important at the same time to differentiate psychopathic youths from other aggressive youths since not all aggressive youths will become high-rate offenders.

Most clinicians and researchers would agree that many psychopathic characteristics are first manifested at an early age. Whether these characteristics are similar to the presentation of psychopathy in adults remains to be determined. Nevertheless, researchers measuring psychopathy in children and adolescents implicitly have assumed a continuity across development. This assumption is analogous to research indicating a relation between early temperament and adult personality traits (Henry, Caspi, Moffitt, and Silva, 1996; Kruger et al., 1994). This provides the rationale for using assessment tools developed for use with adults with younger populations.

Despite the tacit assumption of continuity of psychopathy across development, the precise etiology of psychopathy is unknown. Similar to other personality traits, it is likely that a range of genetic and environmental factors influence the onset, development, and presentation of psychopathy. Knowledge of these developmental risk factors, particularly those factors that are changeable, may enhance our ability to provide more appropriate intervention programs.

The only instrument used to operationalize psychopathy in adults with demonstrated reliability and validity (Cooke, 1998; Hare, 1996; 1998a; Hart and Hare, 1997) is the Hare Psychopathy Checklist-Revised (Hare,1991). The Hare Psychopathy Checklist-Revised is a clinical construct rating scale completed on the basis of a semistructured interview and a review of collateral information.

A number of instruments have been adapted from the Hare Psychopathy Checklist-Revised to measure psychopathy in children and adolescents: Psychopathy Checklist: Youth Version (Psychopathy Checklist: Youth Version; Forth, Kosson, and Hare, in press), Psychopathy Screening Device (Psychopathy Screening Device; Frick et al., 1994), and the Childhood Psychopathy Scale (Child Psychopathy Scale; Lynam, 1997). Two strategies have been used in the development of these instruments. The first strategy extends the adult version into adolescence and, depending on its validity, extends it further into childhood. The second strategy attempts to adapt the adult version for use with children. The Psychopathy Checklist: Youth Version was based on the former strategy whereas the Psychopathy Screening Device and the Child Psychopathy Scale were based on the latter strategy.

In this chapter, we review the empirical research relevant to understanding the manifestation of psychopathy in youth. First, we describe the instruments that have been adapted from the Hare Psychopathy Checklist-Revised for use with children and adolescents. Second, we consider the association between psychopathy and criminal conduct in adolescence. Third, we review research on developmental correlates of psychopathy. Finally, we describe studies on the effectiveness of interventions with psychopathic youth.

Assessment of Psychopathy

Although the etiology and conceptual boundaries of psychopathy have yet to be fully understood, there is consensus across mental health professionals, experimental psychologists, criminal justice personnel, and the lay public that the core features of psychopathy comprise both personality and behavioral characteristics (Albert, Brigante, and Chase, 1959; Cleckley, 1976; Rogers, Dion, and Lynett, 1992; Tennent, Tennent, Prins, and Bedford, 1990). To assess these characteristics among children and adolescents, three instruments have been adapted from the Hare Psychopathy Checklist-Revised.

Psychopathy Checklist: Youth Version. Forth, Hart, and Hare (1990) were the first to examine the construct of psychopathy in adolescent offenders. Since the Hare Psychopathy Checklist-Revised was designed for use in the assessment of adult offenders, it was necessary to revise the scale to make it more appropriate for use with adolescents. Since adolescents typically have a limited work history and few marital relationships, Items 9 (parasitic lifestyle) and 17 (many short-term marital relationships) were deleted. Furthermore, because adolescent offenders have had less opportunity to come into contact with the judicial system than adult offenders, it was necessary to modify two other items: Item 18 (juvenile delinquency) and Item 20 (criminal versatility). Referred to as the 18-item Hare Psychopathy Checklist-Revised, this scale has been used in several of the studies discussed in this chapter.

As researchers gained experience using the 18-item Hare Psychopathy Checklist-Revised with adolescents, they made three modifications that would further take into account the restricted life experience of adolescents. First, a scoring system was developed that reflected the greater involvement of peers, family, and school in the lives of adolescents. Second, Items 9 and 17 were reintroduced but were modified so that it was possible to assess these characteristics in youth. Third, when scoring individual items, the focus is on enduring features of the youth displayed across settings and situations. For example, when assessing poor anger control, if the adolescent displays anger towards specific people (such as parents or authority figures) or in limited contexts, this would not be sufficient evidence to score this item as high. This modified version of the Hare Psychopathy Checklist-Revised was named the Psychopathy Checklist: Youth Version (Forth et al., in press). A draft version of the Psychopathy Checklist: Youth Version has been made available to researchers for use in a variety of research studies.

Two studies have investigated the factor structure of the Hare Psychopathy Checklist-Revised and the Psychopathy Checklist: Youth Version (Brandt, Kennedy, Patrick, and Curtin, 1997; Forth, 1995). Both studies reported a similar two-factor structure replicating that found with adult offenders (Hare et al., 1990). Factor one reflects the interpersonal and affective characteristics, such as grandiosity, glibness, manipulativeness, callousness, and lack of remorse. Factor two reflects behavioral features associated with an impulsive, irresponsible, and antisocial lifestyle.

Both the Hare Psychopathy Checklist-Revised and Psychopathy Checklist: Youth Version are reliable instruments. Indices of internal consistency (alpha coefficient, mean interitem correlation) and interrater reliability are high (Bauer, 1999; Brandt et al., 1997; Forth, 1995; Gretton, 1998; McBride, 1998). The Psychopathy Checklist: Youth Version has very high interrater reliabilities with correlations between independent raters of .90 or above (see Forth and Burke, 1998). The issue of interrater reliability is of particular importance when assessment instruments developed in research settings are used for clinical assessment.

Psychopathy Screening Device. The Psychopathy Screening Device (Psychopathy Screening Device; Frick et al., 1994) is the only instrument to date that has been developed specifically to assess psychopathy in childhood. As a twenty-item scale, ratings are completed based on observations made from parents or teachers. Factor analysis of the Psychopathy Screening Device in a sample of ninety-five clinic-referred children (ages six to twelve years) revealed a two-factor solution that the authors concluded were similar to the two-factor structure found with adults (Hare et al., 1990). The first factor, labeled impulsivity/conduct problems (I/CP), consisted of ten items (for example, brags about accomplishments, acts without thinking). The second factor, labeled callous/unemotional (C/U), consisted of six items (for example, does not show emotions, lack of guilt).

Various discrepancies between the factor structure found in children and adults have been noted (Frick et al., 1994; McBride, 1998). For example, items relating to grandiosity (brags about accomplishments, thinks he or she is more important than others), callousness (teases others), and failing to take responsibility for actions (blames others) were associated with the impulsivity/conduct problems factor, whereas in adults and adolescents, these are associated with factor one of the Hare Psychopathy Checklist-Revised/Psychopathy Checklist: Youth Version. In addition, three items relating to manipulation and lying, which are also associated with factor one of the Hare Psychopathy Checklist-Revised/Psychopathy Checklist: Youth Version, were associated with both factors in the children. Finally, an item (does not plan ahead) that should have been related to the impulsivity/conduct problems factor was more strongly related to the callous/unemotional factor (this item was not included in the callous/unemotional factor). Subsequent research by Frick and his colleagues (Christian, Frick, Hill, Tyler, and Frazer, 1997; Frick, 1998; Wootton, Frick, Shelton, and Silverthorn, 1997) and Blair (Blair, 1997; Blair and Fisher, 1997) have used these two scales of the Psychopathy Screening Device to investigate the differential pattern of associations with a variety of external variables. To date, no study has yet attempted to replicate this factor structure in children.

Research has demonstrated a relatively low interrater agreement between parent and teacher ratings on the callous/unemotional factor (r = .29 in the Frick et al., 1994 study and r = .34 in the Christian et al., 1997 study; in contrast Blair, 1998 found a relatively good interrater agreement between two teachers r = .64). Moreover, a recent study has found that the Psychopathy Screening Device demonstrated poor concurrent validity with the Psychopathy Checklist: Youth Version. McBride (1998) had seventy-five mothers of adolescent offenders complete the Psychopathy Screening Device and compared this to Psychopathy Checklist: Youth Version scores obtained from file ratings.

The total Psychopathy Screening Device was correlated $r = .35$ with the Psychopathy Checklist: Youth Version total scores. Both the callous/unemotional ($r = .28$) and impulsivity/conduct problems ($r = .43$) scales were correlated with factor two of the Psychopathy Checklist: Youth Version but were not significantly correlated with factor one ($r = .16$ and .19, respectively).

In addition to the low interrater agreement, the failure of the callous/unemotional scale to be strongly related to factor one of the Psychopathy Checklist: Youth Version has raised considerable concern about how well this subscale captures the personality features it was designed to measure. These findings may be due to inherent differences in the item content between the Psychopathy Checklist: Youth Version and the Psychopathy Screening Device. For example, each item on the Psychopathy Checklist: Youth Version consists of a one-page description, including examples of that characteristic and explicit criteria for coding the item. In contrast, the Psychopathy Screening Device items are simple statements derived from the Hare Psychopathy Checklist-Revised items but which are not anchored in operational definitions (for example, Thinks he or she is more important than others; His or her emotions seem shallow and not genuine).

Child Psychopathy Scale. More recently, Lynam (1997) developed the thirteen-item Childhood Psychopathy Scale (Child Psychopathy Scale) also based on the Hare Psychopathy Checklist-Revised. This scale was based on archival data of child behavior and personality that were completed by mothers as part of a large-scale study of 430 boys aged twelve to thirteen years. To measure psychopathy, items were drawn from the Child Behavior Checklist (Achenback, 1991) and the Common Language Q-sort (Block and Block, 1980).

Only thirteen of the twenty Hare Psychopathy Checklist-Revised items could be operationalized using items from these two scales (each of the thirteen items consisted of two or more items). Factor analysis of the thirteen-item scale also revealed a two-factor structure similar to that found using the Hare Psychopathy Checklist-Revised with adults. However, since the two factors were so highly correlated ($r = .95$), only the total score was used. A variety of variables were used to assess the validity of the Child Psychopathy Scale including self-reported antisocial behavior at age ten and thirteen. The Child Psychopathy Scale was positively correlated with serious thefts, violent acts, serious delinquency at age ten, measures of self-reported and teacher-ratings of impulsivity, and negatively correlated with internalizing problems. In addition, boys who engaged in serious delinquency at both age periods (ten and twelve to thirteen) had significantly higher scores on the Child Psychopathy Scale than did the other boys. Although initial results from the Child Psychopathy Scale are promising, Lynam (1997) acknowledges that due to the archival nature of the study, the optimal range of psychopathy traits could not be measured (only thirteen of the twenty Hare Psychopathy Checklist-Revised items). Moreover, he notes that there was an overreliance on behavioral descriptors and that some of the items, such as glibness/superficial charm and shallow affect, did not adequately capture the intent of Hare Psychopathy Checklist-Revised item.

In summary, research with the Psychopathy Screening Device and the Child Psychopathy Scale provides some evidence that the construct of psychopathy can be assessed in children and young adolescents. However, both scales appear to focus primarily on behavioral descriptors without adequate coverage of the core affective and interpersonal features that most clinicians consider fundamental to psychopathy in adults. The Psychopathy Checklist: Youth Version is much more closely related to the Hare Psychopathy Checklist-Revised, using a similar methodology to assess psychopathic traits (a review of case history information and when possible, clinical interviews) and providing for the assessment of the full range of relevant symptoms (affective, interpersonal, and behavioral). The remainder of this review will focus on research conducted using both the modified eighteen-item Hare Psychopathy Checklist-Revised scale and the Psychopathy Checklist: Youth Version.

Prevalence of Psychopathic Characteristics

Research conducted with the Hare Psychopathy Checklist-Revised in adult offenders has reported considerable cross-group consistency in the prevalence of psychopathy. In North America, similar Hare Psychopathy Checklist-Revised scores have been obtained across male and female offender samples (Hare, 1991; Mailloux, 1999; Neary, 1991; Strachan, 1993), Native Canadians offenders (Wong, 1985), Francophone Canadian offenders (Hodgins, Côté, and Ross, 1992), and African-American offenders in the United States (Kosson, Smith, and Newman, 1990). Although similar scores are obtained in samples of North American offenders, mean Hare Psychopathy Checklist-Revised scores do differ across samples. For example, lower scores are found in adult male European offenders (for review *see* Cooke, 1998), forensic psychiatric patients, substance abusers, and noncriminals. The extent to which the prevalence of psychopathy differs across groups of adolescents is presented below.

Males. Incarcerated male adolescents display the most psychopathic characteristics with mean scores ranging from 23 to 26, with a standard deviation from 5 to 7 (Brandt et al., 1997; Forth et al., 1990; Forth, 1995; Gretton, 1998; Hume, Kennedy, Patrick, and Partyka, 1996; Laroche, 1996; McBride, 1998; Pan, 1998; Vincent, Corrado, Cohen and Odgers, 1999). This mean is slightly higher than found in adult male offenders whose Hare Psychopathy Checklist-Revised scores range from about 22 to 24, with a standard deviation from 6 to 8 (Hare, 1991). This relatively high score is not surprising since these youths represent a subset of adolescent offenders who have been convicted of violent offenses or who repeatedly engage in crime. For incarcerated male adolescent sex offenders, the mean score is somewhat lower at 21.40 (SD = 7.30; McBride, 1998). Mean scores for male adolescent psychiatric inpatients range from 14 to 17 (Myers, Burket, and Harris, 1995; Stafford, 1997; Stanford, Ebner, Patton, and Williams, 1994). The lowest mean scores are found in samples of male high school students that range from 4 to 9 (Forth, 1995; Ridenour, 1996). Most of these youths had no significant problems at home, school, or in the community. Research with adult noncriminal samples also has shown a similar low score on measures of psychopathy (Forth, Brown, Hart, and Hare, 1996).

Females. Until recently there has been limited research assessing the manifestation of psychopathic traits in females. Recent research using the Hare Psychopathy Checklist-Revised suggests that female offenders have similar prevalence, factor structures, and correlates as do male adult offenders. Mean Hare Psychopathy Checklist-Revised scores of incarcerated adult female offenders range from 18 to 24 (Mailloux, 1999; Neary, 1991; Strachan, 1993). In substance abusing adult females, the scores are typically around 14 (Rutherford, Alterman, Cacciola, and Synder, 1996; Rutherford, Alterman, Cacciola, and McKay, 1998).

To date, three studies have collected data on the prevalence of psychopathy among female adolescents. In these, scores ranged from 24 (n = 80; Bauer, 1999) for incarcerated female adolescents to 18 for delinquent adolescents in a community-based intervention program (n = 54; Rowe, 1997), and to a low of 10 for female adolescent inpatients (n = 30; Stanford et al., 1994). Due to the small number of participants in most of these studies, caution is required when interpreting the results. In each study, the female participants scored lower than the male participants, but this difference was only significant in the Stanford et al. (1994) study (female patients obtained scores three points lower than their male counterparts).

Race. Several studies have compared psychopathy scores in adolescents across racial groups. For instance, Forth et al. (1990) found significantly higher scores for white as compared to Native Canadians. On the other hand, in a larger sample assessing psychopathy using only file-information, no significant differences between white and Native-Canadian adolescent sex offenders was found (McBride, 1998). Other studies comparing adolescent whites and African-Americans have reported no significant differences on psychopathy scores between these two groups (Brandt et al., 1997; Hume et al., 1996; Myers et al., 1995; Pan, 1998). In addition, the one study that compared psychopathy score across white, African-American, and Hispanic adolescents also found no significant differences (Pan, 1998).

Age. Three studies have examined the relationship between psychopathy and age at the time of assessment. None of these studies (Brandt et al., 1997; Forth et al., 1990; Forth and Burke, 1998) has found a significant association between age and psychopathy scores. These results indicate that psychopathic traits are expressed in both older and younger adolescents.

In summary, the prevalence of psychopathic characteristics across samples is different (such as incarcerated male adolescents obtaining the highest scores and noncriminal high school students the lowest scores). Nevertheless, the research to date provides evidence that the Psychopathy Checklist: Youth Version/Hare Psychopathy Checklist-Revised is reliable across sex, race, and age groups. However, given the small sample sizes in some of these studies (for example, Pan (1998) had fewer than eighteen participants in each of his racial groups), caution should be exercised when making generalizations.

Self-report Measures of Psychopathy

Self-report inventories are widely used to assess personality and psychopathy. Their appeal stems from their extensive standardization, their objective nature, their relative ease of administration and scoring, the range of personality features they measure, and for many, the inclusion of validity scales to assess invalid profiles and to control for self-presentation strategies. Attempts to use self-report scales to assess psychopathy is primarily motivated by the resource intensive nature of the Psychopathy Checklist: Youth Version. The Psychopathy Checklist: Youth Version ratings are based on an extensive semistructured interview plus a review of available collateral data. It takes upward of two hours to complete a Psychopathy Checklist: Youth Version and in some cases considerably longer if extensive file information is available. Unfortunately, past research has found only low-to-moderate correlations between self-report measures of psychopathy and the Hare Psychopathy Checklist-Revised in adult offenders. These results may be due primarily to the failure of self-report scales to capture the core personality features of psychopathy (Hare, 1996; Harpur, Hare, and Hakstian, 1989; Hart, Forth, and Hare, 1991).

Minnesota Multiphasic Personality Inventories. The Minnesota Multiphasic Personality Inventory (Minnesota Multiphasic Personality Inventory; Hathaway and McKinley, 1943) and the adolescent version (Minnesota Multiphasic Personality Inventory-Adolescent version; Butcher et al., 1992) are among the most frequently used objective self-report personality instruments with adolescents (Archer, 1992). Three studies have examined the association between the Minnesota Multiphasic Personality Inventory/Minnesota Multiphasic Personality Inventory-Adolescent version and psychopathy in adolescent offenders with limited success. Brandt et al. (1997) examined the association between the eighteen-item Hare Psychopathy Checklist-Revised and the Minnesota Multiphasic Personality Inventory in a sample of 130 persistent male juvenile delinquents. The total score was significantly correlated with Scale 4 ($r = .23$) and with Scale 4 + 9 ($r = .26$). Factor two scores were significantly associated with Scale 4 ($r = .23$), scale 9 ($r = .22$) and scale 4 + 9 ($r = .29$).

Sullivan (1996) examined the association between Minnesota Multiphasic Personality Inventory-Adolescent version and the Psychopathy Checklist: Youth Version in a sample of ninety-five incarcerated male adolescent offenders. Significant correlations were found between the Psychopathy Checklist: Youth Version total scores and the Psychopathic Deviate scale ($r = .23$), the Conduct Problems content scale ($r = .29$), the Alcohol/Drug Acknowledgment scale ($r = .34$), and the Anger Content scale ($r = .34$). Consistent with findings obtained from adult offenders, these scales were more highly correlated with factor two than with factor one of the Psychopathy Checklist: Youth Version. In addition, the presence or absence of psychopathy as assessed using the Psychopathy

Checklist: Youth Version could not be accurately predicted by the Minnesota Multiphasic Personality Inventory-Adolescent version.

Hume et al. (1996) reported no significant correlations between the Minnesota Multiphasic Personality Inventory-Adolescent version scales and psychopathy. In addition, no differences between the Minnesota Multiphasic Personality Inventory-Adolescent version scores of psychopaths (score of thirty or greater on prorated eighteen-item Hare Psychopathy Checklist-Revised) and nonpsychopaths (scores of less than thirty) were found. Using discriminant analysis, it was possible to use the fifteen Minnesota Multiphasic Personality Inventory-Adolescent version scores to correctly classify 78 percent of the psychopathic and nonpsychopathic group. However, there was a 60 percent false positive and 40 percent false negative rate.

Self-report Psychopathy Scales. More promising results have emerged when self-report scales that are specially designed to measure psychopathic personality traits are used. For example, the correlations between the Psychopathy Checklist: Screening Version (PCL: SV; Hart, Cox, and Hare, 1995) and the Hare Self-report Psychopathy Scale (SRP-II; Hare, 1991) were moderate to large in magnitude in a sample of adult offenders ($r = .69$, total PCL: SV, $r = 41$, Factor one; $r = .70$, Factor two; Hart et al., 1995). More recently, in a sample of fifty young adult prisoners, Poythress, Edens, and Lilienfeld (1998) found that the Psychopathic Personality Inventory (PPI; Lilienfeld and Andrews, 1996) correlated moderately with a sixteen-item Hare Psychopathy Checklist-Revised total ($r = .54$), Factor one ($r = .56$), and Factor two ($r = .44$) scores.

In summary, these results indicate that the Minnesota Multiphasic Personality Inventory/Minnesota Multiphasic Personality Inventory-Adolescent version are not highly associated with the construct of psychopathy and have limited utility in screening for psychopathy. Although recent self-report inventories show more promise (for example, the Hare Self-report Psychopathy Scale and the Psychopathic Personality Inventory), the magnitude of the correlations with psychopathy continues to be moderate. Moreover, the predictive validity of these self-report scales with important outcome criteria (treatment response, recidivism, institutional maladjustment) has yet to be established. It is therefore recommended that clinicians not use self-report inventories, particularly the Minnesota Multiphasic Personality Inventory/Minnesota Multiphasic Personality Inventory-Adolescent version, to assess psychopathic traits.

Association with Conduct Disorder, Attention Deficit Disorder, Personality, and Substance Abuse

In this section, we review the studies that have looked at the association between psychopathy and the following measures: conduct disorder, attention-deficit disorder, personality, and substance use.

Conduct Disorder. Conduct disorder (CD), as described in the *Diagnostic and Statistical Manual for Mental Disorders* (DSM-IV; American Psychiatric Association, 1994) refers to persistent serious antisocial actions that result in significant problems for the youth. DSM-IV diagnostic criteria require three of fifteen symptoms to be present over the course of the last year. The criteria are separated into four main categories: aggressive conduct (seven symptoms), deceitfulness or theft (three symptoms), destruction of property (two symptoms), and serious violations of rules (three symptoms). Conduct disorder is the most prevalent diagnosis found in delinquent youths (Grisso, 1998). The occurrence of conduct disorder in adolescence is a predictor of adult antisocial behavior (*see* review by Lahey and Loeber, 1997). However, conduct disorder constitutes a heterogeneous group; most youths with conduct disorder do not become antisocial adults (White, Moffitt, Earls, Robins, and Silva, 1990).

A moderate relation consistently has been reported between symptoms of conduct disorder and psychopathy in adolescent offenders. The correlations between psychopathy scores and conduct disorder symptoms are relatively large (range from .48 to .64) in samples of adolescent male and female offenders (Bauer, 1999; Brandt et al., 1997; Forth, 1995; Forth et al., 1990; Gretton, 1998).

However, the prevalence rates vary dramatically. According to DSM criteria, almost all incarcerated adolescent offenders meet the diagnostic criteria for conduct disorder. For example, 97 percent of the adolescent offenders in the Forth (1995) study met the criteria for DSM-IV conduct disorder. This high prevalence is not surprising since the conduct disorder criteria primarily focuses on antisocial behaviors. An asymmetric relation has been reported between antisocial personality disorder as measured by the DSM criteria and psychopathy as measured by the Hare Psychopathy Checklist-Revised (Hare, 1983, 1985; Stålenheim and von Knorring, 1996).

A similar asymmetric relation has also emerged when comparing the DSM conduct disorder and the Psychopathy Checklist: Youth Version. In the Forth (1995) study, all adolescent offenders who met the criteria for psychopathy (cutoff 30 or greater) also met the DSM-IV criteria for conduct disorder. However, only 30 percent of the conduct disordered adolescents met the criteria for psychopathy using the Psychopathy Checklist: Youth Version.

Psychopathic traits are clearly related to conduct disorder symptoms. However, a different pattern of correlations emerged when comparing the correlations between conduct disorder symptoms and the two psychopathy factors. Factor two (about $r = .42$ to .58) is more strongly correlated with the number of conduct disorder symptoms than factor one (about $r = .32$ to .36; Brandt et al., 1997; Forth, 1995; Toupin, Mercier, Déry, Côté, and Hodgins, 1996). Interestingly, this differential pattern of correlations does not emerge when correlating Psychopathy Checklist: Youth Version factor scores and the number of aggressive conduct disorder symptoms. Forth (1995) correlated Psychopathy Checklist: Youth Version total and factor scores with the number of aggressive conduct disorder symptoms. A significant correlation was found between Psychopathy Checklist: Youth Version total score and the number of aggressive conduct disorder symptoms ($r = .47$). However, when focusing on aggressive conduct disorder symptoms, both factors were equally correlated with factor one ($r = .32$) and factor two ($r = .31$).

DSM-IV has proposed two different subtypes of conduct disorder based on the age at onset, with childhood onset type having one symptom prior to age ten and the adolescent-onset type displaying no symptoms prior to age ten. Gretton (1998) compared the prevalence of childhood onset conduct disorder diagnoses across 157 adolescent offenders classified as psychopaths (Psychopathy Checklist: Youth Version score 29 or greater), mixed group (Psychopathy Checklist: Youth Version score between 18 and 28), and nonpsychopaths (Psychopathy Checklist: Youth Version score less than 18). Across these groups, the prevalence of childhood onset conduct disorder was 66 percent, 51 percent, and 21 percent, respectively. Similar results were found in a study by Smith, Gacono, and Kaufman (1997) with forty-eight male conduct disordered adolescent offenders. The psychopathic group (scores of 29 or greater) was more likely to be assessed with childhood onset (58 percent) as compared to the nonpsychopathic group (scores lower than 20; 10 percent).

Attention Deficit Disorder. Several studies indicate that youth who exhibit both conduct disorder and attention–deficit/hyperactivity disorder (ADHD) engage in higher rates of antisocial and criminal behavior and display greater persistence than do those with only one of these disorders (Mannuzza, Klein, Bessler, Malloy, and LaPadula, 1993; Walker, Lahey, Hynd, and Frame, 1987). Lynam (1996) has suggested that children who demonstrate symptoms of conduct problems and a combination of hyperactivity, impulsivity, and attention deficits are at the greatest risk for engaging in persistent antisocial behavior. He also speculates that children who manifest this combination of symptoms are the "fledging psychopaths" who then later will manifest the symptoms of psychopathy in adulthood.

To date, two studies have investigated the association between psychopathy and attention deficit disorder (American Psychiatric Association, 1980). In a sample of 233 sex offenders, McBride (1998) found that psychopathy was significantly related to the presence or absence of attention deficit disorder ($r = .40$). Interestingly, scores on both factor one and two were equally related to attention deficit disorder ($r = 32$ and .34, respectively). Psychopathic offenders (score of 30 or greater) were three times more likely to receive a diagnosis of attention deficit disorder (57 percent) as compared to the nonpsychopathic group (score of 29 or below; 18 percent).

A similar association was found between psychopathy and attention deficit hyperactivity disorder in a sample of eighty incarcerated female offenders (Bauer, 1999). Attention deficit hyperactivity disorder was correlated ($r = .34$) with the total Psychopathy Checklist: Youth Version scores. Given the lack of research in this area, future research must study the co-occurrence of attention deficit hyperactivity disorder and conduct disorder in psychopathic youth.

Personality Assessment. Only one study has investigated the association between psychopathy and Axis II personality disorders. In a sample of thirty adolescent psychiatric inpatients (Myers et al., 1995), youths meeting the diagnostic criteria for conduct disorder and narcissistic personality disorder possessed significantly more psychopathic traits than those patients who did not meet the diagnostic criteria. In contrast, patients who met the criteria for avoidant or self-defeating personality disorder had lower psychopathy scores. These preliminary results replicate research with adults that has demonstrated a relation between psychopathy and antisocial, narcissistic, and borderline personality traits (Hare, 1991; Hart and Hare, 1989).

To date, only one study has examined Rorschach variables in a sample of forty-eight conduct disordered male adolescent offenders assessed for psychopathy (Smith, Gacono, and Kaufman, 1997). Consistent with research with adult psychopaths (Gacono and Meloy, 1994), psychopathic conduct disordered youths produced higher scores on the egocentricity indexes than did the nonpsychopathic conduct disordered youth. There were no other significant differences on the other Rorschach measures. The authors conclude that psychopathic adolescents are more self-centered, self-absorbed, and likely more narcissistic than are nonpsychopathic conduct disordered youth. Although scores on the two factors of psychopathy were obtained, the authors did not report the correlation between these factors and the Rorschach variables. Future research should include an analysis of the two factors with respect to Rorschach variables.

Substance Use. The comorbidity of psychopathy and substance abuse in adult offenders is high (Hemphill, Hart, and Hare, 1994; Smith and Newman, 1990). Mailloux, Forth, and Kroner (1997) examined the association between psychopathy and substance use in forty male adolescent offenders. Psychopathy scores were correlated $r = .42$ with the Michigan Alcohol Screening Test (Selzer, 1971), and $r = .42$ with the Drug Abuse Screening Test (Skinner, 1982). Psychopathic youths started using alcohol and drugs at an earlier age and tried a greater number of drugs than did the nonpsychopathic offenders.

In summary, some clinicians might be tempted to consider conduct disorder in youths as a precursor to adult antisocial personality disorder and psychopathy. However, the majority of youths with conduct disorder do not develop adult antisocial personality disorder or psychopathy. Psychopathic youths resemble youths with severe childhood-onset conduct disorder and youths with comorbid diagnosis of conduct disorder and attention deficit hyperactivity disorder. The primary difference between psychopathic youths and these other subtypes is that the majority of conduct disordered youths do not possess the affective and interpersonal features of the prototypical psychopath. The above research suggests that conduct disorder and adolescent psychopathy, as with antisocial personality disorder and adult psychopathy, are constructs that cannot be used interchangeably.

Association with Criminal Conduct and Violence

The characteristics that define psychopathy are compatible with an antisocial lifestyle and a lack of concern for societal rules and regulations.

Traits that normally help to inhibit aggressive behavior are missing in psychopaths (consideration of the feelings of others, good impulsive control, strong emotional bonds). To examine the association between psychopathy and criminal conduct, research on the following variables will be reviewed: institutional behavior, age onset, frequency and versatility of nonviolent and violent criminal behaviors, severity of violence, offender subtypes, and self-directed aggression.

Institutional Behavior. Psychopathy is associated with aggression both in institutions and in the community. Forth et al. (1990) found the eighteen-item Hare Psychopathy Checklist-Revised was strongly associated with the number of violent or aggressive institutional charges ($r = .46$). Brandt et al. (1997) correlated the eighteen-item Hare Psychopathy Checklist-Revised total and factor scores with the number of institutional infractions. The Hare Psychopathy Checklist-Revised scores were significantly related to the number of verbal and physical aggressive incidents and to the number of times the adolescent was placed in the intensive supervision program (program where residents who are endangering themselves or others are placed for a limited time). Interestingly, only the Hare Psychopathy Checklist-Revised Total and factor two scores were significantly related to more negative monthly evaluations by staff, perhaps because individuals "high on factor one were able to charm their way out of negative reviews" (Brandt et al., 1997, p. 434).

Among adolescent psychiatric patients, psychopathy also has demonstrated a strong association with overall aggression. Stafford (1997) looked at the association between psychopathy and the frequency and types of aggressive acts in seventy-two male and female adolescent psychiatric patients. Psychopathy was correlated with overall aggression ($r = .49$). Psychopathic youths engaged in more peer and staff directed aggression in addition to more covert expressions of aggression (exploiting others for personal gain). Furthermore, youths with fewer psychopathic traits exhibited reactive forms of aggression whereas those with more psychopathic traits exhibited both instrumental (goal directed) and reactive (evoked during emotional arousal) forms of aggression. In the prediction of institutional aggressive acts, psychopathy explained more variability than did criminal or aggression history, seriousness of criminal history, or past hospitalizations.

Among adolescent offenders from a residential treatment program, psychopathy was associated with institutional maladjustment. Rogers, Johansen, Chang, and Salekin (1997) correlated psychopathy scores with two measures of institutional adjustment in eighty-one adolescent offenders. Psychopathy was significantly correlated with physical aggression infractions (r = .28) but not with verbal aggression. Pan (1998) found that, in a sample of forty-nine violent adolescent offenders, the only variables to predict institutional violence (number of violent infractions within the first four months incarcerated) were race and factor two scores.

While psychopathic youths have difficulty adjusting to institutions, they are also at an increased risk to escape from institutions. Gretton (1998) found that 68 percent of psychopathic adolescents had attempted to escape as compared to 26 percent of nonpsychopathic adolescents. This may be due to psychopaths' risk-taking nature, defiance of authority, and impulsivity.

Age of Onset. Psychopathic adolescent offenders start engaging in criminal behaviors at a young age. Forth (1995) assessed a sample of 106 adolescent offenders using the Psychopathy Checklist: Youth Version and found that age of onset for nonviolent and violent offenses were correlated (r = -.33 and r = -.26) with the Psychopathy Checklist: Youth Version, respectively. The mean age of onset of nonviolent criminal behaviors was 11.9 for nonpsychopaths and 9.3 for psychopathic adolescent offenders. A similar age-related difference was found for violent criminal behaviors with the more psychopathic group starting at age 12.1 versus 14.5 for the less psychopathic group. Four other studies have examined the association between psychopathy and age at first arrest and found similar results. Forth et al. (1990), McBride (1998), and Brandt et al. (1997) found a correlation of r = -.25, -.35 and -.46 , respectively. However, Gretton (1998) found no differences among high, mixed, and low-psychopathy groups in age of first arrest (14.7, 14.9, and 15.2, respectively).

Frequency of Criminal Conduct. Psychopathic adolescents engage in a greater amount of nonviolent and violent delinquent behaviors than nonpsychopathic adolescents. Toupin et al. (1996), in their study of fifty-two conduct disordered youths, reported a correlation of r = .46 between psychopathy and number of delinquent acts and r = .30 with the number of aggressive behaviors.

Forth (1995) found that Psychopathy Checklist: Youth Version scores were significantly related to the number of self-reported nonviolent behaviors (r = .31), violent behaviors (r = .25), versatility of nonviolent behaviors (r = .35), and versatility of violent behaviors (r = .28). With respect to types of antisocial behaviors committed, psychopathic youths were more likely to have threatened others with a weapon, been sexually aggressive, and committed robbery and arson. Although psychopathy was not related to the number of physically aggressive acts within dating relationships, it was related to scores on the Psychological Maltreatment of Woman Inventory (Tolman, 1989). Psychopathy Checklist: Youth Version total and factor one scores were significantly correlated with the total, dominance-isolation subscale and the verbal-emotional abuse subscales. Psychopathic youths were more likely to control their partners by limiting their social network, restricting their activities, and demanding obedience from them.

Psychopathic youths commit more violent offenses when in the community than nonpsychopathic youth. In Gretton's (1998) sample of 157 offenders, the Psychopathy Checklist: Youth Version total, factor one, and factor two scores were significantly correlated with violent offenses per year free (r = .23, .19, and .20, respectively) and unrelated to nonviolent or sex offenses. Psychopathic offenders were more likely to have a prior history of violent offending (26 percent) than were nonpsychopathic offenders (7 percent).

Smith et al. (1997) reported that all the psychopathic adolescent offenders in their study had a history of violence, compared with only 33 percent of nonpsychopathic adolescents. Myers et al. (1995) compared adolescent psychiatric inpatients who did and did not engage in specific delinquent behaviors. Psychopathy scores were higher in adolescent inpatients who fought, caused serious injury in a fight, stole, engaged in vandalism, and purposely injured or killed animals.

Across teacher-rated subscales of the Child Behavior Checklist (CBCL: Achenback and Edelbrock, 1983), psychopathy scores were most strongly related to the aggressive subscale (r = .31; Brandt et al., 1997). This indicates that even using nonclinician observer ratings, the link between aggression and psychopathy is evident.

The association between criminality and psychopathy has also been found in adolescent sex offenders. McBride (1998) found that the Psychopathy Checklist: Youth Version Total score was significantly related to the number of prior nonviolent crimes (r = .33), number of prior violent crimes (r = .26) and versatility of crimes (r = .36). Psychopathy was not related to the number of prior sexual crimes (r = .05). The failure to find an association with prior sexual crimes also has been reported by Brown and Forth (1997) in a study of sixty male adult rapists (r = -.02). However, the failure to observe a reliable relationship between sexual offenses and psychopathy may be an artifact due to the low prevalence of sexual offenses.

Severity of Crime. The association between psychopathic characteristics and the severity of crime has been investigated in two studies. Brandt et al. (1997) found a correlation between the eighteen-item Hare Psychopathy Checklist-Revised total and factor one scores and crime severity (r = .25 and .24, respectively). Gretton, McBride, Lewis, O'Shaughnessy, and Hare (1994) reported that adolescent sex offenders with high Psychopathy Checklist: Youth Version scores threatened their victims more and used more severe violence during their sexually assaultive acts than did nonpsychopathic sexual offenders.

Subtypes of Offenders. In another recent study, Dixon, Robinson, Hart, Gretton, McBride, and O'Shaughnessy (1995) examined the association between the Psychopathy Checklist: Youth Version scores and the FBI's Crime Classification Manual (Douglas, Burgess, Burgess, and Resslcr, 1992). The Crime Classification Manual was used to classify fifty male adolescent sexual offenders. Both the Crime Classification Manual and psychopathy were based on a review of case history information. Psychopathy scores were significantly higher for the three juveniles classified as anger and sadistic rapists (mean (M) = 28.8) as compared to those who committed nuisance offenses (M = 18.8), domestic sexual assault (M = 19.5), and entitlement rape (M = 18.8).

In another study using the Crime Classification Manual, Dempster and Hart (1996) classified the motive for offending in forty-three male juveniles charged with attempted murder or murder. Similar to the previous study, both the Crime Classification Manual and the Psychopathy Checklist: Youth Version scores were derived from a review of the offenders' institutional files. Those juveniles meeting the criteria for sexual homicide scored significantly higher on psychopathy than those classified as criminal enterprise, personal cause, or group excitement.

A study by Myers and Blashfield (1997) assessed a sample of thirteen juveniles who committed sexual homicide for psychopathy, DSM-III-R axis 1 disorders, and personality disorders. All but two of the youths were diagnosed with conduct disorder. The mean psychopathy score for these youths was 22.4. Not surprisingly, the four juveniles who met the criteria for sadistic personality disorder had substantially higher psychopathy scores (M = 28.5) compared to those who did not meet the criteria for sadistic personality disorder (M = 19.7).

Self-directed Aggression. Only one study has examined the issue of self-directed aggression among psychopathic adolescents. Gretton (1998) found that psychopathic offenders were more likely to have a history of self-injury (37 percent) compared to nonpsychopaths (21 percent). This

203

finding is not surprising given the link between self- and other-directed aggression (*see* Plutchik and van Praag, 1997). Recent research has suggested that poor impulsive control might mediate this association (Webster and Jackson, 1997). Interestingly, Myers et al. (1995) found that adolescent inpatients with three or more impulsive behaviors had significantly higher psychopathy scores than did less impulsive patients. However, the impulsivity of the behaviors in this study is questionable since the presence or absence of a behavior was coded, not its intentionality. In addition, using the Conners Parent Rating Scales (Conners, 1989), McBride (1998) found a significant and positive correlation ($r = .27$) between the impulsive-hyperactive problems subscale and factor two of the Psychopathy Checklist: Youth Version.

In summary, the association between psychopathy and violence seen across studies suggests that violence is an integral part of the behavioral repertoire of psychopathic youths. However, to develop optimal strategies to lower this psychopathy-violence association, research is needed that explores the motivations and specific antecedents of violent behavior. This more fine-grained approach will lead to better risk management techniques with psychopathic youths.

Stability of Criminal Behavior

There is substantial evidence that desistance from aggressive behavior takes place during adolescence and early adulthood (*see* Loeber and Stouthamer-Loeber, 1998 for review). However, it is also clear that a subsample of aggressive youths do not desist (Loeber and Farrington, 1998). Two studies have examined age-related changes in patterns of offending from early adolescence to early adulthood in psychopathic and nonpsychopathic youths.

Forth and Burke (1998) examined the age-related change in a sample of psychopathic and nonpsychopathic adolescent offenders. Using the eighteen-item Hare Psychopathy Checklist-Revised, offenders were divided into high psychopathy group ($n = 23$, score of > 30) and a low psychopathy group ($n = 40$, score < 24). Official criminal records were used to code the mean number of nonviolent and violent offenses across three two-and-a-half-year age periods from thirteen to twenty and a half. To control for individual differences in the amount of time incarcerated, the offense rate was converted to the number of offenses committed per six months free. There were no significant differences between psychopathic and nonpsychopathic offenders in the rate of nonviolent offending across the age periods. However, psychopathic offenders engaged in significantly more violence in the first and last age period than did the nonpsychopathic offenders.

Results from a larger sample found a similar pattern of age-related change in offending (Gretton, 1998). Participants were 157 adolescent offenders who were followed-up on average for ten years. The Psychopathy Checklist: Youth Version was coded retrospectively using file-information data. The participants were divided into three groups: psychopaths (*n* = 38; score of > 29), a mixed group (*n* = 77; score between 18 and 28) and nonpsychopaths (*n* = 42; score of < 17). Criminal records were used to calculate rates of nonviolent and violent offending per year free in the community across three age periods: early adolescence (thirteen to fifteen), mid-adolescence (sixteen to eighteen), and early adulthood (nineteen to twenty-one).

All three groups committed lower rates of nonviolent offenses in early adolescence as compared to the two older age periods. Psychopathic youths committed significantly more nonviolent offenses only during late adolescence. With respect to violent offenses, the psychopathic and mixed groups were significantly more violent during late adolescence and early adulthood than in early adolescence. The psychopathic group was significantly more violent than the mixed group during early and late adolescence. In early adulthood, the psychopathic group was significantly more violent than the nonpsychopathic group, but no differences were noted when compared to the mixed group.

The results of these studies confirm that the propensity for violence in psychopathic youths remains relatively persistent. Further research following these offenders as they age will determine whether this pattern is chronic. Persistence in offending has particular relevance to issues surrounding the transfer of youths to adult court and will be discussed in more detail below.

Recidivism

Over the past decade, there has been considerable focus on the importance of the construct of psychopathy as a risk factor for violence in adult forensic psychiatric and correctional samples (*see* reviews by Hemphill, Hare, and Wong, 1998; Salekin, Rogers, and Sewell, 1996). Emerging research indicates that psychopathy is also a major risk factor for violence in adolescent samples.

In the first recidivism study, Forth et al. (1990) administered the eighteen-item Hare Psychopathy Checklist-Revised to a sample of seventy-five male adolescent offenders prior to their release from a secure custody facility. This sample was followed-up for an average of 27.2 months to determine failure rates. Any charge or conviction for a new offense subsequent to release was considered a failure. The majority of the sample was released during the follow-up period (94 percent) in which 79 percent of those released recidivated. Psychopathy correlated only with the number of postrelease offenses ($r = .26$).

A retrospective ten-year review of 157 male adolescents (Gretton, 1998) who had been referred by the courts for psychological assessment is the longest period over which recidivism has been evaluated thus far. Overall, 97 percent of this sample committed some offense and 68 percent committed a violent offense during the follow-up period. Psychopaths (84 percent) were more likely to reoffend violently than the mixed group (70 percent), followed by the nonpsychopaths (50 percent). The groups did not differ with respect to nonviolent or overall reoffenses.

In addition, psychopaths committed their violent offense significantly sooner (on average, forty-three months) as compared to the mixed group (on average, ninety-two months) and nonpsychopath group (on average, ninety-five months). Although prior history of violence is a major risk factor, psychopathic offenders in this study who had no prior history of violent offenses were at the same risk for violence in the follow-up periods as psychopaths with a history of violent offenses. This was the only study to date to compare psychopathic youths who violently reoffended ($n = 32$) to those few psychopathic youths ($n = 6$) who did not violently reoffend. The psychopathic youths who did not violently reoffend were older at the time of their first official offense, older at time of assessment, had higher verbal IQ scores, did not display a large difference in verbal versus performance IQ, were less likely to have a history of self-harm, and less likely to have a history of physical abuse as compared to those offenders who did violently reoffend. Additional research is crucial in identifying those protective factors for psychopathic youths who do not engage in violence.

Lewis and O'Shaughnessy (1998) investigated a number of violent risk predictors in a sample of 209 male ($n = 172$) and female ($n = 37$) adolescent offenders who were being assessed in a juvenile forensic psychiatric unit in British Columbia. They found that psychopathy was a better predictor of violence than other standard sociological (for example, violent crime by mother or father, age of onset of drug/alcohol use) and criminological risk factors (for example, age at first arrest, number or prior violent and nonviolent charges and/or convictions). However, using the Psychopathy Checklist: Youth Version, only 65 percent of the offenders were correctly classified.

Brandt et al. (1997) investigated the association between psychopathy and the length of time before rearrest for nonviolent and violent offenses. No group differences were found in the length of time prior to arrest for nonviolent offenses, although the high psychopathy group was rearrested for a violent offense significantly sooner than the low psychopathy group.

These findings demonstrate the utility of psychopathy as a major risk factor for violence. An assessment of psychopathy has practical implications in the decision-making process within the juvenile justice system. For example, assessment of risk of harm occurs at several points within the juvenile justice system (Grisso, 1998; Hoge, 1999). Juveniles can be held in a secure detention facility prior to adjudication. The decision to detain a youth varies from state to state, but typically involves consideration of the following issues: the likelihood the youth will fail to show up for the adjudication proceedings, the likelihood the youth will engage in serious violence towards self or others, or the likelihood the youth may be in danger if not detained. The assessment of psychopathy is most relevant to decisions concerning the likelihood the youth will engage in future aggressive acts against others while in the community.

Another judicial decision where risk of harm is a pertinent factor is a waiver to the criminal/adult court. A youth who has committed a serious offense who is above a certain age (often fourteen or fifteen) may be transferred to an adult court for adjudication. Recent changes in the juvenile laws in both Canada and United States have resulted in the automatic transfer of youths charged with specific serious offenses (murder and other major assaultive offenses) and being of a certain age (often fourteen) to the adult court.

The issues discussed below will still likely be relevant in many of these cases since most states and Canada provide for a hearing to determine whether the case should proceed to trial or whether the case should be remanded to juvenile court. These youths who are transferred and who are found guilty will be sentenced as adults (although in Canada certain restrictions relating to the length of sentence apply). In light of the potential negative consequences of a transfer to adult court ranging from less serious (nonconfidential nature of proceedings, record of conviction on adult record) to extremely serious (lengthy incarceration periods to the death sentence), the highest standards of practice must be used. The focus of a transfer hearing is on the danger the youth poses to society and the juvenile's amenability to rehabilitation (Kruh and Brodsky, 1997).

The issue of danger includes the likelihood of harm to others across a variety of contexts. Grisso (1998) suggests that a youth's potential harm to others be addressed with respect to the likelihood of harm to other youths and staff in juvenile facilities, the likelihood of the youth engaging in violence if he or she escapes from a juvenile facility, and the likelihood that the youth will persist in offending as an adult. The findings summarized earlier in this chapter point to the potential harm posed by psychopathic youths both within institutions and in the community. Moreover, the studies by Forth and Burke (1998) and Gretton (1998) demonstrate the serious and stable nature of a psychopathic youth's offending pattern.

Developmental Correlates of Psychopathy

Considerable research implicates the link between adverse family background and delinquency and the perpetration of violence (Haapasalo and Tremblay, 1994; Loeber and Stouthamer-Loeber, 1986; Widom, 1997). Recent research has focused on the association between psychopathy and factors such as separation from parents, early physical and emotional abuse, parental pathology, and parenting strategies. To date, five studies have examined the relationship between psychopathy and family variables using a retrospective self-report design.

Investigating the relation between family factors and psychopathy in 106 offenders and fifty community male adolescents, Burke and Forth (1996; Forth and Burke, 1998) coded a total of ten variables: childhood (physical, sexual, and emotional abuse and neglect); parental (marital discord, antisocial parents, alcohol history); and family background (lack of supervision, inconsistent discipline, separation from parents during childhood). From an interview and file review, the variables were coded dichotomously (present or absent) and summed to provide a composite score reflecting poor family background. The results indicated that poor family background was positively associated with the Psychopathy Checklist: Youth Version total and both factor scores. However, among the offender's family background, it was only associated with factor two scores. Moreover, although family factors were not meaningful predictors of psychopathy scores among adolescent offenders, they were among the community youth. For example, the Psychopathy Checklist: Youth Version total scores were predicted from a combination of antisocial parent, inconsistent discipline, and parental alcoholism.

On the basis of file information, Gretton (1998) coded the following four family background variables: history of adoption, age of separation from biological mother, age of separation from biological father, and history of physical, sexual, or emotional abuse in a sample of 157 adolescent offenders. Psychopathic offenders were separated at an earlier age both from their biological mothers (M = 7.8) and their fathers (M = 4.2) as compared to nonpsychopathic offenders (M = 10.1 from mothers, M = 7.3 from fathers). The groups did not differ according to the percentage of adolescents adopted or in rates of childhood abuse.

Adolescent psychopathy has been found to correlate positively with biological parental criminality. Watt, Ma, Lewis, Willoughby, and O'Shaughnessy (1997) assessed 155 male juvenile offenders, between the ages of 12 and 17, who were detained at an inpatient psychiatric assessment facility in British Columbia. Parental criminal behavior was determined based on a review of the youths' file and categorized according to whether the offense was violent or nonviolent. The Psychopathy Checklist: Youth Version total scores were found to correlate with maternal criminality (r = .18) and maternal nonviolent offenses (r = .15). Maternal (r = .16) and paternal (r = .19) criminality correlated more strongly with factor two than factor one; however, only paternal violent behavior correlated with factor two (r = .21).

McBride (1998) investigated the association between family background variables and psychopathy in two adolescent offender samples. In the first study, the files of 233 sex offenders were used to code psychopathy and the following nine family background variables: physical abuse, sexual abuse, emotional abuse, maternal criminality, maternal drug abuse, maternal alcohol abuse, paternal criminality, paternal drug abuse, and paternal alcohol abuse. The parental variables were collapsed to form a global maternal and paternal social deviance score. A history of physical abuse and maternal social deviance were related to the Psychopathy Checklist: Youth Version total and factor scores. Furthermore, a history of sexual abuse and paternal social deviance were significantly related to total and factor two scores. No significant correlations were found between psychopathy and emotional abuse.

In the second sample, the association between psychopathy, physical abuse, maternal social deviance, and parental rearing practices was assessed in seventy-four male adolescent offenders and their mothers.

Similar to the previous study, a history of physical abuse by the father (but not the mother) and negative parental rearing practices were found to be significantly related to the Psychopathy Checklist: Youth Version scores. Maternal psychopathy (measured by the Hare Self-report Psychopathy Scale SRP-II completed by the mothers) was significantly related to the Psychopathy Checklist: Youth Version total and factor two scores.

Larroche and Toupin (1996) examined the association between parental characteristics (maternal psychopathology, paternal antisocial personality), parent-child relationships (level of supervision, physical and nonphysical punishment, communication, attachment, rules, and family activities), and psychopathy in a sample of sixty adolescent male offenders. Level of supervision and involvement in family activities were the only variables that differentiated psychopaths from nonpsychopaths. Nonpsychopathic offenders were more likely to be adequately supervised by their parents and participated more in family activities as compared to the psychopathic offenders.

These studies provide evidence that psychopathy is associated with a range of adverse family factors: physical abuse, sexual abuse, parental criminality, parental alcoholism, childhood separation, maternal psychopathic traits, and poor parenting strategies (inadequate parental supervision, inconsistent discipline). However, for many of these variables, the relation with psychopathy has not been consistent across studies. The failure to replicate could be partly due to methodological issues (for example, most are based on retrospective self-reports from the adolescent, others on maternal self-reports) or in the manner in which the variables were operationalized.

It is unlikely that one variable or cluster of variables (for example, family background) acts in isolation in the development of psychopathy. What may be more probable is that the developmental pathways to psychopathy are multiple and varied. More than likely, these pathways are comprised of interactions between genetic, child and parental factors, and environmental stressors.

Intervention Effectiveness

To date, there has been no controlled evaluation of intervention programs for psychopathic youths. Grisso (1998) has recommended assessing the following characteristics as a method to judge the potential responsiveness of a youth to intervention: amount of psychological discomfort experienced, capacity for adult attachment, and chronicity (duration) of personality traits and behaviors. Youths with psychopathic characteristics are likely to exhibit little psychological discomfort, have superficial relationships with others, and often have a lengthy history of antisocial behavior. Thus, from a treatment standpoint, psychopathic youths present a poorer prognosis for rehabilitation than other youths.

A limited number of studies have considered treatment of psychopathic youths. Currently, only one study has examined the motivation of psychopathic youths for treatment. Johansen et al. (1997) found that psychopathy was significantly correlated with treatment noncompliance ($r = .25$) in eighty-one adolescent offenders.

Similarly, only two studies have assessed treatment outcome in youths assessed for psychopathy. The first study provided preliminary data from 220 adolescent sex offenders released after treatment assessed using the Psychopathy Checklist: Youth Version and followed up for an average of 56 months (Gretton, McBride, O'Shaugnessy, and Hare, 1999).

Offenders were divided into three groups based on their Psychopathy Checklist: Youth Version scores: high psychopathy group ($n = 29$), mixed group ($n = 111$), and low group ($n = 80$). Offenders in the high psychopathy group recidivated sooner than the other offenders. On average, the high psychopathic group recidivated within nineteen months versus twenty-seven months for those in the middle group and thirty-six months for those in the low psychopathy group. Furthermore, the rate of nonviolent recidivism was twice as high for the high group (66 percent versus 27 percent for the low group), while the rate of nonsexual violent recidivism was almost triple for the high group (35 percent versus 13 percent, respectively). The rates for sexual recidivism were considerably higher in the high psychopathy group (30 percent) than in the low psychopathy group (16 percent).

The treatment provided to these adolescents was focused on their sexual deviance; however, in light of the relatively high nonsexual reoffending rates of the psychopaths, targeting their more generalized antisocial tendencies may be more important than addressing their sexual deviancy (Hare, 1998).

Ridenour (1996) correlated the eighteen-item Hare Psychopathy Checklist-Revised with three measures of treatment outcome in twenty-six adolescent offenders in a behaviorally based residential treatment unit. Psychopathy was correlated with the number of level one setbacks ($r = .61$; level one is the lowest level of the five -level system), number of offenses committed in one-year follow-up ($r = .36$) and the highest level obtained in the program (r = -.34). Psychopathy identified those offenders who did poorly in treatment versus those who succeeded in the program.

The primary focus of research should be on creating, implementing, and evaluating intervention programs for youths with psychopathic characteristics. Lösel (1998) suggests that the optimal intervention program will be multimodal (school, family, peers, community), long-lasting and early starting, and target both the characteristics of the youth and parental behavior. It is likely that the degree of support that parents provide will be an important influence on how successful the intervention strategy is. However, if psychopathic youths come from homes characterized by poor parent-youth relationships or if the youths' parents exhibit antisocial or psychopathic traits, it is unlikely they will provide the necessary support for rehabilitation. The recent guidelines for the treatment of adult psychopaths developed by Wong and Hare (in press) could be adapted readily to juvenile delinquents.

Conclusions

Research summarized in this chapter provides evidence that the concept of psychopathy can be extended from adults to adolescents. Although the empirical research is still in its early stages, there are a number of conclusions that can be drawn:

1. Psychopathic youths resemble youths with severe conduct disorder with childhood-onset type and youths with comorbid diagnosis of conduct disorder and attention deficit hyperactivity disorder, and impulsivity. However, most youths with childhood-onset type conduct disorder or with comorbid conduct disorder and attention deficit hyperactivity disorder do not possess the affective and interpersonal features of the prototypical psychopath. Any assessment of psychopathy in adolescence should be based on the Psychopathy Checklist: Youth Version.

2. Psychopathy as measured by the Psychopathy Checklist: Youth Version is a dimensional measure of the degree to which the adolescent matches the prototypical psychopath. Although a categorical diagnosis of psychopathy is useful for some research and clinical applications, it is not possible to specify an optimal cutoff that would maximize diagnostic efficiency across all situations. For clinical applications (for example, risk

assessment, treatment planning), dimensional ratings of psychopathy provide the most relevant information for decision-making purposes. In addition, dimensional ratings permit clinical users to make distinctions among adolescents even in settings where the base rate of psychopathy is very high or very low.

3. Assessing psychopathic traits in adolescence provides meaningful information about the long-term risk for violence. Studies have shown that psychopathic adolescent offenders engage in more serious and more frequent offending, and are more stable in their offending across time as compared to their nonpsychopathic counterparts.

4. Assessment of risk for violence should include psychopathy as a risk factor but also should include other risk factors that have been empirically demonstrated as relating to violent behavior in youths (see Bartel and Forth, 1999), such as frequency and severity of past violent behaviors, substance use, association with deviant peers, attitudes that condone violence, poor social involvement, and poor parent-youth relations.

5. Psychopathic adolescents engage in more disruptive behavior within institutions, respond poorly to supervision, and are more likely to escape than are nonpsychopathic adolescents. To facilitate individual case management planning, clinical staff should be knowledgeable about psychopathic characteristics in the youth (for example, level of security, amount of supervision required).

6. Youths with psychopathic features likely will be resistant to intervention; however, this does not mean that intervention will not have an impact on their behaviors. Moreover, in light of the poor prognosis for these youths, the challenge facing researchers and clinicians is to develop, implement, and evaluate intervention programs.

This chapter has amply demonstrated the importance of the construct of psychopathy to the juvenile criminal justice and mental health systems. There are some legitimate concerns over the potential for misuse of any scale designed to assess psychopathy in youths, in particular with respect to accessibility to intervention (Ogloff and Lyon, 1998; Zinger and Forth, 1997). Concerns about the potential misuse of the Hare Psychopathy Checklist-Revised have been described by Hare (1998b). In adult court proceedings, a diagnosis of psychopathy is typically equated with a high risk of violent recidivism and an inability to benefit from treatment (Zinger and Forth, 1997). Moreover, once diagnosed as psychopathic, the label is likely to stick, with long-term negative repercussions for the individual. The ultimate goal for developing an assessment instrument to detect characteristics of psychopathy in younger people is to provide appropriate intervention programs proactively. Given the persistent nature of this disorder, the personal, social, and financial costs of not investing in early intervention are not ethically acceptable alternatives.

References

Achenback, T. M. 1991. *Manual for the Child Behavior Checklist and 1991 Profile.* Burlington, Vermont: University of Vermont, Department of Psychiatry.

Achenback, T.M. and C. Edelbrock. 1983. *Manual of the Child Behavior Checklist and Revised Child Behavior Profile.* Burlington, Vermont: University of Vermont, Department of Psychiatry.

Albert, R. S., T. R. Brigante, and M. Chase. 1959. The Psychopathic Personality: A Content Analysis of the Concept. *Journal of General Psychology.* 60:17-28.

American Psychiatric Association. 1980. *Diagnostic and Statistical Manual of Mental Disorders*, 3rd ed. Washington, D.C.: American Psychiatric Association.

————. 1994. *Diagnostic and Statistical Manual of Mental Disorders*, 4th ed. Washington, D.C.: American Psychiatric Association.

Archer, R. P. 1992. *MMPI-A: Assessing Adolescent Psychopathology.* Hillsdale, New Jersey: Lawrence Erlbaum Associates, Inc.

Bauer, D. 1999. Psychopathy and Adolescent Females: Personality, Cognition, and Behavior. Unpublished doctoral dissertation. Finch University of Health Sciences/Chicago Medical School, Chicago, Illinois.

Blair, R. J. R. 1997. Moral Reasoning and the Child with Psychopathic Tendencies. *Personality and Individual Differences.* 22:731-739.

Block, J. and J. H. Block. 1980. *The California Q-Set.* Palo Alto, California: Consulting Psychologists Press.

Brandt, J. R., W. A. Kennedy, C. J. Patrick, and J. J. Curtin. 1997. Assessment of Psychopathy in a Population of Incarcerated Adolescent Offenders. *Psychological Assessment.* 9:429-435.

Brown, S. L. and A. E. Forth. 1997. Psychopathy and Sexual Assault: Static Risk Factors, Emotional Precursors, and Rapist Subtypes. *Journal of Consulting and Clinical Psychology.* 65:848-857.

Burke, H. C. and A. E. Forth. 1996. Psychopathy and Familial Experiences as Antecedents to Violence: a Cross-sectional Study of Young Offenders and Nonoffending Youth. Unpublished manuscript, Carleton University, Ottawa, Ontario, Canada.

Butcher, J. N., C. L. Williams, J. R. Graham, R. Archer, A. Tellegen, Y. S. Ben-Porath, and B. Kaemmer. *1992. MMPI: A Manual for Administration, Scoring, and Interpretation.* Minneapolis, Minnesota: University of Minnesota Press.

Christian, R. E., P. J. Frick, N. L. Hill, L. Tyler, and D. R. Frazer. 1997. Psychopathy and Conduct Problems in Children: Implications for Subtyping Children with Conduct Problems. *Journal of the American Academy of Child and Adolescent Psychiatry.* Jci:33 2/1 1

Cleckley, H. R. 1976. *The Mask of Sanity.* St. Louis, Missouri: Mosby.

Conners, C. K. 1989. *Conners' Parent Rating Scales-48.* Toronto, Ontario: Multi-Health Systems.

Cooke, D. J. 1998. Psychopathy Across Cultures. In D. J. Cooke, A. E. Forth, and R. D. Hare, eds. *Psychopathy: Theory, Research, and Implications for Society*, pp. 13-45. Dordrecht, The Netherlands: Kluwer.

Dempster, R. J. and S. D. Hart. 1996, March. Utility of the FBI's Crime Classification Manual: Coverage, Reliability and Validity for Adolescent Murderers. Paper presented at the Biennial Meeting of the American Psychology-Law Society (APA Div. 41), Hilton Head, South Carolina.

Dixon, M., L. Robinson, S. D. Hart, H. Gretton, M. McBride, and R. O'Shaugnessy. 1995. Crime Classification Manual: Reliability and Validity in Juvenile Sex Offenders [Abstract]. *Canadian Psychology.* 36:20.

Douglas, J. E., A. W. Burgess, A. G. Burgess, and R. K. Ressler. 1992. *The Crime Classification Manual: A Standard System for Investigating and Classifying Violent Crimes.* New York: Lexington.

Fisher, L. and R. J. R. Blair. 1997. Cognitive Impairment and its Relationship to Psychopathic Tendencies in Children with Emotional and Behavioral Difficulties. *Journal of Abnormal Child Psychology.* 26:511-519.

Forth, A. E. 1995. *Psychopathy and Young Offenders: Prevalence, Family Background, and Violence*. Program Branch Users Report. Ottawa, Ontario: Ministry of the Solicitor General of Canada.

Forth, A. E., S. L. Brown, S. D. Hart, and R. D. Hare. 1996. The Assessment of Psychopathy in Male and Female Noncriminals: Reliability and Validity. *Personality and Individual Differences*. 20:531-543.

Forth, A. E. and H. Burke. 1998. Psychopathy in Adolescence: Assessment, Violence, and Developmental Precursors. In R. D., Cooke, A. E. Forth, and R. D. Hare, eds. *Psychopathy: Theory, Research, and Implications for Society*, pp. 205-229. Dordrecht, The Netherlands: Kluwer.

Forth, A. E., S. D. Hart, and R. D. Hare. 1990. Assessment of Psychopathy in Male Young Offenders. *Psychological Assessment: A Journal of Consulting and Clinical Psychology.* 2:342-344.

Forth, A. E., D. S. Kosson, and R. D. Hare (in press). *The Psychopathy Checklist: Youth Version*. Unpublished test manual. Toronto, Ontario: Multi-Health Systems.

Frick, P. J. 1998. Callous-unemotional Traits and Conduct Problems: Applying the Two-factor Model of Psychopathy to Children. In D. Cooke, A. E. Forth, and R. D. Hare, eds. *Psychopathy: Theory, Research, and Implications for Society*, pp. 161-187. Dordrecht, The Netherlands: Kluwer.

Frick, P. J., B. S. O'Brien, J. M. Wootton, and K. McBurnett. 1994. Psychopathy and Conduct Problems in Children. *Journal of Abnormal Psychology*. 103:700-707.

Gacono, C. B. and J. R. Meloy. 1994. *Rorschach Assessment of Aggressive and Psychopathic Personalities*. Hillsdale, New Jersey: Lawrence Erlbaum.

Gretton, H. M. 1998. Psychopathy and Recidivism in Adolescence: A Ten-year Retrospective Follow-up. Unpublished doctoral dissertation. University of British Columbia, Vancouver, British Columbia.

Gretton, H., M. McBride, K. Lewis, R. O'Shaughnessy, and R. D. Hare. 1994. Predicting Patterns of Criminal Activity in Adolescent Sexual Psychopaths [Abstract]. *Canadian Psychology*. 35:50.

Gretton, H. M., M. McBride, R. O'Shaugnessey, and R. D. Hare. 1999. Psychopathy and Recidivism in Adolescent Sex Offenders. Manuscript in preparation.

Grisso, T. 1998. *Forensic Evaluation of Juveniles*. Sarasota, Florida: Professional Resource Press.

Haapasalo, J. R., and E. Tremblay. 1994. Physically Aggressive Boys from Ages 6 to 12: Family Background, Parenting Behavior, and Prediction of Delinquency. *Journal of Consulting and Clinical Psychology*. 62:1044-1052.

Hare, R. D. 1980. A Research Scale for the Assessment of Psychopathy in Criminal Populations. *Personality and Individual Differences*. 1:111-119.

————. 1983. Diagnosis of Antisocial Personality Disorder in Two Prison Populations. *American Journal of Psychiatry*. 140:887-890.

————. 1985. Comparison of Procedures for the Assessment of Psychopathy. *Journal of Consulting and Clinical Psychology*. 53:7-16.

————. 1991. *The Hare Psychopathy Checklist - Revised*. Toronto, Ontario: Multi-Health Systems.

————. 1996. Psychopathy: A Clinical Construct Whose Time Has Come. *Criminal Justice and Behavior*. 23:25-54.

————. 1998a. Psychopaths and Their Nature: Implications for the Mental Health and Criminal Justice Systems. In T. M. Millon, E. Simonsen, M. Birket-Smith, and R. Davis, eds. *Psychopathy: Antisocial, Criminal and Violent Behavior*, pp. 188-212. New York: Guilford Press.

————. 1998b. The Hare Psychopathy Checklist-Revised: Some Issues Concerning its Use and Misuse. *Legal and Criminological Psychology*. 3:101-122.

Hare, R. D., T. J. Harpur, A. R. Hakstian, A. E. Forth, S. D. Hart, and J P. Newman. 1990. The Revised Psychopathy Checklist: Reliability and Factor Structure. *Psychological Assessment: A Journal of Consulting and Clinical Psychology*. 2:388- 341.

Harpur, T. J., R. D. Hare, and A. R. Hakstian. 1989. Two-factor Conceptualization of Psychopathy: Construct Validity and Assessment Implications. *Psychological Assessment: A Journal of Consulting and Clinical Psychology*. 1:6-17.

Hart, S. D., D. N. Cox, and R. D. Hare. 1995. *Manual for the Psychopathy Checklist: Screening Version (PCL: SV)*. Toronto, Ontario: Multi-Health Systems.

Hart, S. D., A. E. Forth, and R. D. Hare. 1991. The MCMI-II as a Measure of Psychopathy. *Journal of Personality Disorders*. 5:318-327.

Hart, S. D. and R. D. Hare. 1989. Discriminant Validity of the Psychopathy Checklist. *Psychological Assessment: A Journal of Consulting and Clinical Psychology*. 1:211-218.

————. 1997. Psychopathy: Assessment and Association with Criminal Conduct. In D. M. Stoff, J. Brieling, and J. Maser, eds. *Handbook of Antisocial Behavior*, pp. 22-35. New York: Wiley.

Hathaway, S. R. and J. C. McKinley. 1943. *The Minnesota Multiphasic Personality Inventory*, Revised Edition. Minneapolis, Minnesota: University of Minnesota Press.

Hemphill, J. F., R. D. Hare, and S. Wong. 1998. Psychopathy and Recidivism: A Review. *Legal and Criminological Psychology*. 3:139-170.

Hemphill, J., S. D. Hart, and R. D. Hare. 1994. Psychopathy and Substance Use. *Journal of Personality Disorders*. 8:169-180.

Henry, B., A. Caspi, T. E. Moffitt, and P. A. Silva. 1996. Temperamental and Familial Predictors of Violent and Nonviolent Criminal Convictions: From Age 3 to Age 18. *Developmental Psychology*. 32:614-623.

Hodgins, S., G. Côté, and D. Ross. 1992. Predictive Validity of the French Version of Hare's Psychopathy Checklist [Abstract]. *Canadian Psychology*. 33:301.

Hoge, R. D. 1999. An Expanded Role for Psychological Assessments in Juvenile Justice Systems. *Criminal Justice and Behavior*. 26:251-266.

Hume, M. P., W. A. Kennedy, C. J. Patrick, and D. J. Partyka. 1996. Examination of the MMPI-A for the Assessment of Psychopathy in Incarcerated Adolescent Male Offenders. *International Journal of Offender Therapy and Comparative Criminology.* 40:224-233.

Kosson, D. S., S. S. Smith, and J. P. Newman. 1990. Evaluation of the Construct Validity of Psychopathy in Black and White Male Inmates: Three Preliminary Studies. *Journal of Abnormal Psychology*. 99:250-259.

Kruger, R. F., P. S. Schmutte, A. Caspi, T. E. Moffitt, K. Campbell, and P. A. Silva. 1994. Personality Traits Are Linked to Crime among Men and Women: Evidence from a Birth Cohort. *Journal of Abnormal Psychology*. 103:328-338.

Kruh, I. P. and S. L. Brodsky. 1997. Clinical Evaluations for Transfer of Juveniles to Criminal Court: Current Practices and Future Research. *Behavioral Sciences and the Law*. 15:151-165.

Lahey, B. B. and R. Loeber. 1997. Attention-Deficit/Hyperactivity Disorder, Oppositional Defiant Disorder, Conduct Disorder, and Adult Antisocial Behavior: A Life Span Perspective. In D. M. Stoff, J. Brieling, and J. Maser, eds. *Handbook of Antisocial Behavior*, pp. 51-59. New York: Wiley.

Laroche, I. 1996. Les Composantes Psychologiques et Comportementales Parentales Associées À La Psychopathie du Contrevenant Juvénile. Unpublished doctoral thesis. University of Montreal, Montreal, Quebec.

Laroche, I., and J. Toupin. 1996, August. Psychopathic Delinquents: A Family Contribution? Paper presented at the XXVI International Congress of Psychology. Montreal, Quebec.

Lewis, K. and R. O'Shaughnessy. 1998, June. Predictors of Violent Recidivism in Juvenile Offenders. Poster presented at the annual convention of the Canadian Psychological Association, Edmonton, Alberta.

Lilienfeld, S. O. and B. P. Andrews. 1996. Development and Preliminary Validation of a Self-report Measure of Psychopathic Personality Traits in Noncriminal Populations. *Journal of Personality Assessment.* 66:488-534.

Loeber, R. and M. Stouthamer-Loeber. 1986. Family Factors as Correlates and Predictors of Juvenile Conduct Problems and Delinquency. In M. Tonry and N. Morris, eds. *Crime and Justice* (Vol. 7), pp. 29-149. Chicago: University of Chicago Press.

————. 1998. Development of Juvenile Aggression and Violence: Some Common Misconceptions and Controversies. *American Psychologist.* 53:242-259.

Lösel, F. 1998. Treatment and Management of Psychopaths. In D. Cooke, A. E. Forth, and R. D. Hare, eds. *Psychopathy: Theory, Research, and Implications for Society*, pp. 303-354. Dordrecht, The Netherlands: Kluwer.

Lynam, D. R. 1996. Early Identification of Chronic Offenders: Who Is the Fledgling Psychopath? *Psychological Bulletin.* 120:209-234.

————. 1997. Pursuing the Psychopath: Capturing the Fledgling Psychopath in a Nomological Net. *Journal of Abnormal Psychology.* 10:425-438.

Mailloux, D. 1999. Victimization, Coping, and Psychopathy: Associations with Violent Behaviour among Female Offenders. Unpublished master's thesis. Carleton University, Ottawa, Ontario, Canada.

Mailloux, D. L., A. E. Forth, and D. G. Kroner. 1997. Psychopathy and Substance Use in Adolescent Male Offenders. *Psychological Reports.* 81:529-530.

Mannuzza, S., R. G. Klein, A. Bessler, P. Malloy, and M. LaPadula. 1993. Adult Outcome of Hyperactive Boys: Educational Achievement, Occupational Rank, and Psychiatric Status. *Archives of General Psychiatry.* 50:565-576.

McBride, M. 1998. Individual and Familial Risk Factors for Adolescent Psychopathy. Unpublished doctoral dissertation. University of British Columbia, Vancouver, British Columbia.

Myers, W. C. and R. Blashfield. 1997. Psychopathology and Personality in Juvenile Sexual Homicide Offenders. *Journal of the American Academy of Psychiatry and the Law.* 25:497-508.

Myers, W. C., R. C. Burket, and H. E. Harris. 1995. Adolescent Psychopathy in Relation to Delinquent Behaviors, Conduct Disorder, and Personality Disorders. *Journal of Forensic Sciences.* 40:436-440.

Neary, A. 1991. DSM-III and Psychopathy Checklist Assessment of Antisocial Personality Disorder in Black and White Female Felons. *Dissertation Abstracts International.* 51(7-B):3605.

Ogloff, J .R .P. and D. R. Lyon. 1998. Legal Issues Associated with the Concept of Psychopathy. In D. Cooke, A. E. Forth, and R. D. Hare, eds. *Psychopathy: Theory, Research, and Implications for Society,* pp. 401-422. Dordrecht, The Netherlands: Kluwer.

Ogloff, J., S. Wong, and A. Greenwood. 1990. Treating Criminal Psychopaths in a Therapeutic Community Program. *Behavioral Sciences and the Law.* 8:81-90.

Pan, V. 1998, March. Institutional Behavior in Psychopathic Juvenile Offenders. Poster presented at the Biennial Conference of the American Psychology-Law Society, Redondo Beach, California.

Plutchik, R. and H. M. van Praag. 1997. Suicide, Impulsivity, and Antisocial Behavior. In D. M. Stoff, J. Brieling, and J. Maser, eds. *Handbook of Antisocial Behavior,* pp. 101-108. New York: Wiley.

Poythress, N. G., J. F. Edens, and S. O. Lilienfeld. 1998. Criterion-based Validity of the Psychopathic Personality Inventory in a Prison Sample. *Psychological Assessment.* 10:426-430.

Rice, M.E., G. T. Harris, and C. A. Cormier. 1992. An Evaluation of a Maximum Security Therapeutic Community for Psychopaths and Other Mentally Disordered Offenders. *Law and Human Behavior.* 16:399-412.

Ridenour, T. A. 1996. Utility Analyses of the Psychopathy Checklist, Revised and Moffitt's Taxonomy for a Rehabilitation Program for Juvenile Delinquents. Unpublished doctoral dissertation. Bell State University, Muncie, Indiana.

Rogers, R., K. L. Dion, and E. Lynett. 1992. Diagnostic Validity of Antisocial Personality Disorder: A Prototypical Analysis. *Law and Human Behavior.* 16:677-689.

Rogers, R., J. Johansen, J. J. Chang, and R. T. Salekin. 1997. Predictors of Adolescent Psychopathy: Oppositional and Conduct-disordered Symptoms. *Journal of the American Academy of Psychiatry and the Law.* 25:261-271.

Rowe, R. 1997. Unpublished raw data. Carleton University, Ottawa, Ontario, Canada.

Rutherford, M. J., A. I. Alterman, J. S. Cacciola, and J. R. McKay. 1998. Gender Differences in the Relationship of Antisocial Personality Disorder Criteria to Psychopathy Checklist-revised Scores. *Journal of Personality Disorders.* 12:69-76.

Rutherford, M. J., A. I. Alterman, J. S. Cacciola, and E. C. Snyder. 1996. Gender Differences in Diagnosing Antisocial Personality Disorder in Methadone Patients. *American Journal of Psychiatry.* 152:1309-1316.

Salekin, R. T., R. Rogers, and K. W. Sewell. 1996. A Review and Meta-analysis of the Psychopathy Checklist and Psychopathy Checklist-Revised: Predictive Validity of Dangerousness. *Clinical Psychology: Science and Practice.* 3:203-215.

Selzer, M. L. 1971. The Michigan Alcoholism Screening Test: The Quest for a New Diagnostic Instrument. *American Journal of Psychiatry.* 127:89-94.

Skinner, H. 1982. The Drug Abuse Screening Test. *Addictive Behavior.* 7:363-371.

Smith, A. M., C. B. Gacono, and L. Kaufman. 1997. A Rorschach Comparison of Psychopathic and Nonpsychopathic Conduct Disordered Adolescents. *Journal of Clinical Psychology.* 53:289-300.

Smith, S. S., and J. P. Newman. 1990. Alcohol and Drug Abuse/Dependence Disorders in Psychopathic and Nonpsychopathic Criminal Offenders. *Journal of Abnormal Psychology.* 99:430-439.

Stafford, E. 1997. Psychopathy as a Predictor of Adolescents at Risk for Inpatient Violence. Unpublished doctoral dissertation. University of Virginia, Charlottesville, Virginia.

Stålenheim, E. G. and L. von-Knorring. 1996. Psychopathy and Axis I and Axis II Psychiatric Disorders in a Forensic Psychiatric Population in Sweden. *Acta-Psychiatrica-Scandinavica.* 94:217-223.

Stanford, M., D. Ebner, J. Patton, and J. Williams. 1994. Multi-impulsivity within an Adolescent Psychiatric Population. *Personality and Individual Differences.* 16:395-402.

Strachan, C. 1993. Assessment of Psychopathy in Female Offenders. Unpublished doctoral dissertation. University of British Columbia, Vancouver, British Columbia.

Sullivan, L. E. 1996. Assessment of Psychopathy Using the MMPI-A: Validity in Male Adolescent Forensic Patients. Unpublished master's thesis. Simon Fraser University, Burnaby, British Columbia.

Tennent, G., D. Tennent, H. Prins, and A. Bedford. 1990. Psychopathic Disorder: A Useful Clinical Concept? *Medicine, Science, and the Law.* 30:38-44.

Tolman, R. M. 1989. The Development of a Measure of Psychological Maltreatment of Women by their Partners. *Violence and Victims.* 4:159-177.

Toupin, J., H. Mercier, M. Déry, G. Côté, and S. Hodgins. 1996. Validity of the Hare Psychopathy Checklist-Revised for Adolescents. In D. J. Cooke, A. E. Forth, J. P. Newman, and R. D. Hare, eds. *Issues in Criminological and Legal Psychology: No. 24, International Perspectives on Psychopathy*, pp. 143-145. Leicester, England: British Psychological Society.

Vincent, G. M., R. R. Corrado, I. M. Cohen, and C. Odgers. 1999, July. Identification of Psychopathy in Young Offenders: The Utility of Two Measures. Paper presented at the International Law and Psychology meeting, Dublin, Ireland.

Walker, J. L., B. B. Lahey, G. W. Hynd, and C. L. Frame. 1987. Comparison of Specific Patterns of Antisocial Behavior in Children with Conduct Disorder with and Without Coexisting Hyperactivity. *Journal of Consulting and Clinical Psychology*. 55:910-913.

Watt, K., S. Ma, K. Lewis, T. Willoughby, and R. O'Shaughnessy. 1997, June. The Relationship between Parental Criminal Behavior and Youth Psychopathy. Poster presented at the Annual convention of the Canadian Psychological Association, Toronto, Ontario.

Webster, C. D. and M. A. Jackson. 1997. *Impulsivity: New Directions in Research and Clinical Practice*. New York: Guilford Press.

White, J. L., T. E. Moffitt, R. Earls, L. Robins, and P. A. Silva. 1990. How Early Can We Tell? Predictors of Childhood Conduct Disorder and Adolescent Delinquency. *Criminology*. 28:507-533.

Widom, C. S. 1997. Child Abuse, Neglect, and Witnessing Violence. In D. M. Stoff, J. Brieling, and J. Maser, eds. *Handbook of Antisocial Behavior*, pp. 159-170. New York: Wiley.

Wootton, J. M., P. J. Frick, K. K. Shelton, and P. Silverthorn. 1997. Ineffective Parenting and Childhood Conduct Problems: The Moderating Role of Callous-Unemotional Traits. *Journal of Consulting and Clinical Psychology*. 65:301-308.

Wong, S. 1985. *The Criminal and Institutional Behaviors of Psychopaths*. Ottawa, Ontario: Programs Branch User Report, Ministry of the Solicitor General of Canada.

Wong, S. and R. D. Hare (in press). *Program Guidelines for the Institutional Treatment of Violent Psychopaths*. Toronto, Ontario: Multi-Health Systems.

Zinger, I. and A. E. Forth. 1998. Psychopathy and Canadian Criminal Proceedings: The Potential for Human Rights Abuses. *Canadian Journal of Criminology*. 40:237-276.

Effective Family-based Treatments for Juvenile Offenders: Multisystemic Therapy and Functional Family Therapy

8

Scott W. Henggeler, Ph.D.
Director, Family Services Research Center
Medical University of South Carolina
Charleston, South Carolina

The fields of family therapy and family-based services are replete with treatment models that are not operationalized and have no or minimal empirical support (Henggeler, Borduin, and Mann, 1993). Though focusing on the family, these approaches rarely address the known determinants of adolescent criminal behavior and have poor track records in overcoming barriers to service access.

The purpose of the present review is to examine the two family-based treatment models which, based on criteria set by respected reviewers, have significant empirical support in treating juvenile offenders. More specifically, Elliott's series on *Blueprints for Violence Prevention* (1998) reviewed more than 450 delinquency, drug, and violence prevention programs and concluded that only 10 met criteria of effectiveness. These criteria included (a) evaluation with strong research designs, (b) observed decreases in antisocial behavior that were sustained beyond treatment termination, and (c) program replication across multiple sites. Of these ten programs, two, multisystemic therapy and functional family therapy, provided treatment for juvenile offenders and their families, while the others focused on younger children or provided services that were not family based.

The decision to focus this paper on multisystemic therapy (Henggeler, Schoenwald, Borduin, Rowland, and Cunningham, 1998) and functional family therapy (Alexander and Parsons, 1982) is supported by the conclusions of other respected reviewers. For example, in Farrington and Welsh's (1999) review of delinquency prevention using family-based interventions, multisystemic therapy was the only approach used directly with juvenile offenders that was deemed effective. Similarly, Kazdin and Weisz (1998) and Tate, Reppucci, and Mulvey (1995) have concluded that multisystemic therapy is a highly promising treatment for youths presenting serious clinical problems.

This paper examines the clinical interventions provided by multisystemic therapy and functional family therapy, their respective service delivery models, the clinical outcomes observed for each approach, and their cost effectiveness. Finally, the fundamental characteristics of multisystemic therapy and functional family therapy that are hypothesized to account for their effectiveness are summarized. These characteristics represent signposts for the development of effective family-based services. First, however, the empirical foundations for the development of the interventions used in multisystemic therapy and functional family therapy are briefly examined.

Empirical Foundations

The development of multisystemic therapy and functional family therapy has benefitted from decades of basic and applied research. The basic research generally has examined the correlates or predictors of antisocial behavior, often using complex longitudinal and multivariate designs. The applied research consists of numerous controlled outcome studies that have been synthesized by reviewers conducting meta-analyses. Together, these research literatures suggest the necessary foci and the nature of effective interventions for youthful antisocial behavior.

Determinants of Adolescent Criminal Behavior

The empirical literature strongly supports a social-ecological view (Bronfenbrenner, 1979) of antisocial behavior in children and adolescents. The central tenet of this view is that behavior is multidetermined through the reciprocal interplay of the child and his or her social ecology, including the family, peers, school, neighborhood, and other community settings. Consistent with this perspective, associations have been observed between various forms of antisocial behavior and key characteristics of individual youths and the social systems in which they are embedded. In general, these correlates are relatively constant, whether the examined antisocial behavior is conduct disorder (Kazdin, 1987; McMahon and Wells, 1989), delinquency and violence (Elliott, 1994; Loeber and Farrington, 1998), or substance abuse (Hawkins, Catalano, and Miller, 1992; Office of Technology Assessment, 1991).

A generic list of identified correlates includes:

- Individual: low verbal skills, favorable attitudes toward anti social behavior, psychiatric symptoms, cognitive bias to attribute hostile intentions to others

- Family: lack of monitoring; ineffective discipline; low warmth; high conflict; parental difficulties such as drug abuse, psychiatric conditions, and criminality

- Peer: association with deviant peers, poor relationship skills, low association with prosocial peers

- School: low achievement; dropout; low commitment to education; aspects of the schools, such as weak structure and chaotic environment

- Neighborhood and community: high mobility; low support available from neighbors, church, and so forth; high disorganization; and criminal subculture

In light of the multiple known determinants of antisocial behavior, at least twenty research groups have conducted sophisticated causal modeling studies in an attempt to describe the interrelations among these correlates. Findings from the fields of delinquency (Henggeler, 1991) and substance abuse (Henggeler, 1997) have been relatively clear and consistent. First, association with deviant peers is virtually always a powerful direct predictor of antisocial behavior. Second, family relations either predict antisocial behavior directly (contributing unique variance) or indirectly through predicting association with deviant peers. Third, school difficulties predict association with deviant peers. Fourth, neighborhood and community support characteristics add small portions of unique variance or have an indirect role in predicting antisocial behavior. Across studies, investigators have consistently shown that antisocial behavior of youths is linked directly or indirectly with key characteristics of youths and of the systems in which they interact.

The clinical implications of these findings seem relatively straightforward. If the primary goal of treatment is to optimize the probability of decreasing rates of antisocial behavior, then treatment approaches must have the flexibility to attenuate the multiple known risk factors for antisocial behavior, while enhancing protective factors. That is, effective treatment must have the capacity to intervene comprehensively, at individual, family, peer, school, and possibly even neighborhood levels. Indeed, at least in the area of delinquency, several reviewers have rejected similar conclusions (Henggeler, 1989; Melton and Pagliocca, 1992; Mulvey, Arthur, and Reppucci, 1993; Tolan and Guerra, 1994).

General Characteristics of Effective Offender Rehabilitation

Clear parallels are evident between the characteristics of effective services for adult offenders and those for juvenile offenders. Regarding adult offenders, Gendreau (Gendreau, 1996a, 1996b; Gendreau and Goggin, 1997) has summarized the findings of meta-analyses. *Effective* interventions tend to:

- use behavioral strategies

- provide services in the natural environment

- provide comprehensive services to address multiple needs

- deliver intensive services, albeit for a limited time

- emphasize the development of prosocial relations

- target known risk factors

- provide individualized services

- provide access to aftercare

- maintain high levels of quality assurance

In contrast, *ineffective* services tend to:

- include intrapsychic, nondirective, and medically oriented interventions

- address risk factors that are weak predictors of criminal behavior

- emphasize punishment (for example, boot camps, home confinement)

Similarly, meta-analyses for treatments of juvenile offenders (Lipsey and Wilson, 1998) have shown that more effective services use behavioral interventions, provide comprehensive services, and address a variety of risk factors in the offender's social ecology. In contrast, less effective services were narrow in focus (for example, vocational programs), were delivered with little regard for the youth's natural environment (for example, wilderness training), and were punishment oriented. As discussed subsequently, multisystemic therapy and functional family therapy are characterized by those types of interventions linked with favorable outcomes and eschew the types of interventions associated with weak outcomes.

Multisystemic Therapy

Treatment Theory

The treatment theory underlying multisystemic therapy draws upon the causal modeling studies of serious antisocial behavior noted previously and social-ecological (Bronfenbrenner, 1979) and family systems (Haley,1976; Minuchin,1974) theories of behavior. This research and these theories suggest that human behavior is multidetermined and, consequently, problem behavior may be a function of difficulty within any of the pertinent systems (for example, family, peer, school, community) and/or difficulties that characterize the interfaces between these systems (for example, family-school relations, family-neighborhood relations).

Thus, the scope of multisystemic therapy interventions is not limited to the individual adolescent or the family system, but includes difficulties within and between other systems. Indeed, recent research has supported the multisystemic therapy theory of change. Huey, Henggeler, Brondino, and Pickrel (2000) showed that therapist adherence to the multisystemic therapy treatment protocol produced improved family relations, which were linked with decreased association with deviant peers, which, in turn, was associated with decreased antisocial behavior.

Clinical Procedures

A clinical volume (Henggeler et al., 1998) describes multisystemic therapy interventions in detail. In general, these interventions focus on the individual, family, peer, school, and social network variables that are linked with identified problems as well as on the interface of these systems. In designing particular intervention strategies, multisystemic therapy adapts empirically based interventions from pragmatic, problem-focused treatments that have at least some empirical support. These include strategic family therapy (Haley, 1976), structural family therapy (Minuchin, 1974), behavioral parent training (Munger, 1993), and cognitive behavior therapies (Kendall and Braswell, 1993). In addition, and as appropriate, biological contributors to problems are identified and psychopharmacological treatment is integrated with psychosocial treatment.

A frequent goal of treatment at the family level, for example, is to enhance caregivers' capacity to monitor adolescent behavior and whereabouts, and to provide positive consequences for responsible youth behavior and sanctions for irresponsible behavior. Hence, the therapist often will help the caregivers to develop increased family structure, operationalize desired youth behavior, and identify natural reinforcers to be linked with desired behavior.

Importantly, the therapist also identifies barriers to the effective implementation of these new rules and consequences. Such barriers might include parental substance abuse, parental mental health difficulties, high levels of family stress, and so forth. The therapist then helps to design interventions to overcome these barriers to parental effectiveness, understanding that new family rules and contingencies cannot be implemented effectively or consistently until such barriers are removed.

Similarly, at the peer level, a frequent goal of treatment is to decrease the youth's involvement with delinquent and drug-using peers and to increase his or her association with prosocial peers. Interventions for this purpose are optimally conducted by the youth's caregivers, with the guidance of the therapist, and might consist of active support and encouragement of association with nonproblem peers (for example, providing transportation and increased privileges) and substantive discouragement of association with deviant peers (for example, applying significant sanctions). Caregivers are encouraged to use indigenous opportunities for youths to develop relations with prosocial peers under adult supervision. Such opportunities include church youth groups, after-school activities, and community recreational resources.

Likewise, under the guidance of the therapist, the caregivers develop strategies to monitor and promote the youth's school performance and/or vocational functioning. Typically included in this domain are strategies for opening and maintaining positive communication lines with teachers and for restructuring after-school hours to promote academic efforts. Emphasis is placed on developing a collaborative relationship between the parents and school personnel. Hence, the multisystemic therapy model views the caregivers as key to achieving desired outcomes, and interventions typically focus on the family and the family's interface with key social systems.

Staffing and Model of Service Delivery

Multisystemic therapy programs generally include teams of three master's-level clinicians who are supervised by a doctoral-level mental health professional or highly experienced master's-level professional. Most multisystemic therapy dissemination sites have more than one team. Each team is expected to treat approximately fifty families per year, which means that each practitioner is primarily responsible for fifteen-to-sixteen families per year.

The use of a home-based service delivery model has been crucial to the high engagement and low dropout rates obtained in multisystemic therapy studies (for example, Henggeler, Pickrel, Brondino, and Crouch, 1996; Henggeler, Rowland et al., 1999). Essential characteristics of the home-based model include: (a) low caseloads (four-to-six families per clinician) that allow intense services to be provided to each family (two-to-fifteen hours/week), (b) delivery of services in community settings (for example, home, school, neighborhood center), (c) time-limited duration of treatment (four-to-six months), (d) twenty-four hour/day and seven day/week availability of therapists, and (e) provision of comprehensive services.

Importantly, the home-based model of service delivery helps to overcome barriers to service access and provides more valid clinical assessment and outcome data. Although the intensity (for example, families average four months and approximately sixty hours of direct service) and off-site nature of the model lead to a per family cost that is greater than traditional outpatient treatment, the model is highly cost efficient if out-of-home placements are prevented.

Quality Assurance

Findings from recent clinical trials with violent and chronic juvenile offenders (Henggeler, Melton, Brondino, Scherer, and Hanley, 1997) and with substance abusing juvenile offenders (Henggeler, Pickrel, and Brondino, 1999) and structural modeling research (Huey et al., 2000) have shown that therapist adherence to the multisystemic therapy treatment protocol is associated with more favorable long-term clinical outcomes. These established links between treatment fidelity and youth outcomes have reinforced an already strong commitment to quality assurance in multisystemic therapy programs.

Prior to the development of new multisystemic therapy programs, site assessments are conducted by Multisystemic Therapy Services, Inc. to determine whether the necessary organizational and community conditions are in place or can be developed to enable the multisystemic therapy program to be successful. Thus, the site assessment examines the political climate, commitment of the host agency, interagency relations, support from the courts, funding structures, and so forth (Schoenwald and Henggeler, in press). If a site is viable, several ongoing training and quality assurance mechanisms are put in place, all of which aim to promote treatment fidelity and the program's capacity to achieve desired outcomes. These mechanisms include:

(a) an intensive five-day orientation of program administrators, supervisors, and practitioners to the multisystemic therapy model

(b) weekly or twice weekly onsite clinical supervision by a senior-level professional trained in the multisystemic therapy supervisory protocol (Henggeler and Schoenwald, 1998)

(c) quarterly booster training

(d) weekly consultation via conference call with a multisystemic therapy expert who follows a consultation protocol (Schoenwald, 1998) aimed at promoting treatment fidelity and developing strategies for overcoming barriers to favorable clinical outcomes

(e) ongoing tracking of caregiver reports of therapist adherence to multisystemic therapy through an Internet system (www. mstinstitute.org).

In addition, research sites typically collect audiotapes of therapists' family sessions and have a sample of these tapes rated for treatment fidelity by a multisystemic therapy expert. Together, these quality assurance mechanisms aim to provide clinicians with the resources and clinical support needed to be successful with challenging clinical cases.

Clinical and Cost Outcomes

As recently summarized (Henggeler, 1999a, 1999b), rigorous evaluation has been fundamental to the development of multisystemic therapy. Eight randomized clinical trials have been published about youths and their families who presented serious clinical problems, and several others are currently underway. The majority of these trials have been conducted in field settings, and the targeted populations have included inner-city delinquents (Henggeler et al., 1986), three trials with violent and chronic juvenile offenders (Borduin et al., 1995; Henggeler et al., 1997; Henggeler, Melton, and Smith, 1992; Henggeler, Melton, Smith, Schoenwald, and Hanley, 1993), substance abusing or dependent juvenile offenders with high rates of psychiatric comorbidity (Brown, Henggeler, Schoenwald, Brondino, and Pickrel, 1999; Henggeler, Pickrel, and Brondino, 1999; Schoenwald, Ward, Henggeler, Pickrel, and Patel, 1996), youths presenting psychiatric emergencies (in other words, suicidal, homicidal, psychotic) (Henggeler, Rowland et al., 1999; Schoenwald, Ward, Henggeler, and Rowland, 2000), maltreating families (Brunk, Henggeler, and Whelan, 1987), and juvenile sexual offenders (Borduin, Henggeler, Blaske, and Stein, 1990). Most of the studies focused on youths who were truly at imminent risk for out-of-home placements such as incarceration, residential treatment, or psychiatric hospitalization.

Results from these studies support the short- and long-term clinical effectiveness of multisystemic therapy and its potential to produce significant cost savings and capacity to retain families in treatment. In comparison with control groups, multisystemic therapy consistently has demonstrated improved family relations and family functioning, improved school attendance, decreased adolescent drug use, 25 percent to 70 percent decreases in long-term rates of rearrest, and 47 to 64 percent decreases in long-term rates of days in out-of-home placements.

These findings have led reviewers to conclude that multisystemic therapy is a highly cost-effective treatment model (Aos, Phipps, Barnoski, and Lieb, 1999). For example, the average net gain for multisystemic therapy was $61,068 per youth in criminal justice system benefits and crime victim benefits, which contrasts with a net loss of $7,511 observed for juvenile boot camps. Finally, studies with substance abusing or dependent juvenile offenders (Henggeler et al., 1996) and youths presenting psychiatric emergencies (Henggeler, Rowland et al., 1999) have had treatment completion rates of 98 percent and 97 percent, respectively.

In addition to these completed randomized trials, extensive efforts are currently underway to extend the effectiveness of multisystemic therapy to other challenging clinical populations, settings, and models of services delivery. The Family Services Research Center is evaluating the effectiveness of multisystemic therapy within the context of drug courts and as an alternative to out-of-home placements for physically abused children. Studies of neighborhood-based (Randall, Swenson, and Henggeler, 1999) and school-based (Cunningham and Henggeler, in press) multisystemic therapy programs are underway. In addition, multisystemic therapy-based continua of care including multisystemic therapy outpatient, home-based foster care, and short-term residential treatment are being evaluated in two states. Finally, as described by Henggeler, Schoenwald, Rowland, and Cunningham (in press), randomized trials of multisystemic therapy with variations challenging populations are being conducted by approximately ten additional investigators across North America and Europe.

Functional Family Therapy

Treatment Theory

Functional family therapy (Alexander and Parsons, 1982) is based primarily on family systems and social learning conceptualizations of behavior. Emphasis is placed on understanding the functions of intrafamily behavior, especially with regard to the distance/autonomy and connectedness/interdependency of family dyads. As the clinician accurately assesses the functions of problem behavior (for example, running away to decrease dependency), strategies can be implemented to effectively engage families in treatment. Intervention strategies used in functional family therapy (for example, parent training, communication training, and contracting) generally are based on principles of behavior therapy and social learning theory. Hence functional family therapy is considered a behavioral family-systems treatment model.

Clinical Procedures

The most extensive clinical description of functional family therapy is provided by Alexander and Parsons (1982), and a more current overview of the approach was published (Alexander et al., 1998) in Elliott's *Blueprints Series* (1998). Functional family therapy includes five sequential phases of treatment (engagement, assessment, motivation, behavior change, and generalization) with different intervention techniques used to achieve the goals of each phase.

Engagement. The goal of this phase is to enhance the family members' perceptions of therapist responsivity and credibility. Therapists accomplish this goal by behaving responsively and respectfully toward the family and making the family members feel as comfortable as possible through dress, attitude, affect, and availability.

Assessment. Assessment is a multifaceted and ongoing process that attempts to understand the functions and interpersonal impact of the identified problem behavior for family members. In contrast with traditional mental health approaches, functional family therapy assessment is minimally concerned with findings based on diagnoses and psychological testing. Rather, intrafamilial and extrafamilial relations are examined to determine the blend of autonomy/connectedness among family dyads. Such assessments are conducted primarily through therapist observations of family interactions and discussions with family members.

Motivation. The overriding goal of the motivational phase is to create a therapist-family context that is conducive to desired change. To achieve this goal, the practitioner works to reduce anger, blaming, hopelessness, and other negative behaviors and emotions among family members. Techniques used to reduce negative interactions and emotions include reframing (Watzlawick, Weakland, and Fisch, 1974), which generally attempts to change family members' interpretations of noxious behaviors (for example, anger is reframed as an expression of underlying hurt) and other family therapy techniques.

Behavior change. This stage focuses primarily on changing family interactions through building interpersonal and problem-solving skills. As Alexander et al. (1998) noted, functional family therapy change techniques fall under two categories: parent training and communication training. Parent training is usually emphasized with families of younger children and follows relatively well-specified protocols developed in the behavioral parent training literature. Communication skills training is also based primarily on the behavioral literature and emphasizes elements such as brevity, directness, and active listening.

Generalization. The goal of this final phase is to extend positive intrafamily change by incorporating relations with community systems such as mental health and juvenile justice authorities. Here, the therapist acts largely as a case manager or collaborates with a case manager in attempting to anchor the family in a supportive community context. To accomplish this goal, therapists must possess extensive knowledge of community resources and have positive relations with community social service agencies.

Staffing and Model of Service Delivery

The therapists who use functional family therapy may be part-time or full-time and have included students, paraprofessionals, and professionals. Supervisors should have at least a master's degree. Clinicians work with 12-to-16 active cases and are expected to treat 150 families per year.

Functional family therapy usually follows an outpatient, office-based model of service delivery, but functional family therapy has been delivered using a home-based model in several sites. Families receive an average of twelve sessions. Hence, functional family therapy is a relatively nonintensive intervention approach.

Quality Assurance

Historically, functional family therapy quality assurance protocols have been relatively minimal, though consistent with most extant training of specialized interventions in the field of mental health. As described by Alexander et al. (1998), clinicians receive a two-to-three-day didactic workshop with one booster session during the course of the following year. In addition, each clinician receives approximately two hours of telephone consultation during the year. Standardized measures of treatment integrity have not been developed for functional family therapy. As functional family therapy has begun to be more widely disseminated, however, the developers are devoting considerably more attention to determining the conditions needed to promote program fidelity.

Clinical and Cost Outcomes

The effectiveness of functional family therapy has been examined in two published randomized trials. The first study (Alexander and Parsons, 1973; Parsons and Alexander, 1973) was conducted with status offenders who were predominately female and from Mormon families. Results showed that functional family therapy improved family relations and decreased subsequent status offenses, but did not effect criminal behavior. The second randomized trial was conducted with substance abusing adolescents (Friedman, 1989), and findings revealed that functional family therapy increased family involvement in treatment, but no treatment effects were observed for substance use.

Additional evaluations of functional family therapy include unpublished studies and several quasi-experimental studies (Barton, Alexander, Waldron, Turner, and Warburton, 1985; Gordon, Arbuthnot, Gustafson, and McGreen, 1988) in which considerable functional family therapy effects on youth recidivism have been reported. Unfortunately, these latter studies include substantive methodological limitations that hamper confidence in the validity of reported outcomes. Importantly, however, a third well-designed randomized trial of functional family therapy has recently been completed by Waldron at the University of New Mexico (Waldron, Slesnick, Brody, Turner, and Peterson, in press). This study with substance-abusing adolescents supported the efficacy of functional family therapy in short-term reduction of substance use.

Finally, Aos et al. (1999) examined the cost effectiveness of functional family therapy and concluded that the model produced a net benefit of $22,739 per offender in criminal justice system benefits and crime victim benefits. This cost-benefit compares quite favorably to those reported for criminal-justice oriented interventions.

Implications for the Design of Effective Services

In general, research findings suggest that multisystemic therapy produces stronger treatment effects and greater cost savings than functional family therapy, and that confidence in the validity of multisystemic therapy findings is greater due to the use of more rigorous research methods (Aos et al., 1999). Nevertheless, as noted previously, functional family therapy remains one of the few intervention models used with juvenile offenders that has produced favorable outcomes in controlled evaluations (Elliott, 1998).

To better understand the bases of the relative success of functional family therapy and the even greater success of multisystemic therapy, these family-based interventions are reconsidered in light of the previously noted conclusions of Gendreau and his colleagues regarding the characteristics of effective services for adult offenders.

- *Use behavioral strategies:* As described extensively in their respective treatment manuals (Alexander and Parsons, 1982; Henggeler et al., 1998), both functional family therapy and multisystemic therapy make extensive use of intervention techniques derived from behavioral and cognitive behavior therapies.

- *Provide services in the natural environment:* Multisystemic therapy practitioners provide virtually all services in home, school, and neighborhood contexts. Therapists who provide functional family therapy offer services primarily in office-based settings unless functional family therapy is being used within a family preservation program. Neither treatment provides institution-based services.

- *Provide comprehensive services to address multiple needs:* Multisystemic therapy explicitly addresses individual, family, peer, school, and social network variables in a comprehensive fashion. Functional family therapy focuses initially on the family, but then addresses extrafamilial factors in the generalization phase of treatment.

- *Deliver intensive services, albeit for a limited time:* Multisystemic therapy provides intensive home-based services for an average duration of four months, including approximately sixty hours of direct clinical contact. Functional family therapy generally provides weekly family therapy sessions for approximately three months.

- *Emphasize the development of prosocial relations:* Primary goals of multisystemic therapy are to develop family relations that promote positive emotional and behavioral adjustment; develop youths' relations with prosocial peers; enhance youths' school and vocational performance; and build indigenous, prosocial support networks around the family. Functional family therapy emphasizes the development of effective family communication and parent-child relationship skills, and subsequently aims to generalize these positive gains to relations with extrafamilial systems.

- *Target known risk factors on an individualized basis:* Multisystemic therapy explicitly targets known risk factors across individual, family, peer, school, and neighborhood contexts. Functional family therapy focuses on family risk factors, and subsequently attends to extrafamilial risk factors.

- *Provide access to aftercare:* Neither multisystemic therapy nor functional family therapy provide access to aftercare. This limitation is currently being addressed by multisystemic therapy continua-of-care studies in which youths and their families receive the intensity of services that is titrated to their need, and these services are provided for extended periods of time within the context of a managed care provider organization.

- *Maintain high levels of quality assurance:* Quality assurance aimed at maintaining treatment fidelity to multisystemic therapy and corresponding outcomes is probably the most stringent in the field. Quality assurance for functional family therapy is similar to prevailing mental health practices, but efforts are currently being made to bolster the intensity of quality assurance.

In sum, the success of multisystemic therapy and functional family therapy in comparison with a multitude of other intervention models for juvenile offenders is most likely due to their incorporation of known characteristics of effective programs. The relative advantage of multisystemic therapy is probably the result of its greater intensity, increased attention to quality assurance, consistent focus on the natural environment, and more explicit emphasis on the extrafamilial factors linked with antisocial behavior of youth.

Policy Implications

Multisystemic therapy, and to a lesser extent functional family therapy, have proven to be clinically effective and cost-effective alternatives to out-of-home placement of youths presenting serious clinical problems. Such outcomes coupled with the nature of these family-based treatments have clear implications for mental health and juvenile justice policy. First, because the vast majority of mental health and juvenile justice financial resources are devoted to costly, ineffective, and often iatrogenic (for example, boot camps) out-of-home placements, a sizable portion of these resources should be shifted to the development of intensive, evidence-based community interventions.

Second, consistent with the conclusions of reviewers, these community-based interventions should be intensive, comprehensive, and individualized; provide time-limited treatment with access to aftercare; deliver behavioral interventions in youths' natural environments; and maintain high levels of quality assurance.

Third, favorable outcomes with challenging clinical populations are not likely to result from the prevailing "train and hope" approach to quality assurance. Hence, in the dissemination of effective treatment models, considerable attention must be devoted to building, promoting, and maintaining program fidelity.

References

Alexander, J. F. and B. V. Parsons. 1973. Short Term Behavioral Intervention with Delinquent Families: Impact on Family Process and Recidivism. *Journal of Abnormal Psychology*. 81:219-225.

————. 1982. *Functional Family Therapy*. Monterey, California: Brooks/Cole.

Alexander, J., C. Barton, C., D. Gordon, J. Grotpeter, K. Hansson, R. Harrison, S. Mears, S. Mihalic, B. Parsons, C., Pugh, S. Schulman, H. Waldron, and T. Sexton. 1998. *Functional Family Therapy*. D. S. Elliott, series ed. University of Colorado, Center for the Study and Prevention of Violence. Boulder, Colorado: Blueprints Publications.

Aos, S., P. Phipps, R. Barnoski, and R. Lieb. 1999. *The Comparative Costs and Benefits of Programs to Reduce Crime: A Review of National Research Findings with Implications for Washington State, Version 3.0*. Olympia, Washington: Washington State Institute for Public Policy.

Barton, C., J. F. Alexander, H. Waldron, C. W. Turner, and J. Warburton. 1985. Generalizing Treatment Effects of Functional Family Therapy: Three Replications. *American Journal of Family Therapy*. 13:16-26.

Borduin, C. M., S. W. Henggeler, D. M. Blaske, and R. Stein. 1990. Multisystemic Treatment of Adolescent Sexual Offenders. *International Journal of Offender Therapy and Comparative Criminology*. 35:105-114.

Borduin, C. M., B. J. Mann, L. T. Cone, S. W. Henggeler, B. R. Fucci, D. M. Blaske, and R. A. Williams. 1995. Multisystemic Treatment of Serious Juvenile Offenders: Long-term Prevention of Criminality and Violence. *Journal of Consulting and Clinical Psychology*. 63:569-578.

Bronfenbrenner, U. 1979. *The Ecology of Human Development: Experiments by Design and Nature.* Cambridge, Massachusetts: Harvard University Press.

Brown, T. L., S. W. Henggeler, S. K. Schoenwald, M. J. Brondino, and S. G. Pickrel. 1999. Multisystemic Treatment of Substance Abusing and Dependent Juvenile Delinquents: Effects on School Attendance at Posttreatment and 6-month Follow-up. *Children's Services: Social Policy, Research, and Practice*. 2:81-93.

Brunk, M., S. W. Henggeler, and J. P. Whelan. 1987. A Comparison of Multisystemic Therapy and Parent Training in the Brief Treatment of Child Abuse and Neglect. *Journal of Consulting and Clinical Psychology*. 55:311-318.

Cunningham, P. B., and S. W. Henggeler (in press). Healthy Children through Healthy Schools: Implementing Empirically based Drug and Violence Prevention and Intervention Programs in Public School Settings. *Journal of Clinical Child Psychology*.

Elliott, D. S. 1994. *Youth Violence: An Overview.* Boulder, Colorado: University of Colorado, Center for the Study and Prevention of Violence, Institute for Behavioral Sciences.

Elliott, D. S., series ed. 1998. *Blueprints for Violence Prevention.* University of Colorado, Center for the Study and Prevention of Violence. Boulder, Colorado: Blueprints Publications.

Farrington, D. P. and B. C. Welsh. 1999. Delinquency Prevention Using Family-based Interventions. *Children and Society*. 13:287-303.

Friedman, A. S. 1989. Family Therapy vs. Parent Groups: Effects on Adolescent Drug Abusers. *American Journal of Family Therapy*. 17:335-347.

Gendreau, P. 1996a. Offender Rehabilitation: What We Know and What Needs to Be Done. *Criminal Justice and Behavior*. 23:144-161.

———. 1996b. The Principles of Effective Intervention with Offenders. In A. T. Harland, ed. *Choosing Correctional Options that Work.* Thousand Oaks, California: Sage.

Gendreau, P. and C. Goggin. 1997. Correctional Treatment: Accomplishments and Realities. In P. Van Voorhis, M. Braswell, and D. Lester, eds. *Correctional Counseling and Rehabilitation, 3rd ed.*, pp. 271-279. Cincinnati, Ohio: Anderson Publishing.

Gordon, D. A., J. Arbuthnot, K. E. Gustafson, and P. McGreen. 1988. Home-based Behavioral-systems Family Therapy with Disadvantaged Juvenile Delinquents. *American Journal of Family Therapy.* 16:243-255.

Haley, J. 1976. *Problem Solving Therapy.* San Francisco: Jossey-Bass.

Hawkins, J. D., R. F. Catalano, and J. Y. Miller. 1992. Risk and Protective Factors for Alcohol and Other Drug Problems in Adolescence and Early Adulthood: Implications for Substance Abuse Prevention. *Psychological Bulletin.* 112:64-105.

Henggeler, S. W. 1989. *Delinquency in Adolescence.* Thousand Oaks, California: Sage.

———. 1991. Multidimensional Causal Models of Delinquent Behavior. In R. Cohen and A. Siegel, eds. *Context and Development,* pp. 211-231. Hillsdale, New Jersey: Erlbaum.

———. 1997. The Development of Effective Drug Abuse Services for Youth. In J. A. Egertson, D. M. Fox, and A. I. Leshner, eds. *Treating Drug Abusers Effectively,* pp. 253-279. New York: Blackwell Publishers.

———. 1999a. Multisystemic Therapy: An Overview of Clinical Procedures, Outcomes, and Policy Implications. *Child Psychology and Psychiatry Review.* 4:2-10.

———. 1999b. Multisystemic Treatment of Serious Clinical Problems in Children and Adolescents. *Clinician's Research Digest, Supplemental Bulletin.* 21.

Henggeler, S. W., C. M. Borduin, and B. J. Mann. 1993. Advances in Family Therapy. In T. H. Ollendick and R. J. Prinz, eds. *Advances in Clinical Child Psychology,* Vol. 15, pp. 207-241. New York: Plenum Press.

Henggeler, S. W., G. D. Melton, M. J. Brondino, D. G. Scherer, and J. H. Hanley. 1997. Multisystemic Therapy with Violent and Chronic Juvenile Offenders and their Families: The Role of Treatment Fidelity in Successful Dissemination. *Journal of Consulting and Clinical Psychology.* 65:821-833.

Henggeler, S. W., G. B. Melton, and L. A. Smith. 1992. Family Preservation Using Multisystemic Therapy: An Effective Alternative to Incarcerating Serious Juvenile Offenders. *Journal of Consulting and Clinical Psychology.* 60:953-961.

Henggeler, S. W., G. B. Melton, L. A. Smith, S. K. Schoenwald, and J. H. Hanley. 1993. Family Preservation Using Multisystemic Treatment: Long-term Follow-up to a Clinical Trial with Serious Juvenile Offenders. *Journal of Child and Family Studies.* 2:283-293.

Henggeler, S. W., S. G. Pickrel, and M J. Brondino. 1999. Multisystemic Treatment of Substance Abusing and Dependent Delinquents: Outcomes, Treatment Fidelity, and Transportability. *Mental Health Services Research.* 1:171-184.

Henggeler, S. W., S. G. Pickrel, M. J. Brondino, and J. L. Crouch. 1996. Eliminating (Almost) Treatment Dropout of Substance Abusing or Dependent Delinquents through Home-based Multisystemic Therapy. *American Journal of Psychiatry.* 153: 427-428.

Henggeler, S. W., J. D. Rodick, C. M. Borduin, C. L. Hanson, S. M. Watson, and J. R. Urey. 1986. Multisystemic Treatment of Juvenile Offenders: Effects on Adolescent Behavior and Family Interactions. *Developmental Psychology.* 22:132-141.

Henggeler, S. W., M. R. Rowland, J. Randall, D. Ward, S. G. Pickrel, P. B. Cunningham, S. L. Miller, J. E. Edwards, J. Zealberg, L. Hand, and A. B. Santos. 1999. Home-based Multisystemic Therapy as an Alternative to the Hospitalization of Youth in Psychiatric Crisis: Clinical Outcomes. *Journal of the American Academy of Child and Adolescent Psychiatry.* 38:1331-1339.

Henggeler, S. W. and S. K. Schoenwald. 1998. *The Multisystemic Therapy Supervisory Manual: Promoting Quality Assurance at the Clinical Level.* Charleston, South Carolina: Multisystemic Therapy Institute.

Henggeler, S. W., S. K. Schoenwald, C. M. Borduin, M. D. Rowland, and P. B. Cunningham. 1998. *Multisystemic Treatment of Antisocial Behavior in Children and Adolescents.* New York: Guilford Press.

Henggeler, S. W., S. K. Schoenwald, M. D. Rowland, and P. B. Cunningham (in press). *Multisystemic Treatment of Children and Adolescents with Serious Emotional Disturbance.* New York: Guilford Press.

Huey, S. J., S. W. Henggeler, M. J. Brondino, and S. G. Pickrel. 2000. Mechanisms of Change in Multisystemic Therapy: Reducing Delinquent Behavior through Therapist Adherence and Improved Family and Peer Functioning. *Journal of Consulting and Clinical Psychology.* 68:451-467.

Kazdin, A. E. 1987. Treatment of Antisocial Behavior in Children: Current Status and Future Directions. *Psychological Bulletin.* 102:187-203.

Kazdin, A. E. and J. R. Weisz. 1998. Identifying and Developing Empirically Supported Child and Adolescent Treatments. *Journal of Consulting and Clinical Psychology.* 66:19-36.

Kendall, P. C. and L. Braswell. 1993. *Cognitive-behavioral Therapy for Impulsive Children, Second Edition.* New York: Guilford Press.

Lipsey, M. W. and D. B. Wilson. 1998. Effective Intervention for Serious Juvenile Offenders: A Synthesis of Research. In R. Loeber and D. P. Farrington, eds. *Serious and Violent Juvenile Offenders: Risk Factors and Successful Interventions*, pp. 313-345. Thousand Oaks, California: Sage.

Loeber, R. and D. P. Farrington, eds. 1998. *Serious and Violent Juvenile Offenders: Risk Factors and Successful Interventions.* Thousand Oaks, California: Sage.

McMahon, R. J. and K. C. Wells. 1989. Conduct Disorders. In E. J. Mash and R. A. Barkley, eds. *Treatment of Childhood Disorders*, pp. 73-132. New York: Guilford Press.

Melton, G. B. and P. M. Pagliocca. 1992. Treatment in the Juvenile Justice System: Directions for Policy and Practice. In J. J. Cocozza, ed. *Responding to the Mental Health Needs of Youth in the Juvenile Justice System*, pp. 107-139. Miami, Florida: The National Coalition for the Mentally Ill in the Criminal Justice System.

Minuchin, S. 1974. *Families and Family Therapy.* Cambridge, Massachusetts: Harvard University Press.

Mulvey, E. P., M. W. Arthur, and N. D. Reppucci. 1993. The Prevention and Treatment of Juvenile Delinquency: A Review of the Research. *Clinical Psychology Review.* 13:133-167.

Munger, R. L. 1993. *Changing Children's Behavior Quickly.* Lanham, Maryland: Madison Books.

Office of Technology Assessment, U.S. Congress. 1991. *Adolescent Health—Volume II: Background and the Effectiveness of Selected Prevention and Treatment Services*, pp. 499-578, OTA-H-466. Washington, D.C.: U.S. Government Printing Office.

Parsons, B. V. and J. F. Alexander. 1973. Short Term Family Intervention: A Therapy Outcome Study. *Journal of Consulting and Clinical Psychology.* 41:195-201.

Randall, J., C. C. Swenson, and S. W. Henggeler. 1999. Neighborhood Solutions for Neighborhood Problems: An Empirically-based Violence Prevention Collaboration. *Health, Education, and Behavior.* 26:806-820.

Schoenwald, S. K. 1998. *Multisystemic Therapy Consultation Guidelines.* Charleston, South Carolina: Multisystemic Therapy Institute.

Schoenwald, S. K. and S. W. Henggeler (in press). Services Research and Family Based Treatment. In H. Liddle, G. Diamond, R. Levant, and J. Bray, eds. *Family Psychology Intervention Science.* Washington, D.C.: American Psychological Association.

Schoenwald, S. K., D. M. Ward, S. W. Henggeler, S. G. Pickrel, and H. Patel. 1996. Multisystemic Therapy Treatment of Substance Abusing or Dependent Adolescent Offenders: Costs of Reducing Incarceration, Inpatient, and Residential Placement. *Journal of Child and Family Studies.* 5:431-444.

Schoenwald, S. K., D. M. Ward, S. W. Henggeler, and M. D. Rowland. 2000. Multisystemic Therapy vs. Hospitalization for Crisis Stabilization of Youth: Placement Outcomes 4 Months Post-referral. *Mental Health Services Research.* 2:3-12.

Tate, D. C., N. D. Reppucci, and E. P. Mulvey. 1995. Violent Juvenile Delinquents: Treatment Effectiveness and Implications for Future Action. *American Psychologist.* 50:777-781.

Tolan, P. and N. Guerra. 1994. *What Works in Reducing Adolescent Violence: An Empirical Review of the Field.* Boulder, Colorado: University of Colorado, Center for the Study and Prevention of Violence, Institute for Behavioral Sciences.

Waldron, H. B., N. Slesnick, J. L. Brody, C. W. Turner, and T. L. Peterson (in press). Four- and Seven-Month Treatment Outcomes for Adolescent Substance Abuse. *Journal of Consulting and Clinical Psychology.*

Watzlawick, P., J. Weakland, and R. Fisch. 1974. *Change: Principles of Problem Formulation and Problem Resolution.* New York: Norton.

INDEX

ABOUT THE AUTHORS

Harry E. Allen, the editor of this volume, is Professor Emeritus, Administration of Justice, at San Jose State University in San Jose, California. He is also currently Distinguished Scholar-in-Residence, University of Louisville. He is the co-author of *Corrections In America*, 9th edition (with Clifford Simonsen), and *Corrections in the Community*, 2nd edition (with Edward Latessa).

Francis T. Cullen, Ph.D., is Distinguished Research Professor in the Department of Criminal Justice at the University of Cincinnati, where he also holds a joint appointment in sociology. He received a Ph.D. (1979) in sociology and education from Columbia University. Professor Cullen has published more than 160 works in the areas of rehabilitation, "what works" in corrections, public attitudes about treatment and punishment, criminological theory, white-collar crime, and the measurement of sexual victimization. Among other works, his writings include *Reaffirming Rehabilitation* (1982, with Karen E. Gilbert) and *Offender Rehabilitation: Effective Correctional Intervention* (1997, with Brandon K. Applegate). Professor Cullen is a Fellow of the Academy of Criminal Justice Sciences and of the American Society of Criminology. He has served as President of the Academy of Criminal Justice Sciences and as the editor of *Justice Quarterly*.

Adelle E. Forth, Ph.D., is an Associate Professor in the Department of Psychology at Carleton University in Ottawa, Ontario. She has published in the areas of assessment of psychopathy in youth, offenders, and nonoffenders, emotional processing in psychopaths, and is the senior author of the Hare Psychopathy Checklist: Youth Version.

Robert D. Hare, Ph.D. (1963, University of Western Ontario) is widely considered to be one of the world's foremost experts in the area of psychopathy. He is Emeritus Professor of Psychology, University of British Columbia, where he has taught and conducted research for thirty-five years, and is President of Darkstone Research Group Ltd., a forensic research and consulting firm. He has devoted most of his academic career to the investigation of psychopathy, its nature, assessment, and implications for mental health and criminal justice. He is the author of several books and many chapters and scientific articles on psychopathy, and is the developer of the Hare Psychopathy Checklist-Revised (PCL-R). He is a coauthor of several derivatives of the PCL-R, including the Psychopathy Checklist: Screening Version (PCL: SV), the Psychopathy Checklist: Youth Version (PCL: YV), and the Hare P-Scan. He collaborated in the DSM-IV Field Trial for antisocial personality disorder, and is author of the popular book, *Without Conscience: The Disturbing World of the Psychopaths Among Us*. Dr. Hare consults with law enforcement, including the FBI and the Royal Canadian Mounted Police, and is a member of the Advisory Panel established by the English Prison Service to develop new programs for the treatment of psychopathic offenders. His current research on psychopathy continues to be broad-based, and includes the nature of the disorder, assessment issues, developmental factors, neuroimaging, domestic violence, risk for recidivism and violence, and the development of new treatment and management strategies. In addition, he lectures widely on psychopathy and on the use and misuse of the PCL-R in the criminal justice system. Through Darkstone Research Group (www.hare.org) he provides formal training programs for use of the PCL-R and its derivatives. Dr. Hare's work has been featured in many newspaper and magazine articles and in more than a dozen television programs. Among his recent awards are the 1999 Silver Medal of the Queen Sophia Center in Valencia, Spain; the Canadian Psychological Association 2000 Award for Distinguished Applications of Psychology; the American Academy of Forensic Psychology 2001 Award for Distinguished Applications to the Field of Forensic Psychology; and the 2001 Isaac Ray Award presented by the American Psychiatric Association and the American Academy of Psychiatry and Law for Outstanding Contributions to Forensic Psychiatry and Psychiatric Jurisprudence.

Dr. Stephen Hart is Professor of Psychology at Simon Fraser University. He obtained his Ph.D. in clinical-forensic psychology at the University of British Columbia. His major research interests are assessment of risk for violence, psychopathic personality disorder, and mentally disordered offenders. Dr. Hart has conducted training workshops for mental health, law enforcement, and correctional professionals throughout North America, Europe, and Australasia.

Scott W. Henggeler received his Ph.D. in clinical psychology from the University of Virginia in 1977. Currently, he is Professor of Psychiatry and Behavioral Sciences and Director of the Family Services Research Center at the Medical University of South Carolina. He has published more than 170 journal articles, book chapters, and books; and he is on the editorial boards of nine journals. Recent volumes include *Innovative Approaches for Difficult to Treat Populations* (with A. B. Santos) and *Multisystemic Treatment of Antisocial Behavior in Children and Adolescents* (with several colleagues). Much of Dr. Henggeler's research concerns serious antisocial behavior in adolescents and the development of clinically effective and cost effective treatments for such behavior. In collaboration with several colleagues, he has developed the theoretical rationale and intervention procedures for multisystemic therapy (MST), a family- and home based treatment that has demonstrated long-term reductions in recidivism and out-of-home placements in several studies of youths and their families presenting serious problems. Currently, Dr. Henggeler is conducting an evaluation of the long-term effectiveness of MST with substance abusing delinquents; an evaluation of MST as a family-based alternative to psychiatric hospitalization of youth in crisis; an evaluation of MST and juvenile drug court; and several other studies examining the integration of evidence-based mental health treatments into neighborhood and school settings and the viability of MST-based continua of care. His social policy interests include the development and validation of innovative methods of mental health services for disadvantaged children and their families, and efforts for redistributing mental health resources to services that are clinically effective and cost effective and preserve family integrity.

P. Randall Kropp, Ph.D., is a clinical and forensic psychologist specializing in the assessment and management of violent offenders. He works for the Forensic Psychiatric Services Commission of British Columbia, Canada, is a research consultant with the British Columbia Institute against Family Violence, and is Adjunct Professor of Psychology at Simon Fraser University. He has conducted numerous workshops for mental health professionals, police officers, and corrections staff in North America, Australia, and Europe. This training has focused on risk for violence, psycholegal assessments, and criminal harassment (stalking). He has frequently consulted with provincial, state, and federal government ministries on matters related to violence against women and children, and the assessment and treatment of violent offenders. He has published journal articles, book chapters, and research reports, and he is co-author of two works on risk assessment, *Manual for the Spousal Assault Risk Assessment Guide* and *Manual for the Sexual Violence Risk*.

Donna L. Mailloux, M.A., is a Ph.D. candidate in Forensic Psychology at Carleton University in Ottawa, Ontario and a Research Officer at the Correctional Service of Canada. She has published in the following areas: sex offenders, psychopathy, female and young offenders, and clinical rating scales.

Dr. Melissa M. Moon is an assistant professor at Northern Kentucky University. She received her Ph.D. in criminal justice from the University of Cincinnati. Her research and teaching interests include community corrections, juvenile justice policy, evaluation research, and correctional rehabilitation. Dr. Moon is also qualified to conduct the Correctional Program Assessment Inventory,$^{©}$ an instrument used to determine the extent to which correctional programs are following known principles of effective intervention.

David S. Timken, Ph.D., is President and Senior Research Scientist at Timken and Associates in Boulder, Colorado. He did his graduate work at the University of Colorado at Denver and Columbia Pacific University, San Raphael, California. He is recognized internationally for his work in the areas of diagnosis and treatment for substance abusing drivers and has more than thirty years of experience in the field. He developed the assessment, education, and treatment system for alcohol/drug-related traffic offenders in Colorado and has published numerous technical manuals. He has conducted research with DUI offenders and has been involved in the development of both screening and differential assessment instrumentation and procedures for other substance abusing populations. Dr. Timken has more than fifty publications to his credit and has presented at numerous national and international conferences. He is a member of many professional organizations including the International Council on Alcohol, Drugs, and Traffic Safety. He has extensive background as a trainer and consultant, and he has served as an adjunct professor at several institutions of higher learning. Dr. Timken also maintains a small private practice in the area of diagnosis and treatment of substance abuse.

Pamela M. Yates, Ph.D., R.Psych, is the National Manager of Sex Offender Programs for the Correctional Service of Canada. She was formerly a psychologist and clinical director of a high risk sexual offender treatment unit and senior researcher for the Assessment and Treatment of Sex Offenders Research Team at the Muriel McQueen Fergusson Centre for Family Violence Research at the University of New Brunswick. She has researched sex offender risk, recidivism, and treatment and has collaborated on and co-authored reports in the areas of sexual abuse, assessment of sexual offenders, treatment of sexual offenders, and phallometric assessment. She has worked within Canadian Federal and Provincial correctional systems and in the community with victims of familial and sexual violence. She has been involved in the development of accredited sexual offender treatment and violence prevention programs for the Correctional Service of Canada.